The Shadow Self in Film

ALSO BY GERSHON REITER

Fathers and Sons in Cinema (McFarland, 2008)

The Shadow Self in Film

Projecting the Unconscious Other

GERSHON REITER

McFarland & Company, Inc., Publishers
Jefferson, North Carolina

LIBRARY OF CONGRESS CATALOGUING-IN-PUBLICATION DATA

Reiter, Gershon, 1945–
　　The shadow self in film : projecting the unconscious other / Gershon Reiter.
　　　p.　　cm.
　　Includes bibliographical references and index.

　　ISBN 978-0-7864-7664-0 (softcover : acid free paper) ∞
　　ISBN 978-1-4766-1247-8 (ebook)

　　1. Other (Philosophy) in motion pictures.　2. Projection (Psychology) in motion pictures.　I. Title.
PN1995.9.O77R45 2014
791.43'653—dc23　　　　　　　　　　　　　　　　　　2013050570

BRITISH LIBRARY CATALOGUING DATA ARE AVAILABLE

© 2014 Gershon Reiter. All rights reserved

No part of this book may be reproduced or transmitted in any form or by any means, electronic or mechanical, including photocopying or recording, or by any information storage and retrieval system, without permission in writing from the publisher.

On the cover: Brad Pitt (left, as Tyler Durden), Edward Norton (as Narrator) in *Fight Club*, 1999 (Twentieth Century–Fox/Photofest); background (iStockphoto/Thinkstock)

Manufactured in the United States of America

McFarland & Company, Inc., Publishers
　Box 611, Jefferson, North Carolina 28640
　　www.mcfarlandpub.com

Table of Contents

Introduction: From Enkidu to Mr. Hyde ... 1

1. *Dr. Jekyll and Mr. Hyde*: Envisioning the Other ... 11
2. *Shadow of a Doubt*: The Other by Numbers ... 22
3. *Strangers on a Train*: Playing Doubles ... 35
4. *Cape Fear* (1962): Picturing the Other ... 51
5. *Cape Fear* (1991): The Other Wronged ... 64
6. *In the Line of Fire*: The Knowing Other ... 82
7. *Blood Work*: Double Feature ... 98
8. *Something Wild*: The Other Half ... 110
9. *Sea of Love*: The Feminine Other ... 125
10. *Fight Club*: The Imagined Other ... 140
11. *Desperately Seeking Susan*: Seeking the Other ... 159
12. *Apocalypse Now*: The Other Story ... 169
13. *The Lives of Others*: The Others of Our Lives ... 187

Chapter Notes ... 203
Bibliography ... 207
Index ... 209

Introduction:
From Enkidu to Mr. Hyde

> *Even before you come out of the mountains*
> *Gilgamesh, in the heart of Uruk, will have seen you in dreams.*
> — *Court courtesan to Enkidu*
>
> *The thing that was projected was Edward Hyde.*
> — *Dr. Henry Jekyll*

The Unconscious Other

Call it what we will, double, shadow, *Doppelgänger*, Other, all are outer personifications of an inner split; all mean the denied part of ourselves that appears in our dreams as a shadowy and menacing figure; all refer to the unconscious personality we all too often project on others.

Still, if we seek to call this unconscious personality by what denotes a relationship of binary opposites, of Self and Other, we're best off with the Other. In effect, we all but call it such by how we "relate" to it, by our denial. Rather than calling it "my double," or "my shadow," which implies ownership, in the back of our minds we say to ourselves, "It's not me, it's the *other*," the same other on whom we project our unconscious Other.

The unconscious Other is hardly a new concept. Whether embodied by a monster or a witch, criminal or *Doppelgänger*, the Other was part of mankind's imagination, part of his mythical stories, long before the advent of modern psychology. It was already the central subject matter in what is arguably mankind's first-known story, the five-thousand-year-old *Epic of Gilgamesh*, the "most sig-

1

nificant literary work to come out of ancient Mesopotamia."[1] In this literary work the unconscious Other is embodied by Enkidu, a wild man "out of the mountains," whose advent is foreshadowed by King Gilgamesh's two dreams.

Discovered in 1853 and translated in 1872, the long-buried Babylonian *Epic of Gilgamesh* emerged in the heyday of the Gothic period, a time when the literary double was more popular than ever before. Not only that, as if finding its double, the ancient tale shared with the period's most popular tale of the double, Robert Louis Stevenson's *The Strange Case of Dr. Jekyll and Mr. Hyde*, much more than their respective Others, Enkidu and Mr. Hyde.

But that was only the half of it. Some years later, with the advent of cinema, which became the new century's most popular storyteller, these two tales set the stage for films of the unconscious Other, films that adhered to either the *Gilgamesh prototype* or the "Jekyll and Hyde" *exception* that proved it. Either way, with their uncanny ability to replicate dreams and project "real life" pictures on the silver screen, these films presented an opportunity to experience the unconscious Other as never before.

Gilgamesh

The Epic of Gilgamesh tells of the all-powerful Gilgamesh, king of the city of Uruk, and his unique relationship with Enkidu. Two-thirds divine, one-third human, Gilgamesh severely oppresses his people, who express their discontent before the gods. In turn, the gods respond by creating Enkidu, a rival intended to offset their king's oppressive tyranny.

Enkidu, a wild man who lives among animals, is spotted one day at their watering place by a hunter, who reports what he saw to his father. The father instructs him to inform King Gilgamesh of the wild man and to request that a "temple courtesan" come and seduce the wild man. Gilgamesh approves, and the hunter and the courtesan wait for Enkidu at the watering place where he was initially spotted. On the third day of their wait, the wild man comes with the other animals and is seduced by the courtesan's strong beauty.

After lovemaking for six days and seven nights, Enkidu, as he realizes when the animals turn away from him, is no longer "the man-as-he-was-in-the-beginning." Seeing his transformation mirrored in the animals' reaction, he's persuaded by the courtesan to come with her to Uruk, where "Gilgamesh lives, completely powerful, and like a wild bull stands supreme, mounted above his people."[2] Upon his arrival, Enkidu challenges Gilgamesh by stationing himself at the entrance to a new bride's house, preventing him from making the first entrance reserved for the king. The two begin a terrible fight, which Gilgamesh barely wins. Afterward, embracing as equals, the two become inseparable friends.

Introduction: From Enkidu to Mr. Hyde

When Enkidu tells Gilgamesh about Humbaba, the terrifying guardian of the cedar forest, Gilgamesh, seeking to make for himself a name everlasting, proposes that they go together and kill the evil one. Enkidu tries to dissuade him, but Gilgamesh is set on going, and not even the cautioning words of the city elders can change his mind. When the two reach the forest, Enkidu hesitates before entering, but Gilgamesh spurs him on. The two's attitudes are switched when they have Humbaba at their mercy. Gilgamesh is tempted to accept his pleading to spare his life, but Enkidu warns him not to listen. The two promptly kill the monster, Enkidu cutting off his head.

Impressed with Gilgamesh's heroics, the goddess Ishtar offers to marry him, but the king refuses, thus insulting the goddess. In revenge, Ishtar initiates the sending of the Bull of Heaven to kill Gilgamesh. But Gilgamesh and Enkidu, combining their forces once again, kill the bull instead. Enkidu, adding insult to injury, hurls a piece of the dead bull in Ishtar's face, for which he's punished by illness and death. Gilgamesh, who deeply mourns his equal's death, is inconsolable. The remainder of the tale, which follows Gilgamesh's search for immortality, is essentially his mourning for his dead friend, after which he returns to Uruk a more complete human being and a more considerate king to his people.

Other than offering proof that even five thousand years ago the Other was part of man's imagination, *Gilgamesh* is a remarkable story in the way it reveals the role this unconscious figure plays in our lives. Like a modern how-to book for dealing with the unconscious Other, this "ancient epic, so pregnant with meaning,"[3] not only illustrates how the Other comes to be, but also what's required to deal with it.

Right from its opening (in the first column of the first of 12 fragmented clay tablets that make up the Standard Babylonian version), in which King Gilgamesh is introduced as an oppressor of his people, the ancient epic makes perfectly clear that what begets Enkidu is Gilgamesh's oppression. This oppression is mostly associated with the walls of Uruk that the self-centered king compels his people to build. As Rivkah Scharf Kluger points out in "The Archetypal Significance of Gilgamesh," the people "symbolize the unconscious, the instinctive forces, which are here shown in a deplorable state of suppression by an ego possessed by an ambitious self-assigned task."[4]

When Uruk's people have had enough of Gilgamesh's oppression and give expression to their discontent before the gods, they respond by creating "a being, Enkidu, to be a companion to Gilgamesh ... somebody whose pull is strong enough to get him out of the possession of this wall-building business."[5] Underscoring Enkidu's role, when he first arrives in Uruk and challenges Gilgamesh at the new bride's doorway, in their struggle they break down part of the wall, thus reversing the "wall-building business." This reversal is part of Enkidu's role as neutralizer of Gilgamesh's oppression. He is Gilgamesh's Other, the creature from his unconscious who personifies what the ego-inflated king denies and disowns, what he represses. As the ancient epic repeatedly suggests, Gilgamesh oppresses others because he represses his Other. In other words, he projects his repressed Other onto others.

This notion of the repressed Other is initially put forward by Gilgamesh's two symbolic dreams of a shooting star and a falling axe. In Gilgamesh's godmother, Ninsun, to whom he goes to interpret his disturbing dreams, the ancient tale even has an early interpreter of the unconscious. As Ninsun reveals to Gilgamesh, the two dreams portend the advent of his unconscious Other.

Somewhat like Ninsun's dream interpretation, in his book *Coming to Our Senses*, Morris Berman explains how the Other comes to be that's remarkably similar to how it's depicted in the Babylonian epic. According to Berman, who never mentions *Gilgamesh* in the course of his book, it "is the phenomenon of mirroring, i.e., the growth of self-recognition through the medium of other people,"[6] that engenders the Other. In *Gilgamesh*, this mirroring plays a crucial role when Enkidu, after he's transformed by mating with the temple courtesan, encounters the other animals who, seeing his transformation, turn away from him. Like a newborn separating from its mother at birth, Enkidu's seeing his transformed self mirrored in the animals is his birth trauma, his separation from Mother Nature. It forever exiles him from his Garden of Eden, separating him from the animal world into which he was born. For Enkidu, the animals' reaction is no different than what Berman calls "self-recognition through the medium of other people." Or as Kluger puts it, through the animals Enkidu "gets a reaction, a mirror.... It is because the animals run away from him that Enkidu realizes that something has happened. He still does not understand it. He is just terribly shocked."[7]

This mirroring, which shocks and baffles Enkidu, creates a binary split of him and them, of Self and Others. His terrible shock is much like the one you get when looking "in the mirror and understanding, for the first time, but in clear and unequivocal sense, that what you are seeing is nothing other than what other people see when they look at you.... The shock is not that an Other exists, but that you realize that *you are an Other for other Others*."[8] In its primeval way, what Enkidu experiences foreshadows Jacques Lacan's crucial "mirror stage," his psychoanalytic theory of the infant's first experiencing the Other upon seeing himself reflected in a mirror (or in his mother's face), which film theorist Christian Metz likened to what the spectator experiences in "that other mirror, the cinema screen."[9]

Countering *Gilgamesh*'s first part that deals with the relationship between Gilgamesh and Enkidu, its second part, which is mostly about Gilgamesh's mourning for the dead Enkidu, demonstrates how one deals with the Other by showing Gilgamesh becoming more and more like his second image. Tearing off his fine clothes like things unclean, he ventures outside the city walls and "enters the wild and becomes one with it. In his grief he becomes indistinguishable from his double, Enkidu."[10] This transformation, of course, is the tale's way of conveying Gilgamesh's assimilating the unconscious Other into his consciousness.

Finally, after a long and arduous process of embracing the dead Enkidu and what he represents, Gilgamesh, as signified by his being washed clean at the washing place (which recalls Enkidu's taming at the watering place), returns to Uruk a new man, a more complete human being. Having assimilated his unconscious Other, his double, the formerly ego-inflated king is no longer driven to elevate himself by oppressing his people, no longer compelled to project his Other on others.

In summing up "The Archetypal Significance of Gilgamesh," the Jungian Kluger writes, "The Gilgamesh Epic as a whole shows in its inner structure a process of transformation in the collective unconscious, an anticipation of the individuation process.... Gilgamesh, in accord with the heroic role, did step into the future, far ahead of the consciousness of his time."[11]

Though not necessarily intended by Kluger, one significant way *Gilgamesh* "did step into the future" was in the way it informs, as an archetype, the films of the unconscious Other.

Dr. Jekyll and Mr. Hyde

Robert Louis Stevenson's *The Strange Case of Dr. Jekyll and Mr. Hyde*, published in 1886, came out midway between the first translation of *Gilgamesh* (1872) and the publication of Freud's *The Interpretation of Dreams* (1900), the first important book on the significance of dreams and the workings of the unconscious. This neat symmetry, coincidental as it may be, is not without its meaningful synchronicity. On the one hand, Gilgamesh's dreams of Enkidu before he appeared in his life is much like Stevenson's dream that inspired the writing of *Dr. Jekyll and Mr. Hyde*; on the other hand, when seen through Freud's groundbreaking book, these two tales become obvious expressions of the unconscious Other.

Somewhat like Gilgamesh's two dreams of his Other, Stevenson wrote two versions of his tale of the Other following his disturbing dream. The first version he finished within three days of his dream; but his wife, believing he could do better, urged him to write a more allegorical work on the dual nature of man, a subject which had preoccupied Stevenson for a good part of his life. Writing intensively for three additional days, he came up with the first draft of what became *The Strange Case of Dr. Jekyll and Mr. Hyde*.

The strange story, which garnered immediate and enormous success, became the Gothic period's best-known tale of the double, striking a dark chord in the public's imagination that rings to this day. This literary success in Victorian England was soon doubled when its stage production was thrilling American audiences in 1887; and with the emergence of man's new cinematic story teller at the end of the century, a dozen or so movie versions were made before 1920. Curiously enough, perhaps because one tale of the Other was ancient (and rather scholarly) and the other contemporary and available to the public (for one shilling), the coming years saw more movies adapted from *Dr. Jekyll and Mr. Hyde* than any other literary tale, while to this day no cinematic feature has been made of *Gilgamesh*.

Notwithstanding this disproportion, nor the five millenniums between them, there are many parallels and similarities between these two tales of the Other. For one, both begin with the same repression that engenders the Other. Gilgamesh's *oppressing* the citizens of Uruk not only parallels the *repressive* Victorian London in which the tale takes place, in Jekyll's "Full Statement of the Case," the last will and testament segment which closes the tale, the city of Uruk is invoked when Jekyll refers to himself as a "city of refuge" for Mr. Hyde. Like the city wall that Gilgamesh and Enkidu partly break down in their first struggle, the transforming drug, as Jekyll wrote, shook "the very fortress of identity." In one tale the walled city mirrors the hero's psyche; in the other the psyche is depicted as a fortified city and as "the prisonhouse of my disposition."

Dr. Jekyll and Mr. Hyde, like *Gilgamesh,* even has its own phenomena of mirroring. Much as Enkidu first sees his transformation mirrored in the animals' reaction, the mirror, a common household fixture in the 19th century, comes into play throughout Stevenson's tale, as when Dr. Jekyll first sees his less upright twin reflected in a looking glass. "That night," he writes, "I looked upon that ugly idol in the glass." On another occasion, Poole, Jekyll's butler, whispers to Utterson, Jekyll's friend, that "'this glass has seen some strange things.'" Jekyll himself imagines that "whatever he had done, Edward Hyde would pass away like the stain of breath upon a mirror." Later, however, upon going to bed as Jekyll and waking up as Hyde, he writes, after "bounding from my bed I rushed to the mirror." And finally, having given up hope of ever returning to being Henry Jekyll, he writes toward the end of his "Full Statement of the Case," "This, then, is the last time, short of a miracle, that Henry Jekyll can think his own thoughts or see his own face (now how sadly altered!) in the glass." Of course, what he sees in the mirror is a creature of his unconscious, his Other.

All the same, however similar *Gilgamesh* and *Dr. Jekyll and Mr. Hyde* may be in giving expression to the unconscious creature, the two tales represent different approaches to the Other. In *Gilgamesh* two persons represent the opposite sides of the projector and his Other; in *Dr. Jekyll and Mr. Hyde* one person has two opposite sides, the Self and the Other. Enkidu is the projected Other of Gilgamesh's repressed unconscious; Mr. Hyde is the embodiment (or personification) of Dr. Jekyll's. Gilgamesh becomes more of a human being by virtue of his relationship with Enkidu; Jekyll becomes "tenfold more wicked" after separating his two opposite sides. One assimilates the Other; the other separates from him.

Along with its difference from *Gilgamesh*, Stevenson's approach to the Other also differs from the other Gothic tales of man's dual nature that preceded his tale, such as Mary Shelley's *Frankenstein* (1818), James Hogg's "Confessions of a Justified Sinner" (1824), and Edgar Allan Poe's "William Wilson" (1839). In all three stories, and as in the tales that followed *Dr. Jekyll and Mr. Hyde*, such as Oscar Wilde's *The Picture of Dorian Gray* (1890) and Joseph Conrad's "Heart of Darkness" (1902) and "The Secret Sharer" (1910), the Other is an autonomous personality, a shadowy figure who mirrors the hero's unconscious. Among these stories whose characters "embody and act out conflicting, subconscious psychic energies,"[12] Stevenson's strange case is the only one in which the two sides of the protagonist share the same body. Rather than remain "committed to a profound duplicity of life" and reconciling the two sides in himself, Jekyll wants the Hyde and the Jekyll too — but as two separate beings. Only the two sides are not as symmetrical or controllable as he imagines. Like the return of the repressed, each time Hyde returns it's with more vigor and autonomy than the time before. Until he begins to take over at will.

This bitter truth about *the return of the repressed* Dr. Jekyll learns firsthand, years before the term was coined by Freud in explaining the workings of the repressed unconscious. As Jekyll writes about the repressed Other, when "the attempt is made to cast it off, it but returns upon us with more unfamiliar and more awful pressure." Unfortunately, in experiencing "that man is not truly one, but truly two," Jekyll learns that you can't have one without the other.

Projecting the Other

Dr. Jekyll and Mr. Hyde, it turned out, was not an exception merely among the Gothic tales of the double. With the advent of cinema at the end of the nineteenth century, the early movies made from Stevenson's novella also proved to be the exceptions among the later movies that dealt with the Other, most of which followed the *Gilgamesh* prototype. Being the exceptions, though, did not exclude the early cinematic adaptations of Stevenson's tale from demonstrating how the new movie medium was made to measure for projecting the unconscious Other. The moving pictures on the silver screen not only mirrored the unconscious images we project on our "mind screen" in dreams, the movie projector itself doubled for our unconscious mechanism of projecting our Other on others.

And yet, even with this uncanny ability to project the Other, many of the movies that adhere to the *Gilgamesh* prototype are not necessarily (or easily) perceived as movies of the Other. Where in the exception of *Dr. Jekyll and Mr. Hyde* the cinematic Other is in plain view and openly discussed, in the *Gilgamesh* prototypes it's suggested by the movie's symbolic subtext, which most of us overlook, especially at first viewing. This phenomenon, as Leo Braudy points out, is the other side of the medium.

> Because we have gotten so much from a film at first viewing, we often balk at any insistence that the understanding of certain canons, methods, and tradition will help us understand more. But we resist especially because films seem so real and therefore so self-sufficient, without need of any critical interloper to explain them to us.[13]

In a way, our tendency to balk or resist understanding what movies harbor is not unlike our denying our projected Other. Much as we're blind to our unconscious projections on others, we generally overlook these movies' "other" stories, the symbolic subtext of the projector and his unconscious Other. But when we do look for this underlying subtext, when we approach it as the protagonist's unconscious story, the movie takes on a whole new meaning. It literally becomes an "other" movie, a movie of the protagonist and how, by dealing with his nemesis in the outer world, he comes to terms with his inner (unconscious) Other.

Of course, it almost goes without saying that when looking for the unconscious Other in movies we can hardly overlook psychoanalysis, which "reveals the role of the other as a psychic projection of the self."[14] In fact, as if fated for each other from the beginning, cinema and psychoanalysis were launched the same year, in 1895. Cinema began with the Lumiere Brothers' first public showing of the short (one shot) movie of a train arriving at the Ciotat Station; psychoanalysis commenced with Sigmund Freud's and Josef Breuer's publication of "Studies on Hysteria," in which the two made public their discovery of the unconscious, the central psychoanalytic concept that inaugurated psychoanalysis.

Seemingly inseparable like the projector and his Other, cinema and psychoanalysis had an ongoing dialogue. On the one hand, as Sharon Packer notes in *Movies and the Modern Psyche*,

Because film reached wider audiences than the written word, it introduced far more people to Freudianism than serious literature"; [On the other hand,] "cinema would not be the same had it not surfaced at the same time as Freudian psychoanalysis. For cinema absorbed Freudian influences like a sponge.[15]

An early appreciation of the kinship between Freudian psychoanalysis and cinema and how it gave expression to the Other was put forward by the Austrian psychoanalyst Otto Rank in his 1914 book, *The Double: A Psychological Study*. Rank, one of Freud's closest colleagues, saw cinema's similarity to the dream-work and its uncanny ability "in visibly portraying psychological events." Rank's seminal book proposes to introduce the double as it appears in literature and anthropology. And yet, as if mesmerized by cinema's "conspicuous imagery" of the double, he begins his psychological study with Stellan Rye's 1913 movie, *The Student of Prague*. "It may perhaps turn out," he writes, "that cinematography, which in numerous ways reminds us of the dream-work, can also express certain psychological facts and relationships ... in such clear and conspicuous imagery that it facilitates our understanding of them."[16] Later, in his closing words to his analysis of Rye's silent movie, Rank reiterates cinema's unique ability to mirror the psyche: "The uniqueness of cinematography in visibly portraying psychological events calls our attention, with exaggerated clarity, to the fact that the interesting and meaningful problems of man's relation to himself—and the fateful disturbance of this relation—finds here an imaginative representation."[17]

However *The Student of Prague* serves Rank as an illuminating "point of departure" for dealing with the double, there's probably no better proof of cinema's "imaginative representation" and our fascination with the unconscious Other than the number of movies inspired by *Dr. Jekyll and Mr. Hyde*. As the makers of these early cinematic adaptations understood all too well, man's dual nature, and the Mr. Hyde more than the Dr. Jekyll, got people to see movies. As Braudy points out in his brief history of "film doubles,"

> Although German films are the first to exploit the double explicitly, its presence in later films shows the attraction it had for filmmakers of all sorts, because it could express something of the special nature of film form.... Film doubles became even more popular in the 1940s, when World War Two created a cultural situation in which almost everyone found themselves leading several lives.... One of the most powerful expressions of the double theme in this period is Alfred Hitchcock's *Shadow of a Doubt* (1943).[18]

With this brief history of the cinematic double in mind, the present work begins exploring how movies envision the unconscious Other with *Shadow of a Doubt*; that is, after Rouben Mamoulian's *Dr. Jekyll and Mr. Hyde* (1931), which functions as a "prelude" to illustrate the exception that proves the *Gilgamesh* prototype. Together with David Fincher's *Fight Club*, Mamoulian's movie is also the exception in that it directly addresses the two selves. The other examined movies, all typifying the *Gilgamesh* prototype, address the Other indirectly, through their visual metaphors and various tropes of binary opposites. On the whole, from first film to last, *The Shadow Self in Film* aims to show how cinema, like no other medium, envisions the unconscious Other we all too often project on others.

1

Dr. Jekyll and Mr. Hyde: Envisioning the Other

> *You're a nuisance. But I don't know what I should do without you.*
> — Dr. Henry Jekyll to Poole

Expovisioning the Other

Rouben Mamoulian's *Dr. Jekyll and Mr. Hyde*, which is "widely regarded as the pre-eminent film adaptation of Robert Louis Stevenson's novella,"[1] may well be the first fully developed movie of the Other. The 1931 film both presents and represents a definitive and clear-cut portrayal of man's dual nature, envisioning the projector and his Other through many of the trappings and tropes of binary opposites employed by subsequent movies of the Other, metaphoric devices such as doubles, pairs, twos, symmetric mise-en-scenes, and reflecting mirrors. The way these devices come into play in *Dr. Jekyll and Mr. Hyde*, the way they envision the Other, is best illustrated by what may be called the movie's *expovision*, the "elliptically swift, scene-setting opening which was to become almost a Mamoulian trade-mark."[2]

Beginning where Stevenson's story ended with Jekyll's personal "Full Statement of the Case," Mamoulian's *Dr. Jekyll and Mr. Hyde* opens with a subjective camera descending in one continuous motion, passing over vertical organ pipes until coming to briefly rest on the player's shadow projected on two pages of the musical score played by the shadow's owner, whose playing of Bach's "Toccata and Fugue in D Minor" doubles for the fugue's orchestrated rendition over the movie's titles. The camera continues its descent, coming to rest on the pianist's hands playing the black and white keys of the organ's three keyboards. While the hands and the black and white keys clearly envision man's two sides, the doubly "addressed" subject matter of the movie, the three keyboard levels may well allude to Freud's three levels of the personality (upper superego, lower Id, and the ego mediating between the two), particularly when bearing in mind the movie's Freudian subtext.

The *three* is underscored when, upon hearing several knocks on the door, the player-camera cuts to the butler, Poole (Edgar Norton), who comes in to remind his master of his scheduled address "at three." In fact, as fits the *expovision*'s numerous twos and threes, Poole *twice* mentions the *three* in the movie's first line: "It's a quarter to three, sir, and your address at the university is at three." Likewise, the two sides are suggested by the unnamed Jekyll (Fredric March) speaking to Poole in two voices. "You know, Poole? You're a nuisance. But I don't know what I should do without you." When Poole reminds him he'll be late, Jekyll, whose shadow is once again shown projected on the double-paged musical score, projects his shadowy Other upon his butler when he says, "I see you want to get rid of me." But as revealed by his subsequent address, it is Jekyll himself who wants "to get rid of" the other side of his dual personality, or at least separate the one from the other. Presently, the two sides are represented by the master and his butler. One is playful; the other dutiful.

As Jekyll rises from his chair to the call of duty, the subjective camera, reversing its opening descent, ascends from the "shadowed" musical score to the organ pipes. In one rather long continuous shot, the final one of this *expovision*, Jekyll follows Poole, all the while revealing the various compositions of pairs and symmetric mise-en-scenes that envision man's two sides. The most obvious of these pairs are the two geometric patterns that dominate the floors of the two spacious rooms. These two patterns, one octagonal, the other round, each consisting of three "rings," once again envision both the *two* sides of man and the *three* Freudian functions. Underscoring the two sides, Poole asks, "Will you wear your overcoat or cape, sir?"

"Give me the cape," Jekyll replies, choosing the same outer attire he wears when transformed into Mr. Hyde.

Still in the same shot, the player-camera stops before a framed mirror, in which we get a glimpse of the person through whose eyes we experience the whole subjective opening. The way he looks at his reflection transforming before his eyes (while he's dressed by Poole), never looking away, seems to foreshadow his transformation into Hyde. When shown in the mirror without the outer attire, he stands straight and upright in his upstanding best; when last shown, attired in cape and top hat, clutching a pair of gloves in one hand, a cane in the other, he is off balance and full of urgency, staring intently into his glaring eyes.

At the very end of this rather long subjective shot, after Dr. Jekyll exits the house through the door opened for him by Poole and climbs into the waiting horse-drawn carriage, another carriage is parked in the street. Significantly, the horse of Jekyll's carriage is black; the other one is white. As a horse represents the sex drive, the two horses may well suggest that Jekyll, who desires to marry his fiancée as soon as possible, is driven to separate his two sides by his repressed sex drive. Dressed in his upright best for his address, the sexually repressed Jekyll must surely feel that he's putting the cart before the horse. Or, as Tom Milne describes this opening in his book on Mamoulian, that he puts the Jekyll before the Hyde.

> At the outset, Jekyll's behaviour, the music, his inconsequential banter with Poole, are a paean of joy of a man in love; but from the moment he is glimpsed in the mirror, the celebrated Dr. Jekyll arrayed for the public eye, the mood changes, constables and doormen bow obeisance, and the soundtrack rings with obsequious phrases, "Good afternoon, Sir," "Yes, Sir," "How do you do, Sir." In effect, what we are watching here is the first transformation scene: not of Jekyll into Hyde, but of Hyde — the man of passion — into Jekyll.[3]

Dr. Jekyll

In what may be called *Dr. Jekyll and Mr. Hyde*'s "other exposition," the public one (particularly as the *expovision* was excised in the movie's re-release shortly after it came out, only to be restored some 40 years later, in the early seventies), both the twos and threes and the subjective camera continue to envision the projector and his Other as Dr. Jekyll arrives at St. Simon to give his address. Dismounting from the carriage, the yet-to-be named speaker encounters three young students who bow to him, the one in the middle greeting him by his name. "How do you do, Dr. Jekyll?" To which the doctor echoes, "How do you do?" In this doubling of the public for the private, as Jekyll moves toward the lecture hall, greeting the doorman by name and tossing to him his cape and top hat and handing over his cane, the doorman doubles for Poole. One opens the front door to the outside; the other opens the back (stage) door to the inside, to where Dr. Jekyll is to give his public address about the twofold soul of man, which was "merely" envisioned in the *expovision*.

The three Freudian levels are envisioned as, still in the same subjective shot, Jekyll walks from the back of the stage toward the speaker's symmetric lectern, setting his sight on three groups of threes in the first three rows, each trio conversing amongst themselves, apparently about the speaker himself. Likewise, man's two sides are envisioned as the camera cuts to a pair of students with similar wavy hair, one light, the other dark, exchanging views on the man about to speak. "I hope Jekyll's in form today," the dark-haired student remarks. "He's always in form," retorts the light-haired one, the same one who greeted Jekyll upon his arrival. "The old codgers are in for another jolt."

The "old codgers," shown in a second "pair" shot, double for the first pair. Where the two students had different-colored hair but the same-colored suits, the two "old codgers" have the same-colored hair but different-colored suits. One of the two is Dr. Lanyon (Holmes Herbert), who doubles for the light-haired student just as the unnamed professor doubles for the other student. Where one hopes Jekyll is "in form today," the other "hope[s] your friend has something up his sleeve again, Dr. Lanyon." Lanyon himself doubles his double's "always" by stating, "Jekyll is always sensational, always indulging in spectacular theories."

No sooner does Lanyon finish his words than Jekyll's voice is heard, as if addressing the two gentlemen still shown in the front row. Rhyming with the twos and threes, Jekyll's address about the two opposing selves that "carry on an eternal struggle in the nature of man" is envisioned in three pairs of shots, each one mirroring his spoken words.

(1a) The first shot shows Jekyll from the audience's point of view (from low angle), between two men in the audience, standing at the lectern between a pair of marble columns and two framed pictures of human skeletons at his back. "London is so full of fog," he begins his address, "that it has penetrated our minds, set boundaries for our vision. As men of science, we should be curious and bold enough to peer beyond it, into the many wonders it conceals." (1b) The second shot, doubling for the first one, shows Jekyll (from high angle) between another pair of men sitting in the upper seats, standing onstage between twin pairs of marble columns. "I shall not dwell today on the secrets of the human body in sickness and in health," he continues. "Today, I want to talk to you of a greater marvel—" the camera cuts to the third shot in mid–sentence.

(2a) The third shot, which again shows Jekyll from low angle (this time from much closer and by himself), envisions him as a pompous and mad scientist, obsessed with "the soul of man." As he addresses his audience, "My analysis of this soul, the human psyche, leaves me to believe man is not truly one, but truly two," he raises two fingers for emphasis. (2b) The fourth shot shows him from backstage, addressing the visible audience below him on mankind's two sides. Mixing the aural and the visual, the camera and Jekyll turn to the left side of the audience as he says, "One of him strives for the nobility. This we call his good self." Then, turning to face the other side of the audience, he speaks of "the other self," the side "we may call the bad."

(3a) The fifth shot, identical to the first, shows Jekyll once again between the two men in the foreground as he continues addressing man's two selves: "These two carry on an eternal struggle in the nature of man, yet they are chained together and that chain spells repression to the evil, remorse to the good." (3b) The sixth and final shot, which shows only Jekyll's face, doubles for the third shot, its low angle once again portraying Jekyll as a "lunatic." "Now, if these two selves could be separated from each other, how much freer the good in us would be. What heights it might scale, and the so-called evil, once liberated, would fulfill itself and trouble us no more. I believe the day is not far off when this separation will be possible."

While Jekyll continues to talk of his experiments, in which he has "found that certain chemicals have the power," the close-up of the mad scientist dissolves to a shot of the audience filing out of the lecture hall in pairs. Shown in two shots, pair after pair exchange views about what they just heard, "pairing" such phrases as "split me in two" with "divide a human being in two," and "other self" with "psyche." The segment ends as it had begun, with twos and threes, as the last-shown pair, Jekyll and Lanyon, are followed by a trio of students, apparently the last to leave.

As Jekyll declared in his address, it's "repression" that engenders the split between the two selves. And as he proclaims to Lanyon afterward, just before his upright friend reminds him of their scheduled dinner at the Carews that evening, "It's the things one can't do that always tempt me." One thing he "can't do," as he finds out at the Carews, is marry Muriel (Rose Hobart) in the immediate future. At the same time, the other thing he's afraid he can't do is to "come back soon" to Ivy (Miriam Hopkins). As she tempts him immediately after his tryst with Muriel, his other side rears its head, with no repression holding him back.

This split between what he can and can't do is given voice in the dispute he has with Lanyon after Jekyll's first encounter with Ivy, while her swinging gartered leg is superimposed on the screen as if to imply that he can't get the image out of his mind.

"I thought your conduct quite disgusting, Jekyll," Lanyon censures him for his behavior with Ivy.

"That's not a matter of conduct but of elementary instincts," Jekyll replies.

"You ought to control those instincts," Lanyon advises his friend. "You sound almost indecent."

"What names you give things," Jekyll shoots back, all but naming his other side. "Why aren't you frank enough to admit that indecent self in you? No, you prefer to hide it."

Mr. Hyde

The segment in which Jekyll first takes the potion that transforms him into Hyde, which doubles for the movie's *expovision* in Jekyll's living quarters, takes place in his laboratory, the *other* side of his home. Then he was shown playing the organ and playfully projecting his Other on Poole; now he's pictured (amidst a bubbling chemistry setup of glass tubes, test tubes, and bottles) as a mad scientist, the same "mad man" Dr. Lanyon called him just before the previous scene ended, when he talked about man's "other self" and his efforts to "separate the two natures in us." Still in the same shot, the camera pans to the right, showing Dr. Jekyll from some distance as it moves towards him, coming to a stop at a mid–close-up before cutting to a close-up of his face. In both shots his upper body is framed by an arching glass tube, which envisions him doubly ensnared, both captive and captivated by his desire to scientifically separate his two sides. Where he was initially shown *playing* the Bach Toccata on the *pipe* organ (art), now he's shown objectively, smoking a pipe and *playing* with various bottles and test *tubes* (science), mixing the potion that will turn him to his Other.

Jekyll's mixing the medicine is interrupted once again by a knock on the door, to which he replies his usual, "Come in." Whereas in the *expovision* Poole reminded Jekyll he was a guest speaker at the university at three, a public obligation, now, after reminding him that he hasn't eaten for three days, he hands him a two-fold scald-invitation from Muriel "for having missed dinner last night," to which Jekyll responds with a message of his own. Once Poole leaves with the message, Jekyll, after writing a parting note to his fiancée, raises his glass before the mirror. Cutting once again to a subjective shot and focusing on his reflection in the mirror, he drinks the concocted potion. When he next sees his reflection, he sees the transformed but unnamed Hyde, whom he names only when, upon being disturbed by Poole a second time, he soon comes to the door as the restored Jekyll, explaining that the "strange voice" his butler had heard was "Hyde, Mr. Hyde," which echoes his first repeated words as Hyde before the mirror: "Free! Free at last!"

Just as Jekyll was initially driven to take the potion as a result of two conflicting influences on his "instincts," sexual frustration with Muriel and sexual excitement with Ivy, he takes it a second time after receiving a second letter from Muriel (who was taken "away" by her father), announcing that her return is delayed for another month, and after Poole suggests that he "ought to amuse" himself. Being a gentleman, however, he "daren't take advantage" of such amusements. But his other self does. Once transformed a second time into Hyde, and with no repression holding back his horses, he immediately goes out in search of the sexually promiscuous Ivy.

Curiously enough, Hyde's seeking out Ivy brings to mind the transformation of Enkidu, but in reverse. Where in *Gilgamesh* the animal-like Enkidu is civilized by a prostitute, forever separating him from the animals and his animal nature, in Mamoulian's movie Jekyll's transformation into the ape-like Hyde comes after he's sexually aroused by the prostitute. Saying much the same, Milne notes, "What interested him [Mamoulian] in Stevenson's story was not so much the conflict between Good and Evil, but between Nature and Civilization."[4] Or as Jekyll foreshadows in his address, "The other self seeks an expression of impulses that binds him to some dim animal relation with the earth."

Dr. Freud and Mr. Oedipus

Besides dealing with man's two sides, Mamoulian's *Dr. Jekyll and Mr. Hyde*, made at a time when Freud's sexual theories were fascinating the American public, mixes cinema and Freudian psychology. In Mamoulian's capable hands, Stevenson's story becomes *Herr Doktor*'s Oedipal drama in which the Other functions as a Victorian Oedipus who carries out Dr. Jekyll's unconscious desires. The Oedipal triad itself, made up of Jekyll, Muriel, and General Carew (Halliwell Hobbes), is initially suggested even before the three are first shown together, when Dr. Jekyll, detained at the hospital, asks Lanyon to "make my excuses to the General and Muriel"; but on second thought, giving expression to his desire to have Muriel for himself, he says, "You make my excuses to the General and I'll make mine to Muriel myself."

That Muriel is the maternal figure in this Oedipal triad is implied by introducing her as one who "must have almond cakes" for her fiancé. Only Jekyll, impatient to marry her, wants more than oral gratification. But Muriel's father, the triad's figure of authority, denies Jekyll this pleasure by rejecting his request to set an earlier date for their wedding. "I waited five years for your mother," he reminds his daughter, giving expression to his displeasure of her mothering Jekyll. "You know you'll spoil that fiancé of yours." When Muriel retorts, "I like spoiling him," he asks, "And what about your father?"

In this Oedipal drama the father-son conflict is introduced when Jekyll arrives late for dinner, as the General, who's never late, redresses him for his tardiness: "Oh, merely a matter of training, my boy." In contrast to the always-late Jekyll, Lanyon, the good son to Jekyll's bad one, is always on time. "Punctual for dinner," the General commends him at the first dinner. "Punctual in everything." Seeing her father's delight in Lanyon's punctuality, Muriel, who naturally favors Jekyll, cynically "commends" him on a second occasion, exclaiming "Oh, we're early." This other father-son relationship between General Carew and Lanyon explains why, upon seeing his other self in the mirror upon his first transformation into Hyde, Jekyll addresses the two: "Mad, Lanyon? Carew? You hypocrites, deniers of life. If you could see me now, what would you think?"

In another of his attempts to come between Jekyll and his daughter, the father sends Lanyon, his errand boy, to Jekyll's home bearing "a letter from General Carew." Delivered between Hyde's first two scenes with Ivy, this paternal obstacle underscores why in this Oedipal drama Jekyll needs Hyde to satisfy his desire for the mother. While Muriel, the drama's "conscious mother," speaks to Jekyll of love, Ivy, the "unconscious mother," speaks to Hyde (in the tavern) in double entendres. By their second encounter (in Ivy's apartment), however, more than anything else, more than sexual gratification, Hyde, the unconscious son, wants to be loved by the unconscious mother. "Come here," he orders Ivy after reading the newspaper announcement of the General and Muriel's return, trying to convince himself that she loves him. "If you don't hate me, you must love me. Isn't that so, my little one? Isn't it?"

Only Hyde is not convinced. Wanting to hear it from the source's mouth, he forces Ivy to say she loves him, as if saying the words makes it so. When she reluctantly agrees but cannot utter the actual three words, he says it for her, pressing his face to her breast, more as a child to a mother than a paramour to his mistress. "Remember, you belong to me, do you hear? You belong to me," he reminds her.

Much as the unconscious seeks to become conscious through double entendres and Freudian slips, both Jekyll and Hyde seek to reveal their other selves through Ivy's garter, the last thing Jekyll sees before him, swinging enticingly on her leg, when first changing into Hyde. The garter, suggesting both repression and sexual excitement, mirrors the opposite sides of Dr. Jekyll and Mr. Hyde, particularly as each of the three references to the garter, one from Jekyll, two from Hyde, are Freudian slips.

The first reference ("By the way, you mustn't wear so tight a garter.... It impedes the circulation.") is Jekyll's unconscious reference to the "other self" impeded by social conventions represented by the father. The other two refererences, laden with sexual innuendos, point to Hyde's seeking to reveal that he's Jekyll, much as the unconscious seeks to become conscious. "Perhaps you prefer a gentleman?" Hyde taunts Ivy. "One of those fine-mannered, virtuous, and honorable gentlemen. One of those canting hypocrites who like your legs but talk about your garter." Mamoulian underscores the double meaning by having Ivy shoot back, "What are talking about?" and by Hyde's letting her *know* what he is "talking about" by once again echoing Jekyll's Freudian slip when gazing at her bare leg, "Look, my darling, how tight your garter is. You mustn't wear it so tight."

With the conscious mother's return, Jekyll, after spending his "last night" with the unconscious mother, decides to finish with the unconscious Hyde. As he informs Poole about the key to the back door used by Hyde, hurling it against the wall, "I have no further use for it. From now on, I'll use only the front door." But despite his resolution, the two sides of the mother remain, as envisioned by the diagonal wipe's split screen of Ivy (after receiving from Poole the payoff from Dr. Jekyll) and of Muriel with the payer himself. Both "mothers," each in her own way, speak to Jekyll of love.

In the scene with Muriel, when Jekyll confesses to his mother-confessor ("I've played with dangerous knowledge. I've walked a strange and terrible road. Help me to find my way back."), she speaks like Mother Earth, saying the words Hyde wanted to hear from Ivy. "When you're all mine to love and keep, I shall be patient as the earth with you." Significantly, at his daughter's behest, Muriel's father agrees to an earlier wedding only after Jekyll decides to renounce both Hyde and Ivy. The ecstatic Jekyll, declaring, "If music be the food of love, play on," plays the same Bach fugue he played in the *expovision*, its orgiastic celebration anticipating what marriage will mean for his manhood. Only unlike the first playing in which he played all three levels of the keyboards, now he only plays the middle one, the one that represents the ego which mediates between the lower Id and the upper superego.

In Jekyll's parallel scene with Ivy, like the return of the repressed, she comes to thank him for the 50 pounds he had sent her as part of his contrition for her mistreatment at the hands of his other self. As suggested by the symmetric shot that shows her approaching Jekyll, her recognizing him from their first encounter, "Why, it's you, sir," may well address his other side, whom she saw last. "So it is," Jekyll owns up, as if finally saying outright what he let slip, as Hyde, through his reference to the garter. Ivy underscores Jekyll's other self when addressing him in another symmetric shot, "Who'd have thought that I'd find the celebrated Dr. Jekyll?" inadvertently (unconsciously) reminding him of their first encounter when baring her back to him to show what his other self had done to her. Promising "I'll love you," what she could not bring herself to say to Hyde, she reminds him, "You liked me once, didn't you?" But all Jekyll can do is assure her, "I give you my word, you will never be troubled by Hyde again.... You'll never see Hyde again, believe me."

"I believe you, sir. I believe you." Ivy leaves a believer in another symmetric shot that doubles her entrance and mirrors Jekyll's two sides.

Jekyll may claim that he "never breaks" his word, but with Hyde now having a mind of his "own accord," instead of going to dinner at the Carews, where his marriage to Muriel is to be "formally announced," he goes to Ivy as Hyde, thus breaking his word at the very first chance. Ivy, shown in her room before Hyde arrives, raises a toast before the mirror: "Here's hoping that Hyde rots wherever he is.... And here's hoping that Doctor Jekyll will think of Ivy once in a while." But just as she finishes her toast, Hyde is shown behind her, reflected in the mirror. He has come to "share" with her "a secret so great that those who share it with me cannot live." "I am Jekyll!" he announces before strangling her while speaking words of love. "There, my dove. There, my little bride. Isn't Hyde a lover after your heart?"

On his return home, unable to enter through the front door as "a friend of Dr. Jekyll's," Hyde leaves a message to Lanyon, relaying his "mortal distress," which doubles for Lanyon's earlier message to Jekyll relaying the General's concern. Revealing more than he consciously intends, Hyde inadvertently sends an unconscious message within his message that begs Lanyon to bring the chemicals he needs to transform himself back into Jekyll. His written instructions, shown in a lingering close-up, "Hasten to my laboratory and there from a cabinet marked E, take the phials listed below and bring them to your home," are clear enough. But when taken together with the "phials marked A, H, S, T, R, M," which appear at the bottom of the paper, the message's capital letters, when rearranged, spell MATHERS, as if alluding to the two mothers in the Oedipal drama.

Reinforcing this notion of the mother, when Hyde comes to Lanyon for the phials ("for Doctor Jekyll"), the paintings on his study wall draw a picture of the Oedipal triad. In the first of the scene's three symmetrical shots, three paintings of paternal figures are shown hanging on the wall as Hyde confronts Lanyon, demanding the phials. In the second shot, when Lanyon draws a gun on the unrelenting Hyde, warning him, "If you take another step towards that door, I'll shoot you," above him hangs a portrait of Queen Victoria, which seems to envision Hyde confronting the royal mother and the threatening father. In the third shot, shown after Lanyon witnesses Hyde changing into Jekyll, the portrait of the queen comes between the two, picturing what comes between father and son. Significantly, in all three symmetrical shots the two friends are divided by a table, on which burns a phallic candle.

Now, with the tables turned, the paternal Lanyon, sitting behind a raised table like a judge in a courtroom, redresses the guilt-ridden Jekyll much as the arrogant Jekyll had addressed Lanyon in his address: "There is no help for you Jekyll.... You are in the power of this monster that you've created." To these words Jekyll can only plead, "Don't judge me." Having revealed to Lanyon his monstrous crime against the unconscious mother, the guilt-ridden Jekyll abandons his Oedipal desire for the conscious mother, as must every boy. And he's determined to tell her so himself.

While in Muriel's first appearance she wanted "almond cakes" for her fiancé, in her last appearance, recalling Jekyll's quotation, "If music be the food of love," she plays the piano, which clearly agitates her father as he reads a newspaper on the other side of the room. This symmetric (but less-than-harmonious) picture is interrupted by the butler's announcing, "Doctor Jekyll is calling." True to form, the General will "have nothing to do with it!" But

Muriel finally stands up to her father: "Neither of us have the right to judge him. You tried to bend him to your will." She ends the matter by instructing the butler to "show him in."

But rather than seal their love, the self-judging Jekyll, like the guilt-ridden Oedipus who tore out his eyes after realizing his crime, has come to inform the stunned Muriel, "I must give you up." Underscoring her role in the Oedipal drama, Muriel tries to calm the distressed Jekyll by caressing and holding him in her arms like a mother holding a baby, rocking him to sleep. But Jekyll cannot dismiss his other half and the crime he has committed against the unconscious mother. "I give you up because I love you," he declares before Muriel, adding twice, as if for both his sides, "This is my penance."

A man of his word, Jekyll departs. But just as the son doesn't give up his desire for the mother so easily (if ever), his other half doesn't give up Muriel. Shown outside the house looking in, he gazes through a window at Muriel slumped over the piano keys, weeping miserably, which moves him to tears. To his horror, it also moves the Hyde in him, who silently opens the side door, sneaking up on the weeping Muriel from behind, embracing her as if still Jekyll. Thinking it's her fiancé who's returned despite himself, which indeed he has, Muriel starts with "My dar—." But as she turns around, she's horrified to see Hyde's face, now more horrifying than ever. "Father! Father!" she screams wildly, as Hyde assaults her.

In the ensuing scuffle, Hyde, the unconscious son, slays the father, using his cane as Oedipus used his sword, after which he's shown escaping through the streets and entering Jekyll's home through the front door. Once inside, he desperately mixes the chemicals to change him back into Jekyll as the camera cuts to the scene of the crime, showing Lanyon kneeling over General Carew's dead body, recognizing Jekyll's broken cane, the same cane Jekyll "sticks" through Ivy's discarded garter, thus connecting his "patricide" with the unconscious mother. "I know whose cane it is," he informs the police. "I can take you to the man."

Much as Oedipus's true identity was revealed to him after killing his father, Jekyll now transforms into the guilty Hyde before all who have followed him home: Poole, Lanyon, and the police. With the police inspector shooting the ape-like Hyde, he turns back into Jekyll, moving Poole, his seemingly impervious Rock of Gibraltar, to weep uncontrollably for the dead "Dr. Jekyll," at peace at last with his other self, the shadowy Mr. Hyde.

2

Shadow of a Doubt:
The Other by Numbers

> *"Oh, are you—?" Young Charlie hesitates when greeting her uncle at the train station.*
> *"Charlie," Uncle Charlie allays her doubt, though it's not clear who he means.*

Hide and Seek

In an overview of "most of his forties films," Thomas Leitch notes in *Find the Director and Other Hitchcock Games*, "each of Hitchcock's heroes and heroines during this period ends by defining himself or herself in terms of an enigmatic Other, a shadow-self which can never, even after the final revelation, restore the initial sense of security the films had worked to undermine. This pattern is clearest in *Shadow of a Doubt*."[1]

Though never stated explicitly as in Mamoulian's *Dr. Jekyll and Mr. Hyde*, Alfred Hitchcock's *Shadow of a Doubt* is indeed about the "enigmatic Other," about Young Charlie (Teresa Wright) and her shadowy double, Uncle Charlie (Joseph Cotton). Except for the two Charlies being of opposite genders, the 1943 movie adheres to the *Gilgamesh* prototype in which two autonomous persons embody the projector and his Other. This curious digression from the prototype, from the "rule" of Jung's shadow, may well suggest that the shadow in *Shadow of a Doubt* is a red herring, the movie's "real" McGuffin, what Hitchcock called the throwaway device of no real consequence to the movie's subtext. After all, much more than sharing their names, the two Charlies are mirrored doubles in their shared desire to replace the father and "twins," as Young Charlie calls the two, in their illicit desire for one another. This doubled Oedipal desire is the movie's real shadowy double.

Just as he used the device of the double to deal with *Shadow of a Doubt*'s Oedipal subtext, Hitchcock, as countless articles and books point out, kept returning to the unconscious Oedipal drama in his later movies. One book, Paul Gordon's aptly titled *Dial "M" for Mother*, subtitled *A Freudian Hitchcock*, even confines its analysis to Hitchcock's string of films that, starting "with *Shadow of a Doubt* and ending with *Frenzy* [1970], involve characters, both male and female, who are caught up in the impossible desire to recover the 'mother' as the first love object."[2]

In *Shadow of a Doubt*, the "impossible desire" is perhaps best envisioned by the shot of Uncle Charlie reclining in Young Charlie's bed, blowing a ring of smoke from his cigar. This smoky "nightcap," which wraps up his first day at the Newton's home, is an unconscious smoke signal, revealing the real Charlie he tries to hide. The ring of smoke, of course, recalls the ring he had given Young Charlie earlier that evening, an act brimming with incestuous connotations. More subtly perhaps, the ring of smoke also envisions, and alludes to, the more than a hundred verbal "Oh's" that crop up in the course of the movie, as if to say that one "O" is worth a hundred "Oh's." What's more, just as sometimes a cigar is *not* just a cigar, the "O" may not just be an "O," just as it wasn't 16 years later in *North by Northwest* (1959), when the woman who replaces the hero's mother inquires about the middle initial in his business card, "What does the 'O' stand for?"

Taken together with the round ring and the scores of "Oh's," the "O" Charlie Oakley orally forms from the smoke of his phallic cigar may well stand for Oedipus, particularly as the first syllable of "Emma," the name of both Hitchcock's and the Oedipal drama's mother, forms the letter "M," as in "'M' for Mother," not to mention the second syllable "ma." And if "M" is for Mother, why not, as in *North by Northwest*, "O" for Oedipus? It certainly fits Hitchcock's "notorious" playfulness, his playing hide-and-seek with the audience, challenging us to seek what he hides in plain sight. As Robin Wood sees it, a "double incest theme runs through the film: Uncle Charlie and Emmy, Uncle Charlie and Young Charlie. Necessarily, this is expressed through images and motifs, never becoming verbally explicit; certain of the images depend on a suppressed verbal play for their significance."[3]

One of *Shadow of a Doubt*'s recurring cases of "suppressed verbal play," no doubt, is "expressed through" its many verbal "Oh's." Hidden in the movie's dialogue in a variety of seemingly meaningless interjections, they don't draw attention and, consequently, are not easily "hitched" to the visible "O," let alone to Oedipus. But like the one visual "O" and the countless *twos* and *pairs* that Hitchcock planted in the movie, the deliberate and exorbitant number of verbal "Oh's" seems to suggest that the movie is a picture-by-numbers formed by penciling in the "Oh's." Farfetched as this notion may seem, it's the only one that explains Ann's (Young Charlie's younger sister) curious fascination with pencils and Roger's (her little brother) peculiar preoccupation with numbers. It's another one of his "Hitchcock Games," in which the playful director seems to say that in order to see the overall Oedipal picture, we only have to pencil in the dialogues' "Oh's."

Though not necessarily meaning the numerous "Oh's," in his book *Hitchcock—The Murderous Gaze*, William Rothman reinforces the notion when cautioning about the movie's dialogue: "Getting to know *Shadow of a Doubt* is partly a matter of coming to recognize how every line of dialogue is charged with multiple meanings and functions.... This film contains no line of dialogue that is merely conventional or 'ordinary.'"[4] So why not "Oh's" for Oedipus? The mere number of "Oh's" speaks for itself, or for *themselves*. Besides, as countless critics have shown, one should never underestimate the notoriously playful Master. Why else would he have Young Charlie greet Uncle Charlie upon his arrival at Santa Rosa with "Oh, are you—?" if not to have her greet him by his name just as he greets her by hers?

Hitchcock's hiding the "Oh's" in plain sound fits right in with what Gordon points out about *Shadow of a Doubt*: "Hitchcock can be most interesting from a psychoanalytic perspective when he is least explicit about it."[5] The picture formed by penciling in the "Oh's," together with the movie's other revealing family photographs, offers "a psychoanalytic perspective" of Uncle Charlie as Uncle Oedipus. For when closely examined, *Shadow*'s "least explicit" scores of "Oh's" reveal a deliberate and well-laid pattern, especially when linked to the movie's Oedipal drama. The more the two Charlies give expression to their Oedipal desires, the more "Oh's" are uttered.

There's only one "Oh" in the opening scene in Philadelphia, in which Uncle Charlie goes by the name of Spencer; in the parallel segment in Santa Rosa, in the home where the Oedipal drama unfolds, there are 13 "Oh's," which also happens to be the street address at which Uncle Charlie stays in Philadelphia. On the day he arrives at Santa Rosa, Thursday, which ends with the shot of his forming the "O" in Young Charlie's bed, there are 31 (13 mirrored) "Oh's." On Friday, the day the Oedipal desires are most apparent, which ends with Young Charlie discovering Uncle Charlie's other identity, no less than 40 "Oh's" come up. Following this peak, in the days that follow the "Oh's" are considerably diminished, just as Young Charlie distances herself from Uncle Charlie. On Saturday, there are merely nine "Oh's." On the next three days there are 13 "Oh's" altogether. The day Uncle Charles departs, Wednesday, after a seven-day stay, has no "Oh's," as fits the day in which Uncle Oedipus meets his death.

Penciling In the "Oh's"

Shadow of a Doubt's very first "Oh" comes up in its opening segment, which shows "Mr. Spencer" lying in bed stroking a suggestive cigar, as the boardinghouse's landlady interrupts his "rest" to inform him that two men are looking for him. Seeing the bills of money on the floor, she confides in him, "Oh, it makes me nervous to see money lying around. Everybody in the world isn't honest, you know." As the only "Oh" in this segment, it links "Mr. Spencer" to money, while also suggesting that he "is not honest." But, more significantly, considering it's said by the scene's maternal figure to a man who goes by his mother's maiden name, and that for Uncle Charlie money represents patriarchal authority, the landlady's words may be read as the mother confiding in the son, "Oedipus, it makes me nervous to see how you feel about your father."

In the mirrored segment at the Newtons' home in Santa Rosa, the first "Oh" comes as Ann (Edna May Wonacott) receives the phone call regarding Uncle Charlie's telegram: "Oh, hello, Mrs. Henderson. This is Ann. Mother isn't home yet." Perhaps intuiting what the message is about, just as she seems to sense that Uncle Charlie is "different" from how she remembers him, Ann doesn't take down the message on the pretext that she can't find a pencil, which doubles for Uncle Charlie's cigar.

Continuing with Ann's penchant for pencils, the subsequent two "Oh's" come up in the brief exchange between her and her father (Henry Travers), who returns home after another workday at the bank. "Oh. Then how about a kiss?" the father seems to console himself when Ann informs him that Mother (Patricia Collinge) is "out" and that she doesn't know what the telegram is about, adding "I would have taken it down, only I couldn't find a pencil." ("When I have a house," Ann later informs her mother, "it's going to be full of well-sharpened pencils.") The scene ends with another "Oh," the father's response to the bookish Ann's informing him she that she's reading *Ivanhoe*, cutting him down to size by saying, "Here I am, practically a child, and I wouldn't read the things you read." Like Ann's berating her father, the lack of a pencil, mentioned twice in this scene, draws a picture of the father's phallic authority, which the cigar-smoking Uncle Charlie usurps as soon as he enters the Newton home.

Where the downstairs scene has three "Oh's," in the one that transpires upstairs, underscoring its significance in the Oedipal drama, the number of "Oh's" is tripled. As this scene mirrors the one between Uncle Charlie and his landlady in Philadelphia, the tone and content of Young Charlie, who has "just been thinking for hours," seems to give voice to her uncle's thoughts, which were interrupted by the landlady's message just as her father interrupts hers. In effect, her talking about her mother ("She works like a dog, just like a dog.") seems to come straight from Uncle Charlie's mouth when he later talks about the "merry widows." Whereas downstairs Ann reprimands her father for what he reads, upstairs Young Charlie "throws the book" at him for how "this family's just gone to pieces," which recalls Uncle Charlie's throwing the glass against the sink, shattering it to pieces. This connection of the visual and the verbal is another sign of the two Charlies' shared antagonism toward the father.

As if guilty as charged, the father links himself with money when feebly trying to defend himself with three "Oh's." The first one: "Oh, come now, Charlie, things aren't as bad as that. The bank gave me a raise last January." To which Young Charlie counters, dismissing her father as the breadwinner of the family: "Money. How can you talk about money when I'm talking about souls?"

"Oh, now, Charlie, you're right," the father replies. "I'll figure out something." To his daughter's "Oh, I don't believe in good intentions anymore. All I'm waiting for now is a miracle," he has two words to his defense: "Oh, Charlie." Of course, being doubles, he can also mean the other Charlie, especially as he's the miracle Young Charlie is waiting for.

While Young Charlie feels "perfectly all right," she clearly has a score to settle with her father. When he mentions "work," for instance, she never considers that he's the one who works to support the family, literally making money. Rather, she takes pity on her mother, outwardly projecting on her what inside she feels about herself. When the mother herself comes to the doorway from the backstairs, like the father (and Uncle Charlie's landlady) before her, she asks "What's the matter, Charlie?" Only then, when the mother is present, does Young Charlie, not forgetting her "Oh," begin to talk directly about her self, about what really troubles her: "Oh, I've become a nagging old maid." She sits up in bed as the mother sits down by her feet, immediately proceeding to berate her mother when once again talking about herself.

The mother and father, overheard from Young Charlie's room as they walk downstairs, try to convince themselves (with one "Oh" apiece) that there's nothing wrong with their Charlie. "Oh, it's nothing. Charlie's a bit under the weather," the father says explaining her mood.

"Oh. Well, she'll be all right," the mother says dismissively, tucking it away. But as their "Oh's" seem to suggest, their daughter is "a bit under the" Oedipus complex, albeit in its feminine version, what Freud called the Electra complex. Unhappy with her father, Young Charlie fantasizes about his replacement, the dashing Uncle Charlie, the "miracle" who will "shake us all up," making her Oedipal dreams come true. As Gordon notes, "If young Charlie's bedroom scene suggests that she is stifled by desires which she is unable to direct outside the family, the same can be said of Uncle Charlie as he lies in bed, half-conscious and motionless except for the stroking of his cigar."[6]

After a dozen "Oh's," the last two of the Santa Rosa segment belong to the mother and daughter, the two love objects of Uncle Charlie, and to whom the telegram announcing his coming was sent. The mother's "Oh, nothing, Operator," whom she calls to connect her to Mrs. Henderson at the telegraph office, not only recalls Ann's words when she received the message about the telegram, it also repeats Young Charlie's words to her father's question what she's thinking of doing for her mother, "Oh, nothing, I suppose."

What Young Charlie thinks of doing, as shown next, is to send Uncle Charlie a telegram. Her correcting Mrs. Henderson at the telegraph office, "Oh, not telegraphy. Mental telepathy," wraps up what the two segments in Philadelphia and Santa Rosa have been about. As she explains to Mrs. Henderson, "It's all mental," the two mirrored bedroom scenes are indeed "all mental." Reflecting one another, they envision Young Charlie projecting her unconscious Other on Uncle Charlie. In his essay "All in the Family," James McLaughlin even suggests that "there is a sly hint that what Charlie and her uncle are thinking about while lying in bed is of the other in bed, i.e., of being with the other in bed."[7]

In the subsequent scene on the train that brings Uncle Charlie to Santa Rosa, there are no "Oh's" just as there are none when he leaves. However, this brief three-shot sequence does have an "O" in "Mr. Otis," which the porter calls Uncle Charlie behind the curtain. His "Mr. Otis? Mr. Otis?" not only rhymes with Young Charlie's words to herself that close the Santa Rosa segment ("He heard me. He heard me."), the "O" and the sound of the name may well suggest that the name under which Uncle Charlie is traveling is Otis for Oedipus, particularly as it follows his going by his mother's maiden name, also uttered twice by the maternal landlady. Moreover, just like the landlady and Young Charlie's father and mother, the porter asks Uncle Charlie, "How you feelin', Mr. Otis?"

Appearing in two shots in this brief train segment, Hitchcock diverges from his customary one-shot cameo appearances while keeping with the double motif that informs *Shadow of a Doubt*. Both shots, showing the back of his head, may well envision that he's showing us what's at the back of his mind. Particularly as the doctor sitting opposite him, against whom he's playing bridge, addresses him directly, linking him to the sick "Mr. Otis." Suggesting that he's no less sick than Uncle Charlie, or that the movie is his story, Hitchcock shows the doctor taking off his glasses for a closer look at the man before him, observing, "Well, you don't look very well either."

When Young Charlie meets Uncle Charlie at the train station, she makes a similar observation about his health. "I thought you were sick … You aren't sick, are you?" That Young Charlie's observation is right on the money is corroborated by Ann, whose glasses recall the doctor's on the train. Countering Uncle Charlie's "I bet you don't remember me," Ann says, "I remember you, sort of. You look different." Perhaps she recognizes him as the fictional character she's currently reading about (Count Dracula).

Where to Ann Uncle Charlie may be Dracula, to Young Charlie, as suggested by her two "Oh's" that begin and end his arrival at Santa Rosa ("Oh, are you —?" and "Oh, no. It's nothing."), he looks different because, mirroring her own desires, he's Uncle Oedipus. This notion is reinforced by the boy riding a bicycle in the background on the other side of the street, crossing the screen from left to right in the space that divides Emma and Uncle Charlie precisely when, seeing her, he calls out, "Emma, don't move. Standing there, you don't look like Emma Newton. You look like Emma Spencer Oakley of 46 Burnham Street, St. Paul, Minnesota, the prettiest girl on the block." The juxtaposition of the boy riding the bicycle with Uncle Charlie freeze-framing Emma as she was when he (apparently) had his traumatic bicycle accident after which he was never "the same," suggests that his visit is a *re*visit to the traumatic accident that's still etched in his psyche. As if linking the Newtons' home with the bicycle accident, not only is there another boy on a bicycle in the background, going the opposite direction, when the house is first shown from across the street (before showing Young Charlie in her bedroom), two boy cyclists cross the screen from opposite directions, doubling for the boys playing ball in the street outside Uncle Charlie's boardinghouse in Philadelphia. Tying it all together, Young Charlie's greeting Uncle Charlie at the train station is doubled by Emma when the two are singled out together. "Oh, Charles, it's so wonderful to have you here."

Once inside the Newtons' home, Uncle Charlie immediately goes against Joe's expressed warning by throwing his hat on the Young Charlie's bed ("It's bad luck.") right after he clips a rose bud from a vase and inserts it through the buttonhole of his lapel. The suggestive clipping itself is sandwiched between his seeing Young Charlie in the picture on the bureau, which receives a brief close-up, and his looking out the window at two older women, potential merry widows no doubt. While the picture of Young Charlie, in graduation gown with two other girls (in the front) and two boys in the back, mirrors the Newton family of three females and two males, "The widows Uncle Charlie seduces, marries, and then kills are all identifiable as 'mother surrogates'; not only are they significantly older than Charlie but also as widows they are in a sense still married to the father figure."[8]

That same evening, around the dinner table, Uncle Charlie literally takes Joe's place at the head of the table. "Oh, dear now," Joe mutters to himself the scene's first "Oh" when Uncle Charlie hands Ann and Roger his gifts, just before he receives his own gift like the other two children. His reaction to his gift, shown together with Ann's and Roger's silent reaction, "Say, I've never had a wristwatch," complements his putting it on like a child. "Fellows at the bank'll think I'm quite a sport," he talks as if it makes him look younger.

That Uncle Charlie has the mother in mind is underscored by his twice speaking directly to Emma, who is singled out in two solo shots. But even more so, he expresses his love for her through his two gifts, "One old and one new." Emma herself is all "Oh's," once again linking it to "Charles" when asking, "Oh, Charles. What is it?" Or when she exclaims, "Oh, Charles," upon seeing the "new" mink stole, which he probably *stole* from one of the widows. "Oh, how beautiful," she doubles the first two "Oh's" when taking it out of the package. "Oh, I've always wanted one," she says as she puts the stole around her shoulders.

Uncle Charlie's second gift to Emma, the twin pictures of their two parents that he has kept "all these years, safe in a deposit box, no matter where I was," suggests that he wants to get rid of the mental picture by giving it to his sister, who's shown against a background of two windows that mirror the twin pictures she's holding. Young Charlie, seeing it all with the same admiring eyes she had looked at the two when they met, chimes in, "Oh, mother, it's exactly right. It's what you should have." Then, when seeing the twin pictures, she asks, "Oh, Grandpa and Grandma?"

Next day, Uncle Charlie's second in Santa Rosa, the first bedroom shot not only doubles for the movie's opening bedroom shots, the sequence also repeats the scene of Young Charlie lying in her bed. Only now Uncle Charlie, in a double-breasted pajama top, has taken her place, just as Emma, entering the room with breakfast, replaces the father. That she functions as his mother is underscored by her mentioning that she had her "meals in bed after the children came," and by her "pampering" her brother, who first greets her, "Oh, coffee, Emmy," which rings like "Mommy."

Appropriately enough, in this key scene between the boy and his mother, the "Oh's" come in pairs. Following a rather long shot of the two sharing the bed and facing each other, when the camera cuts to Emma, she utters two "Oh's," followed by two more, while Charlie repeats his own "Oh," thus also making it two. In fact, his second "Oh" includes the number two ("Oh, there were two."), referring to the two survey men who, like him, are not what they appear to be. After that, as in two times two, Emma utters four additional "Oh's."

In this scene, with the symmetric head of the bed functioning as a pair of black wings, Uncle Charlie is repeatedly envisioned as a vampire, but only until Young Charlie comes into the room. However, he *speaks* like a member of the undead when objecting to being photographed by the survey men, saying, "I've never been photographed in my life and I don't want to be," inadvertently opening a Pandora's box that he forgot existed.

"Oh, Charles, how can you talk that way?" Emma corrects him. "I had a photograph of you. I gave it to Charlie."

"I tell you, there are none," he continues his denial. "I guess you've forgotten this one," Emma asks Young Charlie to bring the photograph. "You sure you don't remember?" Emma, playing a maternal therapist, asks her brother. But Uncle Charlie doesn't remember what he had repressed. "Of course I don't remember ever being photographed," he petulantly insists. In a close-up of the photograph, in which he's shown as a child, all he remembers is "46 Burnham Street," the very words he had said when first meeting Emma on the street. In the sequence's longest shot by far, Uncle Charlie and his two objects of desire are shown in a closer shot, admiring the picture and talking about the traumatic accident that forever changed his life. "It was taken the Christmas you got your bicycle," Emma reminds her brother. "Just before your accident." As she remembers it, after the accident their mother "wondered if he'd ever look the same. If he'd ever *be* the same."

Significantly, Emma's reminiscing about the pictured boy just before the accident comes after he had given her a picture of their parents when they were "beautiful." Bearing in mind that the father had given the boy the bicycle (for Christmas, when the streets are generally icy in St. Paul, Minnesota), the manly *handlebar* mustache he sports in the picture seems to suggest that he wanted to get rid of him much as King Laius wanted to get rid of his son. In fact, Emma all but accuses their father of this life-changing accident: "Papa never should have bought you that bicycle. You didn't know how to handle it." As Gordon sees it, "A fundamental change in Charlie's relationship with his mother did in fact occur about this time, for Charlie's later obsession with seducing and killing mother figures first manifested itself upon sexual maturation (symbolized by Charlie's first experience riding a bicycle!) as a powerful expression and equally powerful repression of his Oedipal desires."[9]

Other Pairs

Shadow of a Doubt's Oedipal drama doesn't only remain within the family home. It's also played out in the public arena, through such American institutions as the police and the bank, representing the father, and to a lesser extent, the library and the church, representing the mother. Highlighting this point, the police and the bank are paired in our very first glimpse of Santa Rosa, in two of the town's six establishing shots that show a policeman directing traffic with a big sign of Bank of America (on the roof of the bank) in the background, the same bank in which Joe Newton works. The policeman is singled out in the second shot's medium close-up, shot from below to emphasize his authority. Pairing the two, the bank is in the background in all the traffic directors' appearances, four in all, the same number of times the "Merry Widows" are shown waltzing.

The second pairing comes after the morning scene in the bedroom, when Uncle Charlie, accompanied by Young Charlie, walks to Joe's bank to deposit a handsome sum of $40,000. "Oh, Uncle Charlie, I love to walk with you," she once again links Uncle Charlie with Oedipus when they cross the street, after two of her girlfriends look at them as if they're a couple. "I want *everybody* to see you."

Once in the bank, Uncle Charlie, walking directly to Joe's window, immediately starts berating him, and once again, the numerous "Oh's" reveal his Oedipal problem: "Hello, Joe. Can you stop embezzling a minute and give me your attention?"

The embarrassed Joe, pencil in hand, responds in a lower tone,

"Oh, Charles, we don't joke about such things here." "Oh, what's a little shortage in the books at the end of the month?" Uncle Charlie shoots back.

Reacting to her uncle's unrelenting arrogance, Young Charlie remarks, "Oh, Charlie, you're awful. Everyone can hear you," which comes, ironically enough, right after she told him on the street that she wanted "everybody to see you." On the other hand, recalling her own belittling comments to her father about money, part of the reason Young Charlie doesn't like what she hears is because it gives expression to how *she* really feels about money and her father. Much as Young Charlie projects her unconscious Other on Uncle Charlie, he can't help projecting his Other on the figure representing the father in his psyche, especially after Emma reminds him of his traumatic accident: "We all know what banks are. Look all right, but no one knows what goes on when the doors are locked." Significantly, his words come after he was twice shown behind the closed door of Young Charlie's bedroom.

Finishing with one father figure, Uncle Charlie projects his shadowy contempt on a second one, the bank's president, Mr. Greene, who "doesn't care much for jokes about banks," and not only because his name is the color of money. In another example of the "Oh's" deliberate design, the first three "Oh's" linked with one father figure are doubled in the second part of the segment by a second set of three "Oh's," with two maternal figures added for good measure.

"Oh, dear. I'm sorry," a woman's voice is heard off camera while Uncle Charlie is signing his new account in Mr. Greene's office. "I didn't know you were busy." Introduced by Young Charlie as "Mrs. Greene and Mrs. Potter,"

Uncle Charlie greets the two as "Mrs. Greene, *Miss* Potter." "*Mrs.* Potter," the other woman, charmed by this debonair snake, corrects him, to his obvious pleasure.

"Oh, there was something about you made me think —," Uncle Charlie quits while he's ahead.

But Mrs. Potter catches his drift. "There's one good thing in being a widow, isn't there?" she speaks directly to Uncle Charlie. "You don't have to ask your husband for money." Just then Mrs. Greene thanks her husband for the money he gives her, "Oh, thank you," as the two depart more happily than when arriving, each for her own reasons.

Later that evening, when Young Charlie rushes to the library before it closes, to check the article that Uncle Charlie had torn out of her father's newspaper, the same policeman stops her from crossing the street against his directives. "Get back there! Get back! Get back!" he orders Young Charlie, as if trying to stop her from discovering her uncle's shadowy side. This notion is suggested by the big "STOP" sign by his left arm in the foreground and by his catching her by her arm when she starts crossing. "Just a minute Charlie. What do you think I am out here for?"

"Oh, I'm sorry, Mr. Norton," she apologizes to the figure of authority whose name sounds like Newton. Once she acknowledges his authority, he allows her to cross the threshold beyond which her view of Uncle Charlie changes overnight.

Arriving at the Free Public Library just after closing time, Young Charlie is all "Oh's": "Oh, Miss Corcoran, please let me in," she pleads with the librarian. "Oh, please." Despite her lateness, the maternal figure of authority, like the policeman before her, gives in to Charlie. "Oh, thank you," Young Charlie says to the librarian when she reluctantly opens the door for her, assuring her, "Oh, I'll only be a minute."

The next day, Saturday, after Young Charlie supposedly sleeps late (like Uncle Charlie the day before) to postpone her facing the "merry widows murderer" she knows him to be, Uncle Charlie, holding the open newspaper, calls out when she appears for dinner, "Oh, here she is." Mirroring Young Charlie, who "doesn't look quite herself," as her mother describes her to Uncle Charlie (recalling their own mother wondering "if he'd ever look the same"), Ann asks not to sit next to her uncle. Then, as if to humor her when trying to change the subject of Young Charlie saying she had nightmares about Uncle Charlie leaving on a train, he turns to her and asks patronizingly, "Oh, Ann, would you like to see the funnies?"

That same evening, when Young Charlie avoids dinner with her family and flees from the house because she cannot stomach Uncle Charlie's presence, she once again runs into the same policeman. With Uncle Charlie catching up and standing next to her, holding her by her arm, Young Charlie is envisioned as trapped between paternal law and the shadowy father in her psyche. "You're always running along the street at night," the lawman reprimands young Charlie again, this time for literally running into him. As if in cahoots with the shadowy father, he inquires about her nocturnal excursion to the library, "Say, where were you going in such a hurry last night?" When she introduces Uncle Charlie, the policeman advises him, "Better keep your eye on your niece."

"I'll take care of her," Uncle Charlie assures the policeman as he ominously takes hold of Young Charlie's arm.

Now that Young Charlie has learned the horrifying truth about Uncle Charlie, and just before she lays it all on the table, ring and all, the figure of patriarchal authority isn't shown again. Likewise, Young Charlie no longer utters, "Oh, Charlie," as she did like her mother so many times before. In fact, her only other "Oh" in connection with her uncle is "Oh, yes, there is. I want you all to go," when she insists that her family attend Uncle Charlie's lecture, after her father tries to call it off because of the "accident" in the garage that almost took her life.

Signaling that the movie now returns to the *double* motif with which it opened, the "Oh's" decrease drastically after Young Charlie returns Uncle Charlie his incriminating ring, merely two nights after he had given it to her in the Newton's kitchen. Underscoring this two-fold return, the ring's return transpires at the "'Til Two" bar, where twos come in doubles.

Sitting in one of the bar's booths opposite Young Charlie, Uncle Charlie orders two drinks (including a double brandy) from a waitress from Young Charlie's high school class, who's been working there for two weeks, after she had "been in half the restaurants in town." As the waitress departs for the drinks, Uncle Charlie appeals to his niece: "Now look, Charlie. Something's come between us. I don't want that to happen. Why, we're old friends. More than that, we're like twins. You said so yourself." Uncle Charlie may be able to control his words, but he cannot control his two hands with which he *wrings* the napkin, as if, like the shadow itself, they have a mind of their own. "Oh, Charlie, now, don't start imagining things," he says, trying to return matters to their former state. Just when she returns his ring, placing the "smoking gun" between them in the middle of the table, the phlegmatic waitress returns with the drinks, asking, "Whose is it?" Not waiting for an answer, she adds, "I'd just die for a ring like that. Yes, sir, for a ring like that, I'd just about die."

While Young Charlie replaces her "Oh's" to Uncle Charlie with "go away" at practically every opportunity, on two occasions she transfers her "Oh's" to his replacement: Jack Graham (Macdonald Carey), one of the two detectives shadowing her uncle. "Oh, I am relieved," she says in connection to the police finding "that other fella, the one they call the Merry Widow Murderer" on the other side of the country, which she and Uncle Charlie initially overhear together when a neighbor relays the news to Joe. Young Charlie's second "Oh" to Graham comes after he confesses that he loves her and that perhaps he'll come back for her.

"Oh, please come back," she says as earnestly as she had wanted Uncle Charlie only a few days before. This second "Oh" is doubled by Uncle Charlie in the movie's very last interjection, when, not unlike the return of the repressed, he assures Emma, who can't bear the idea of his leaving, "Oh, Emmy, I'll be back."

Uncle Charlie indeed comes back, but in a coffin, not unlike Dracula. As generally happens to the cinematic Other by the movie's end, he's killed by his projector after a violent struggle, such as the one between the two Charlies on the train leaving Santa Rosa. In psychological terms, the Other's death symbolizes his ceasing to exist as an autonomous figure in its projector's unconscious by its integration in the protagonist's consciousness. In *Shadow of a Doubt*, this integration is confirmed by the movie's closing scene.

Opening with an establishing shot of the church, which replaces the bank in Santa Rosa's opening sequence, Young Charlie is shown "united" with Jack Graham within one of the church's twin vestibules, while inside, Uncle Charlie is eulogized for the side he had presented to the citizens of Santa Rosa. As the camera closes in on Young Charlie and Jack, she gives him her hand, speaking to him as she had formerly spoken to Uncle Charlie. Where earlier, upon telling her of his suspicion of her uncle, she had told Graham to "go away," she now confides to him, "I'm glad you were able to come, Jack. I couldn't have faced it without someone I knew."

When speaking of Uncle Charlie, Young Charlie may well be speaking about herself as she spoke before he came to Santa Rosa, when she was "talking about souls" and complaining to her father of their being "in a terrible rut." "He thought the world was a horrible place. He couldn't have been very happy, ever. He didn't trust people. He seemed to hate them. He hated the whole world. You know, he said that people like us had no idea what the world was really like." The overheard closing words of the minister's ironic eulogy ("the beauty of their souls, the sweetness of their characters, live on with us forever") surely speak to Young Charlie more than to the others inside the church, particularly when recalling her reply to Ann's question about how long Uncle Charlie would be staying, "Forever, I hope."

3

Strangers on a Train:
Playing Doubles

> *I suppose you're going to Southampton for the doubles.*
> — Bruno Anthony to Guy Haines on the train where they first meet.

Double Crossing

In *Strangers on a Train*, his second movie on the double, Alfred Hitchcock created an early cinematic exemplar of the projector and his Other that adhered to the *Gilgamesh* prototype of autonomous doubles of the same gender. Hitchcock, after all, as many of his movies bear out, was clearly fascinated, if not obsessed, by man's dark side, and the double offered him the perfect means with which to give it expression. As Donald Spoto points out about the "motif of the double," Hitchcock "required no training in psychology to be aware of this common creative currency and its imagery: it was one of the major recurring motifs in the art and literature of his time, and inevitably the cinema, *his* cinema, capitalized on the forms and patterns of this device."[1]

More so than in *Shadow of a Doubt*, the device of the double allowed Hitchcock to be at his playful best when making *Strangers on a Train*. The movie's protagonist, Guy Haines (Farley Granger), may be "going to Southampton for the doubles," which we never see him play, but it's Hitchcock who plays endless sets of doubles in the course of the movie. The most prominent double, of course, is the movie's double, Bruno Anthony (Robert Walker). He's "a character in his own right, realized in detail with marvelous precision; but he also represents the destructive, subversive urges that exist, though suppressed, in everybody: he is an extension, an embodiment, of desires already existing in Guy."[2]

From start to finish, from the opening train scene to the one that doubles it in the end, all that transpires in *Strangers on a Train* is linked to the doubles of the projector and his Other. And once again, nothing illustrates this better than the movie's exposition, the inevitable meeting between the two strangers, the protagonist and his unconscious Other.

Envisioning Guy before, during, and after Bruno encroaches himself into his life, *Strangers on a Train* opens with an establishing shot of Union Station in Washington, D.C., a stationary shot that shows (over the opening credits) the passage of time by changing from daylight to nighttime and back to daylight. The projector and his Other are introduced by cross-cutting parallel shots that show their arriving at the station one after the other, their pairs of shoes striding toward the entrance from opposite directions. One stranger is distinguished by his sporty shoes, the other by his two tennis racquets. Besides envisioning their being doubles, the pairs of shoes suggest the lower realm of Guy's unconscious, from which Bruno emerges.

Foreshadowing the Other and his projector crossing paths on the train, its shadow is shown moving forward over crossing tracks as it pulls out of the station. Cutting inside the train, the two pairs of shoes are shown again, in the lounge car, walking from opposite directions toward the same table. One after the other, they "double" cross their legs as they sit down, with Guy's right shoe accidentally (unconsciously) striking the other man's matching shoe. "Excuse me," he apologizes, thinking nothing of it as he proceeds to leaf through the book in his hands. But the other man recognizes him, and not only from seeing him "in South Orange last season," where he "made the semifinals." "I beg your pardon," he says, "aren't you Guy Haines?" Rising from his seat on the other side of the table, he goes to Guy's side, trapping his hand in a double clasp. "By the way, my name is Bruno. Bruno Anthony. See?" He points to the tie pin that spells his name, which receives a close-up, revealing the tie's twin-clawed lobsters. "Well, I suppose you think it's corny," he says taking a step back, "but my mother gave it to me, so I had to wear it to please her." As envisioned in this symmetric shot, Bruno penetrates Guy's side, at least into the dark partition in the background that separates the two. Guy, on the other hand, never crosses from his side.

Like the lobster's twin claws that adorn his tie, Bruno sinks his claws into Guy, whose politeness and innocence of his Other makes him easy prey. As Robin Wood notes about this "chance meeting,"

> Hitchcock makes it clear that Bruno has not engineered the meeting, despite that he knows all about Guy … it is rather as if he is waiting for a chance meeting he knew would come. This gives us, from the outset, the

sense of some not quite natural, not quite explicable link between the two men.³

The "not quite explicable link between the two," of course, is between the projector and his unconscious Other, which explains the *strangers* in the title and their inevitable meeting. This projection of the Other is envisioned by the venetian blinds' shadow projected, like prison bars, on Bruno, never on Guy.

With Hitchcock playing doubles (and double bass), the introduction's "other" double meaning emerges when juxtaposing the tie pin and the pair of lobster claws below it with a couple of lines from T.S. Eliot's famous poem, "The Love Song of J. Alfred Prufrock":

> "My necktie rich and modest, but asserted by a simple pin"—and "I should have been a pair of claws Scuttling across the floors of silent seas."⁴

The playful Hitchcock, who in his customary cameo appearance boards the train carrying a double bass immediately after Guy gets off (at Metcalf, to see Miriam), may well have in mind "The Love Song of Alfred J. *Hitchcock*," which explains why he has Miriam (Laura Elliot), the woman to whom Guy is hitched, work in a music store. And why the movie's "You and I," Guy and Bruno, visit her and one another like "The Love Song's" "Let us go and make our visit."⁵ Hitchcock's name is clearly suggested when in Bruno's visit to Miriam at Metcalf, he looks for her name and address in the phone book, which receives a close-up, and two names above hers is "Haigwood, Alfred C."

Intended or not, the notion of "The Love Song" gives the cumbersome musical instrument Hitchcock hauls on the train another set of double meanings. On the one hand, Hitchcock, the musical player who replaces the tennis player on the train, is playing with doubles throughout the movie; on the other, his instrument of low-pitched musical notes suits a movie that deals with man's more base (unconscious) desires. As in Elliot's poem, Bruno's talk is always full of "insidious intent," and the "pair of claws" at the bottom "of silent seas" envision him as an unconscious creature from the lower depths, giving voice to Guy's unconscious desires. Particularly as up to now, like the "silent seas," Guy hasn't uttered a word, thus inadvertently (unconsciously) allowing his Other to claw himself into his life.

In his first words to his Other, the "merely" polite "How do you do?" Guy not only inadvertently asks the man who "admire[s] people who do things" how he *does* it, his double "do's" mirror Bruno's obsessive talk about *doing*. Despite his assuring Guy that "I don't talk much," as if he *does* rather than talk, the shifty Bruno talks nonstop. But only to set up Guy for what he has in mind to *do*, and for Hitchcock to set up the two as doubles, as projector and his Other. And with the projector unconscious of his Other, Bruno, sensing the easy prey that has fallen into his claws, leads the unsuspecting Guy straight into his crafty trap. "You know, it must be exciting to be so important," he says obsequiously.

"Tennis player isn't so important," Guy says modestly, unaware of Bruno's "insidious intent."

"But people who do things are," Bruno insists. "Me, I never do *anything*."

When Guy offers Bruno his monogrammed lighter with the crossed tennis rackets, which doubles for his tie clip, his Other alludes to their being two of a kind while sinking his claws deeper than Guy would like. As the lighter receives a close-up, Bruno initiates a verbal match without a net. "From A to G. I'll bet I can guess who 'A' is," Bruno says, serving Guy an ace. But when he pitches what he knows about him from "the sports page," the clearly uncomfortable Guy lobs back, "You're quite a reader, Mr. Anthony." With Bruno getting his game going, talking about Guy's love life, Guy hits back a bit harder: "Perhaps you read too much."

Realizing he had overplayed his part, Bruno changes tactics. "Oh, there I go again. Too friendly. It always happens. I meet somebody who I like and admire, and I open my mouth too much." Guy once again plays it down: "Forget it," he says apologetically. "I guess I'm a little jittery."

But Bruno doesn't relent: "Oh, there's a new cure for that." He means the pair of doubles he orders when already thinking of another "double" cure for their shared problems. This double entendre is underscored by his adding, "The only kind of doubles I play."

Guy, not wanting anything more to do with Bruno, replies, "You'll have to drink both." But needing a drink after Bruno's ceaseless insinuations about his traveling companion's personal life, especially about his getting off at Metcalf for "a little chat with your wife about divorce," Guy changes his mind when the drinks arrive.

Having succeeded with his "double" strategy, Bruno makes a move to draw Guy into his dragon's den. "Drink up, and we'll have lunch sent to my compartment."

The weary Guy, downing his double, declines: "Thanks, but I'll go to the dining car." But despite Bruno's proposed toast, "Here's to luck," Guy is unlucky as the dining car is full for the next 20 minutes. With his prey practically in his claws, Bruno proposes a second toast: "Here's a toast to the next Mrs. Haines," his opening serve for the real match he has in mind to play.

The second part of the meeting, underscoring their growing intimacy, takes place in Bruno's compartment, with its opening shot emphasizing the soles of Bruno's pair of shoes, which doubles for the shoes in the earlier shot. Bruno even calls attention to the shoes by saying he "got kicked out of three" colleges for "drinking and gambling," adding, "Not like you, huh?" He even refers to himself as "a bum."

Guy downplays Bruno's self denigration by asking, "Who said you were?"

This is all Bruno needs to start giving expression to his dark desires. "My father. He hates me. What do you think of a character like that?" he asks Guy, speaking for him when answering, "Yes, I hate him, too." Clenching his hand like a claw, he adds, "I tell you, I get so sore at him sometimes, I want to kill him."

"What are you trying to prove?" Guy asks. "I'm not like you, Guy." Bruno compares the two once again, pairing his hated father to Guy's estranged wife when claiming that "some people are better off dead." In one serve he once again brings up Guy's love life about "marrying the boss's daughter"; he then takes back his words, with double meaning: "I'm your friend, remember? I'd do anything for you." This ominous statement, coming so soon after his revelation of what he would like to *do* to his father, can only spell double trouble. "Wanna hear one of my ideas for a perfect murder?" he says suddenly.

Guy laughs off Bruno's idea to "swap murders" by repeating his words, but Bruno conveniently interprets it as his consent. With Guy about to change trains, he reveals his game plan, "You do my murder, I do yours. For example, your wife, my father. Crisscross." But what the insidious Bruno, armed with Guy's forgotten lighter in his hands, really means is *double cross*.

Messages and Visits

However unconsciously, Guy has Bruno in mind when, visiting Miriam at the music store in Metcalf, he reminds her who *did* what in the "family quarrel" that develops between the two: "You little double-crosser! *I* didn't want this divorce—*you* did." In her response, while alluding to how the two first made contact on the train, Miriam speaks for Bruno as Guy's inescapable Other: "You can't throw me away like an old shoe." Subsequently, envisioning what Guy would really like to *do*, the shot showing him calling "the next Mrs. Haines," admitting to her that he could "strangle" Miriam, dissolves into a shot of Bruno's pair of hands strangling an imagined neck.

"I do wish you'd keep your hands quiet," Bruno's mother (Marion Lorne) says when manicuring his hands, in essence sharpening his claws. In this family scene, which reveals Bruno's Oedipal relationship with both his parents, the mother comments on their "naughty boy" while the father, dressed in a double-breasted suit, maintains that his unstable son needs to be "put under restraint." But this naughty boy, who can't keep his claws to himself, is already making a long-distance call to Guy at the Southampton tennis club, reminding him of their meeting on the train. Disconnecting the phone after Bruno's two questions, "Are you getting a divorce?" and "Are you going to see her again?" Guy does neither, as his Other sees her first and does what Guy is dying to *do* but does not allow himself.

That in strangling Miriam Bruno *does* what Guy unconsciously desires is underscored by the name of the boat, *Pluto*, which takes him to the amusement park's Magic Isle, where he carries out his crime. The name Pluto, god of the underworld, points to the unconscious that the Magic Isle represents, a notion reinforced by envisioning both Bruno and Miriam as shades when they pass through the Tunnel of Love. As Spoto notes, "Hitchcock drew on the tradition of the fairground as the place where the demented aspects of life are concentrated and expressed ... where Bruno actualizes the metaphorical and the surrogate, unleashing the forces of madness and death."[6]

Showing the strangling reflected in one of the lenses from Miriam's fallen glasses is certainly another way to "see her." Moreover, seeing it from below suggests the lower underworld of Guy's unconscious, particularly as his lighter, given to him by "the next Mrs. Haines," is shown right next to the present wife's glasses. This "seeing" is underscored by the subsequent shot of Bruno, perhaps thinking that one bad deed deserves a good one, escorting a blind man across the street, and by his consulting his *watch*, another word for "see."

Connecting Guy to Bruno's *lower* crime, he's subsequently shown checking his watch on the train going *south* to Washington while sharing the *observation* car with a professor *under* the influence, who doubles for the blind man. One is blind; the other is blind drunk. What's more, his having "just made a speech in New York on integration" surely alludes to the projector's integration of his unconscious Other, which is why the professor, believing that Guy understands his theory of integration, asks surprisingly, "You do?" And why he twice sings a "love song" (in the brief scene's beginning and ending) with double meanings that emphasizes the "did": "He loved that goat, He loved that goat. Indeed he did. He loved that goat just like a kid." Goat not only represents the devil, Bruno is also Guy's scapegoat, and vice versa. Presently, however, the two are divorced from one another, a divorce which allows the autonomous Other to carry out the crime that takes place during this "other" shared ride on the train. While Guy, in a light suit, leafs through *Fortune* magazine, his Other, wearing a dark suit like the professor in the car, is forever changing his fortune.

By the time Guy arrives at his Washington residence, Bruno, proving Guy "can't throw [him] away like an old shoe," is already waiting for him in the shadows, calling out his name as a voice in the night from the *other* side of the street. Having put his Other out of his mind, Guy is confused by this nocturnal visit. "What are you doing here? At this time of night?" Bruno tries to break the news gently by handing Guy Miriam's glasses, their broken lens suggesting that he *did* his half of the crisscross. "Why, you maniac!" the horrified Guy exclaims when realizing what he *did*.

"But, Guy, you wanted it," Bruno gives voice to his unconscious desire. "We planned together on the train, remember? You're just as much in it as I am. We planned it together. Crisscross."

Recalling the venetian blinds' projected shadow in the lounge car, where up to now only Bruno is shown behind the fence's iron bars, after Guy threatens to call the police, he too is shown behind them, imprisoned in his Other's trap. As Bruno explains to Guy why he cannot go to the police, "You see, *you* have the motive." And indeed, when the police arrive at his residence (to inform him of his wife's murder), Guy is shown hiding behind the fence's bars together with Bruno, remaking, "You've go me acting like I'm a criminal." But after the police depart (because Guy isn't home), when Bruno insists that he carry out the other half of the plan, Guy walks out on him, denying his Other: "I never saw you before! I never want to see you again!"

Guy's desire to get rid of one Mrs. Haines for another is envisioned by showing him with Anne (Ruth Roman) only after Miriam's death. On the other hand, that he cannot get rid of her so easily, just as he cannot rid himself of his Other, is underscored by the presence of Anne's sister, Barbara (Patricia Hitchcock, the director's real-life daughter), who doubles for Miriam, especially for Bruno.

When Senator Morton (Leo G. Carroll), the father of the two sisters, informs the three of Miriam's death, Guy tries to hide his knowledge of the murder by turning away and sitting down. But his shadow, projected on the wall behind him, gives him away. While Anne consoles him by saying, "It's not as though anyone can see that you had anything to do with it," her father advises him, "Never lose any sleep over accusations. Unless they can be proven, of course." Not to be outdone, Barbara, who says what others think, just as Bruno *does* what Guy desires, chimes in, "I still think it'd be wonderful to have a man love you so much he'd kill for you."

The doubling continues at the Metcalf police station, as the professor from the train, rather than providing Guy with an alibi, denies ever having seen him, which doubles for Guy's denying his projected Other. With this lack of a reliable alibi casting doubt over Guy's innocence, he is shadowed by two detectives, Hennessy and Hammond. The pair's shadowing is doubled by Bruno, who follows Guy wherever he goes.

Bruno first contacts Guy by calling him at the Mortons after Guy informs them of his "trouble with the police" and his "unconscious" alibi.

"They're acting as if you were guilty," Anne muses as the camera cuts to

Guy, looking up at her with a culpable look on his face, all the while revealing his guilt by holding the coffee cup between his two hands that could easily pass for a pair of claws. Significantly, Bruno's "urgent" call comes immediately after Anne advises Guy, "You mustn't do anything that looks suspicious. You've got to go on acting as though nothing had happened." Hearing it's Bruno on the other end of the line, who only gets in "Hello, Guy," Guy immediately disconnects, once again denying his Other when saying, "It wasn't for me."

Bruno's call is paired by his "visit" in the subsequent scene that opens with an establishing shot of both the Jefferson Memorial and the Washington Monument, another of the movie's many pairs. Guy, in light suit, spots Bruno on the Jefferson Memorial's step while paired with his "shadow," Hennessey, in dark suit. Like his phone call at the Mortons and this encounter, Bruno keeps "pestering" Guy through his pairs of messages and visits, alternating between the two, getting closer with each pair.

The message of the second pair comes when Bruno slips a note under Guy's door, reminding him, "We must get together and make plans." The corresponding visit takes place at the Senate, which Guy visits with Anne, and where Bruno blames him for "making me come out into the open," suggesting the unconscious Other is becoming more conscious.

Always one to speak his mind, Bruno comments upon seeing Anne, "Slight improvement over Miriam, huh, Guy?"

Anne, growing suspicious, notices Bruno's monogrammed tie pin. "Who is it, Guy?" she asks, only to have Guy dismiss him as "just some tennis fan." But the more Bruno pesters Guy, the more Anne gets involved in their relationship. This, after all, is Bruno's function. Through him, through his unconscious Other, Guy swaps his unconscious marriage to Miriam for a conscious one to Anne.

In the message of the third pair, just as Guy opens the "special delivery" envelope, "marked 'personal,'" which contains the key to Bruno's house and the map showing his father's room (second floor, second door), Barbara comments (over a close-up of the map) about the "shadow" detective outside. "I think it's a shame Daddy won't let us have him in." Of course, as this line is uttered by the director's real-life daughter, it harbors double meanings about the projector and his Other.

Barbara also appears in Bruno's corresponding visit to Guy's tennis club, which picks up where Guy's last words to Anne about his being "just some tennis fan" left off. But before that, as Guy waits at courtside to start his own practice game, Bruno is singled out among the spectators watching the on-going game of mixed doubles. Rather than follow the ball like all the other spectators, he stares intently at Guy, who once again seems to feel as if "asserted by a simple pin," particularly as Bruno is once again wearing one. Worse yet, when Guy finishes his own game and walks up to the terrace overlooking the court, he sees Bruno sitting at a table with Anne and another couple, another kind of mixed doubles. When the unsuspecting Anne introduces the two rivals, Bruno once again double clasps Guy's hand. "I've been a fan of yours for a long time, Mr. Haines," he echoes Guy's own words to Anne from his last visit while reminding him of his shadowy role in their relationship. "In fact, I follow everything you do." As Bruno proceeds to ingratiate himself with the other couple, Anne notices his monogrammed tie pin once again, and, looking up at Guy, begins to connect the two.

Even more than Anne, when she introduces Barbara to Bruno, the two lock looks as if recognizing each other from a previous meeting. Barbara's first words to Bruno, "How do you do?" double for Guy's first words to him on the train and recall their first meeting. Her glasses, on the other hand, remind the entranced and speechless Bruno of Miriam. With the camera moving toward Barbara, herself entranced by Bruno's look, he re-experiences his approaching Miriam at the amusement park. He "sees her" just as he had "seen" Miriam, which doesn't go unseen by Anne, who's shown looking inquisitively at the spellbound Bruno in two identical shots.

In the last pair of his messages and visits, Bruno sends Guy a package containing his gun and makes an uninvited visit to the Morton's party, which he had overheard Barbara mention at the tennis club. Whereas up to this point one police "shadow" (Hennessy) was repeatedly paired with Guy, with his receiving the potential instrument of murder, the other "shadow" is evoked as Hennessy informs him, "Hammond will be on duty in a couple of hours." In response, Guy speaks of both Hammond and his Other when remarking, "He sticks so close, he's beginning to grow on me." In return, when Guy turns his back toward the drawer in which he hid the gun, Hennessy speaks of both Bruno and his shadow (Hammond) when replying, "He thinks you're a very suspicious character," and then adds, "But then he doesn't trust anybody, not even himself," as Guy is shown opening the drawer that holds the gun.

Before Bruno's visit, the scene of Morton's party opens with another pair of matching shots of Anne as she and her father receive the arriving guests. Shown gazing at Guy standing by himself, nervously holding an empty champagne glass between his two hands, which doubles for his holding the coffee cup in an earlier scene, Anne is visibly anxious. Having seen Bruno's tie pin for the second time, she begins to view Guy differently.

Anne relaxes momentarily when seeing Barbara take Guy's empty glass for a refill, but her troubled look returns when she spots Bruno come in and walk directly toward Guy, extending his hand, which Guy refuses, as if one handshake is more than enough. Recalling his words to Guy, in this last visit, Bruno really does "come out into the open," revealing the unconscious Other he personifies. What was merely suggested by Guy's cupping the champagne glass, now takes place when, overhearing Bruno's words to a guest judge about how "few murderers are caught," a lady dressed in black, Mrs. Cunningham (Norma Varden), who shares a sofa with a lady dressed in white, addresses Bruno, "Mr. Anthony, you seem very interested in the subject of murder."

"No more than anyone else," Bruno responds charmingly. He then proceeds to discuss the subject as he had done with Guy on the train, giving expression to Guy's unconscious once again when saying, "Everyone has somebody that they want to put out of the way." Bruno makes it more particular when adding, "Surely, madam, you're not going to tell me that there hasn't been a time that you didn't want to dispose of someone. Your husband, for instance? ... How are you going to do it?"

"Well, I suppose I'll have to get a gun from somewhere," she replies gaily.

"Oh, no, Mrs. Cunningham," he corrects her. "Bang, bang, bang, all over the place? Blood everywhere?" Coming soon after he had sent Guy the gun with which to dispose of his father, Bruno's words reveal what he had in mind for his rival, particularly when he proceeds to demonstrate what he considers "the best way and the best tools" with which to *do* it.

"Simple, silent, and quick," Bruno holds out his hands like a pair of claws ("of silent seas?"). "The silent part being the most important. Let me show you what I mean," his hands are itching to wring the woman's neck. "You don't mind if I borrow your neck for a moment, do you?"

"Well, if it's not for long," replies Mrs. Cunningham, whose flowery shawl and necklace recall Miriam's when Bruno borrowed *her* neck. All that's missing are her eyeglasses.

Divorce and Integration

Providing the missing eyeglasses, Barbara comes into the picture precisely when Bruno wraps his hands around the neck of the motherly version of Miriam. With Barbara behind Mrs. Cunningham, Bruno's attention shifts from his pair of hands around one woman's neck to the other's pair of bespectacled eyes. Doubling for their first recognition of one another at the tennis club, the two can't take their eyes off each other. Bruno once again starts hearing the merry-go-round's pipe organ, seeing Miriam in Barbara while abreacting her murder when strangling Mrs. Cunningham.

As suggested by Bruno falling unconscious when his hands are forcibly removed from Mrs. Cunningham's "borrowed" neck, this double strangling, of the symbolic mother and Guy's wife, signals the beginning of Guy's divorcing himself from his unconscious Other. "Let's get him out of here," he says to the man helping him lift Bruno. It also marks the end of Bruno's pairs of *messages* and *visits*.

Guy's divorcing himself from his unconscious Other is acted out when, alone together in the Morton's study, he pushes Bruno down on the couch when he regains consciousness and starts standing up. "You mad, crazy maniac! You ought to be locked up," his words echoing what Bruno's father had said. Growing more assertive, when Bruno tries getting up a second time, Guy hits him on the jaw, driving him back down to the sofa and admonishing, "Will you get out of here and let me alone?"

Guy's commencing to divorce himself from his unconscious Other runs parallel to his acknowledging Bruno's role in his life when sharing what he knows about him with Anne. But Guy's acknowledgment comes only after Anne, who finally puts two and two together from what Barbara shares with her ("He looked at me. His hands were on her throat and he was strangling me. He thought he was murdering me."), confronts him with a series of questions: "You didn't meet him for the first time the other day, did you?" "What did Miriam look like?" "She wore glasses, didn't she, Guy?" "She looked something like Barbara, didn't she?" With Guy declining to answer, Anne gets to the point with two more questions: "How did you get him to do it?" "He killed Miriam, didn't he?" Once Guy comes clean, once he acknowledges his unconscious Other, he begins to integrate him in his consciousness. As Wood points out, "The removal of doubts between the lovers marks a necessary stage in the action. Their relationship is now on a surer footing, giving Guy the strength to take steps to extricate himself."[7]

That Guy is beginning to integrate his unconscious Other is reinforced by the first appearance of Hammond, who joins Hennessy on the other side of the street when coming to take over the night shift. With one "shadow" associated with Guy and the other with Bruno appearing together for the first time, Hennessy warns Hammond, "You better keep on your toes. Something funny's going on."

That "something," as we see next, is Guy's own *message* and *visit* to Bruno. "I've decided to do what you want," he informs Bruno over the phone, which doubles for his call to Guy before killing Miriam. "I'll make that little visit to your father." Unlike Bruno's earlier call, however, in which both are shown on either side of the telephone line, now only Guy is shown, suggesting Bruno's diminishing presence in his life. Doubling for Bruno's visit to Miriam, Guy is shown walking down the fire escape with the gun tucked inside his coat's breast pocket as if descending to the underworld of death and the unconscious.

In his "little visit" to the Anthony home, Guy encounters a Great Dane, a Cerberus of sorts, which doubles for the boat called Pluto in Bruno's visit to the underworld of the amusement park, particularly as it seems as if he intends to use the gun to kill Bruno's father. Only things are not as they seem. Stationed at the top of the stairs, the Great Dane, known as the Apollo of dogs, proves to be more growl than bite as Guy passes by him without a hitch by letting him sniff the same hand that held Bruno's gun. Just before he crosses the threshold to the father's bedroom, Guy, accompanied by his projected shadow on the wall, takes the gun out of his breast pocket and puts it in the outer pocket, giving the impression that he really intends to carry out his part of the "crisscross."

But inside is a double surprise. Not only does Guy have no intention to carry out his part of the one-sided agreement, but rather to talk to Mr. Anthony about his son, instead of finding one Mr. Anthony in bed, he finds the other.

"Yes, Mr. Haines?" Bruno, in black tuxedo and white tie, formally welcomes Guy after switching on the light, his enormous shadow projected on the wall behind him. Confronting his Other head on, Guy tells Bruno what he intended to tell his father: "I thought he'd be interested to know he has a lunatic son." With these words Bruno rises to his feet as if to strike Guy, but then, sensing his resolve, sits back down. In fact, envisioning who's on top and who's down, in most of the encounter Bruno is lying or sitting down, while Guy is always standing above him. For once, when Guy makes it clear that he has "no intention of going ahead with our arrangement," that he "never had," all the usually verbose Bruno can say is "I see."

After returning the key, and the gun, Guy speaks more freely. "Look, Bruno. You're terribly sick. I don't know much about these things, but why don't you go some place where you can get some kind of treatment?"

Bruno hits back, "I don't like to be double-crossed." He follows his implied threat by explaining to Guy, who doesn't "know much about these things," "I have a murder on my conscience, but it's not *my* murder. It's *yours*," he points the gun at the unconscious culprit. "And since you're the one to profit by it, I think you're the one to pay for it."

"We have nothing further to discuss," Guy divorces himself from Bruno, whose bigger-than-life shadow is projected on the wall behind him, and proceeds to descend the stairs. Bruno follows him with his drawn gun, standing on the landing between the two flights of stairs together with the Great Dane, his enormous shadow once again projected on the wall. Scared as he may be, Guy continues his descent, perhaps intuiting that Bruno doesn't intend to shoot him, which Bruno himself confirms: "Don't worry. I'm not going to shoot you, Mr. Haines. It might disturb Mother."

Guy's descent back to the unconscious is a necessary stage in dealing with his Other because, as Bruno informs him, he may have lost a set, but the match is far from over. "I'm a very clever fellow," he says in the voice of the ingenious unconscious. "I'll think of something better than that. Much better." As demonstrated by Bruno repeatedly calling Guy "Mr. Haines," the two have grown apart. Moreover, that he's become a less threatening Other is illustrated by the fact that no shadow appears when Guy repeatedly looks up at Bruno on the landing in their last exchange.

This segment of Guy's *message* and *visit* to Bruno ends as it had started, with Hennessy and Hammond, whose brief exchange mirrors the divorce between the projector and his Other. The hot-headed Hammond, who unknowingly let Guy "give him the slip," wants him "taken in," assuming they will "probably hear of another dame murdered"; the more levelheaded Hennessy tells Hammond to "shut up," that they "have nothing conclusive on Haines." As the "shadow" paired with Guy, Hennessy reminds his partner, "There's no evidence he was ever at the scene of the crime." Of course, providing the evidence is precisely what the clever Bruno has in mind to *do*.

Doubling for Guy's "little visit" to the Anthony home, and trying to *do* her part in clearing his name, Anne is subsequently shown sharing the couch with Bruno's mother. As one woman to another, she appeals to her "to make him do something about this." But Mrs. Anthony dismisses her son's culpability with the same approach he takes in his one-sided deal with Guy: "Miss Morton, really. I know Bruno has been in some very awkward scrapes but nothing so ridiculous as a murder." Anne, to her dismay, quickly realizes her host is totally "confused," as Bruno describes her. After all, she knows Bruno merely as her "naughty boy," not as Guy's unconscious Other. "Don't you understand, Mrs. Anthony?" Anne asks. "Your son is responsible for a woman's death."

Mrs. Anthony replies, "Did Bruno tell you this?"

"Well, of course not."

"Well, there you are," Mrs. Anthony rests her case.

Immediately after, Mrs. Anthony excuses herself to go back to her painting. "Come see us again sometime," she says pleasantly.

Bruno, having heard their exchange, comes out of the woodwork. Speaking non-stop to the mostly silent and horrified Anne, much as he had first spoken to Guy on the train, he turns everything around, beginning by projecting his lunacy on his mother. Then, standing behind Anne as he lights a small cigar with the lighter she had given Guy, which receives a close-up, he says calmly, "You know, I'm very upset with Guy. He shouldn't have sent you on an errand like this."

In her only line in the exchange, Anne corrects him: "Guy doesn't know I'm here, Mr. Anthony."

But that doesn't faze Bruno, who tries to turn the tables on Guy as he had turned the tables on him. "He must be very desperate to try to involve me. I've been protecting him ever since that conversation on the train when he told me how much he hated his wife."

Putting the "smoking gun" back into his robe's pocket, Bruno, sitting on the sofa's armrest next to Anne, continues his projection while she tries to control her emotions. "Would you know, Miss Morton, that he tried to get me to go back to the island one night after dark to pick up his lighter so the police wouldn't find it? He dropped it there, you know, when — Well, that night. You see, all the police are waiting for is one piece of evidence to convict Guy for the murder." While Anne breaks into tears when he claims that going back would make her "an accessory," Bruno, having presented his side of the story, excuses himself like his mother before him. "I have an urgent appointment. I really must go now."

Like the unconscious Other that needs to reveal itself, Bruno provides Anne and Guy with the information they need to make the unknown known, the unconscious conscious. Putting their heads together later that day at the Forest Hills tennis court, they figure out what it all means. "He said if the police ever found your lighter that's all they'd need — something to prove you were at the scene of the murder," Anne relays Bruno's message to Guy.

"That lie about my wanting him to get it back means he's going to put my lighter on that island," Guy says, putting himself in his Other's head, understanding "what's on his mind," becoming, as it were, conscious of his unconscious. As the two realize, they must "get to Metcalf before he does."

With his scheduled match only minutes away, and with Bruno on his way to Union Station for his "urgent appointment," Guy needs to "finish the match in three sets." In other words, he must win the *match* to get the *lighter*. But to achieve this he must change the way he plays the game.

What the game is ultimately about is suggested by two courtside announcements, one visual, the other aural. The visual is stated by the sign at the entrance to center court that hangs above Guy's head as he enters with Anne, which cites a couplet from Kipling's renowned poem "If": "If you can meet with Triumph and Disaster/And treat those two imposters just the same." The aural is announced in a couple of sentences by one of two radio broadcasters during the warm-ups: "On the other hand, Guy Haines is a quiet, methodical player, almost lackadaisical. As a rule, he plays slowly between points, well within himself." One announcement suggests treating the opposing "imposters" of the projector and his Other as two sides of "the same"; the other sets up the transformation Guy undergoes in dealing with the Other "within himself."

Between showing Guy winning the first two serves and first two sets, the radio broadcaster describes his transformation in two sentences: "Guy Haines is hitting harder, hurrying up the play, taking chances I've never seen him take. This is a complete reversal of his usual watch-and-wait strategy." In the repeated cross-cuts from Guy to Bruno, who's first shown leaving his home in a cab to Union Station, he twice lights his cigarettes with Guy's lighter. The first time he's in a cab; the second time he's on a train to Metcalf, where a fellow passenger, sitting next to him, asks for a light. Not wanting to reveal the incriminating lighter, Bruno, to the man's bewilderment, tucks the lighter in one pocket and fishes for a matchbook in the other. Of course, in this peculiar act Bruno, like the unconscious Other who seeks to be acknowledged by his projector, calls attention to both the lighter and himself.

Bruno's going against himself is doubled when, arriving at Metcalf just as Guy loses the third set, he loses the lighter when he takes it out of his pocket only to have a man bump into him, much as Guy had initially bumped his shoe, causing it to fall through a grating and into a street drain. While back in Forest Hills, as the broadcaster announces, "Guy Haines is mighty grim and determined, and he needs but one more game for the entire *match*," Bruno is repeatedly shown reaching for the *lighter* through the grating. Naturally, immediately after he finally manages to grasp the lighter between two fingers, Guy wins, in the announcer's words, "game, set, and match."

All this crosscutting between Guy and Bruno leads to the two's final meeting at the amusement park at Metcalf, realm of the unconscious. As Bruno waits in line to take the boat to the Magic Isle to plant the incriminating lighter, the boatman recognizes him and goes to a nearby pair of lawmen on the lookout for Guy. Seeing Bruno fleeing the police, Guy calls out to him, "Hey, Bruno!" Of course, his calling him by name in the realm of the unconscious and his catching up to him on the merry-go-round, demanding, "Bruno! Give me that lighter!" represents his recognizing him as his unconscious Other. Likewise, that their struggle on the merry-go-round represents Guy's integrating his Other is suggested by the two-fold confusion between the two: the boatman *meaning* Bruno while the police *assuming* Guy; the detective firing at Guy but hitting the merry-go-round's "boatman" instead, killing, as it were, the wrong man.

Envisioning the conscious and the unconscious that has accompanied the story from its very beginning, while Guy and Bruno fight for the lighter on the merry-go-round that's whirling out of control, an elderly man volunteers to try and stop it by crawling underneath to reach the controls at the center. The struggle on top, doubling for the two shots of the man crawling underneath, is divided into two distinct parts, just as was the two's first meeting on the train. What separates the two parts is the brief incident with the boy on the nearby horse beating on Bruno while he struggles with Guy, a boy who doubles for the one whose balloon Bruno, on his first visit to the amusement park, punctured with his cigarette, after he aimed his toy gun at him with "Bang, bang."

Before the incident with the boy, Guy and Bruno are equally matched. But after Bruno knocks the boy off the horse and Guy saves him from falling off the merry-go-round, the tables are turned once again. Now Bruno has the upper hand, or the upper foot, as he repeatedly tries to kick Guy off the merry-go-round, which recalls how the two first met on the train when their shoes bumped into one another. Where up to now Guy wanted to *divorce* himself from his unconscious Other; now, needing to *integrate* him in his consciousness, he clings to him as if his life depends on it, and not only because he needs to get back the incriminating lighter. This integration, the coming together of the two, is doubly suggested by the confusion between the two: by the one detective telling the other detective which of the two men the boatman means: "He says this isn't the man we want. It's the other one"; and by the boatman himself: "I've never seen this man before in my life. I meant the other one."

This two-fold confusion reinforces the notion that more than Bruno saw in Guy a perfect patsy for his "crisscross," Guy saw in Bruno the perfect "lunatic" on which to project his Other, which explains his inadvertently "bumping" into him on the train and his "forgetting" his monogrammed lighter in his compartment. Beyond needing his projected Other to get rid of Miriam, Guy needs Bruno to prepare himself for his marriage to Anne. On the one hand, Bruno is his unconscious collaborator in getting rid of the first Mrs. Haines, which ends his unconscious marriage; on the other hand, in his dealing with his unconscious Other, Guy moves ever closer to a conscious marriage to the "new Mrs. Haines."

Bruno's last words, "I'm sorry, Guy. I want to help you, but I don't know what I can do," sum up what he has *done* for Guy in his dealing with his unconscious Other. What he can now *do*, of course, is release the monogrammed lighter he's clutching in his claw, which can set everything straight. But being who he is, he can only *do* it in death, which represents Guy's withdrawing his projection of his unconscious Other by integrating it in his consciousness.

Wrapping it all up in the movie's last double — the closing scene on the train that doubles for the opening scene — Guy and Anne's enfolded hands not only replace Bruno's claws around Guy's hand, the priest who replaces Bruno when recognizing Guy ("I beg your pardon. But aren't you Guy Haines?") may well mean the other Guy Haines, the one no longer shadowed by his projected Other.

4

Cape Fear (1962): Picturing the Other

> *Hello, Counselor. Remember me?*
> — Max Cady to Sam Bowden

Hitchcock's Shadow

In J. Lee Thompson's own words, Hitchcock's shadow hovers over much of his 1962 *Cape Fear*: "I've studied all his films, and when I come to a scene I can't help it, but I wonder how Hitchcock would do it. Hitchcock almost always liked to let the audience know, and the person on the screen not to know."[1]

For *Cape Fear*, his second Hollywood movie, which followed his highly successful *Guns of Navarone* (1961), Thompson recruited some of the people who had worked with Hitchcock over the years: art director Robert Boyle, who had collaborated with Hitchcock on five movies, which include *Shadow of a Doubt*, *North by Northwest*, and *The Birds*; film editor George Tomasini, who had worked with Hitchcock on all the masterpieces from *Rear Window* in 1954, by way of *Vertigo* (1958) and *Psycho* (1960), to *Marnie* in 1964; composer Bernard Herrmann, best known for his musical scores for almost every Hitchcock movie from *The Trouble with Harry* (1955) to *Marnie*.

Hitchockian as Thompson's *Cape Fear* may be, it lacks the Hitchcock touch that only the Master could give. All the same, with the volatile Robert Mitchum as the movie's Other, Thompson had a truly menacing predator for the shadowy double, much more ominous than either *Shadow of a Doubt*'s Charlie Oakley or *Strangers on a Train*'s rather effeminate Bruno Anthony. Mitchum is clearly in his element in the role of Max Cady, who comes across as the embodiment of evil. Arriving at Sam Bowden's (Gregory Peck) hometown after being locked up in prison for more than eight years, Cady is a classic case of the return of the repressed, an archetypal exemplar of the protagonist's unconscious Other.

Like Hitchcock before him in *Shadow of a Doubt* and *Strangers on a Train*, Thompson introduces *Cape Fear*'s motif of the Other in a meticulously orchestrated exposition replete with twos and doubles and other tropes of the projector and his unconscious Other.

The Repressed Remembered

Opening with the Other, Max Cady is shown over the opening credits, heading toward the downtown courthouse with a relaxed but resolute gait, twice straightening his emblematic Panama hat. His cigar, which adds a menacing touch to his relaxed demeanor, recalls both Charlie Oakley and Bruno Anthony. As he's about to enter the courthouse, he throws a brief glance at two young women.

Once inside the courthouse, the sneer on Cady's face projects a mood of trouble in mind. Climbing the stairs to the second floor, his mere presence seems to make the woman descending the stairs drop one of the stacked books she carries. By the look on her face, she seems surprised that he doesn't bat an eye, let alone not pick up the book. On the second floor, Cady's demeanor draws the attention of another person, a man who looks at him suspiciously, with Cady returning the look as if daring the man to open his mouth.

In the subsequent shot on the second floor, an elderly black man, his head bowed as he sweeps the floor, enters the symmetric screen in the foreground, occupying its right half. Cady, occupying the screen's left half (in the background), calls out to him from the other side of the round gallery: "Hey, Daddy, where does Sam Bowden hang out?" The man, the only black person addressed in the movie, and hence a symbolic "shadow," points with his extended arm and index finger, "In there, sir." Envisioning what's on his mind, as Cady heads to where the "shadow" had pointed, he stops briefly before the courtroom's double doors, crushing his cigar in his hand and flinging it to the floor.

Shown entering the courtroom, Cady comes to life when he hears the counselor arguing his case before the judge. With the camera cutting to Cady's point of view, but hiding Sam from our view by a wooden column, the counselor continues addressing the judge as Cady removes his hat: "Now, granted that this witness is ill, the defense still has 11 important witnesses able to testify —." In Sam's mid-sentence, the camera cuts to a frontal shot of Cady as he sits down among the other spectators in the gallery, thrilled to finally see his nemesis, who seems to be speaking of Cady's own trial (in which he apparently acted as "chief witness" for the prosecution) when arguing "that 11 [witnesses] against one should be enough." Particularly as in the next shot, which shows the two sharing the frame for the first time (with Sam in the foreground and Cady in the background), the "opposing counsel" addresses his courtroom adversary more than the judge he's addressing. With a sly smirk on his face, he cynically slights his other witnesses with "no matter how decrepit those 11 happen to be," his words receiving subdued laughter from the spectators. When the camera cuts to a medium-close-up of Cady, he doesn't find Sam's cynical remark all that funny. The sneer on his face, shown in four identical shots while Sam argues his case before the judge, reveals the deep contempt he harbors for the counselor.

When the court adjourns, the sequence's closing shot follows Sam as he heads toward the exit. Once he's out of the picture, Cady's head comes into the frame as he rises from his seat, his eyes following Sam. This coming into the picture from below, which doubles for the "shadow's" entering the frame from the right, envisions the Other welling up from the lower depths of Sam's unconscious.

Cady's first confrontation with Sam, outside the courtroom, is envisioned in three twin pairs of shots-reverse shots that underscore their being binary opposites. The first twin pairs, the longest of the three, begin after an establishing street shot, as Sam is shown inside his car, when suddenly, from seemingly nowhere, a hand reaches for the car key, pulling it out of the ignition. Together with the camera tilting up, the stunned Sam looks up to see Cady leaning on the car door. "Hello, Counselor. Remember Me? Baltimore. Eight years, four months and thirteen days ago." Bearing in mind the sexual allusion of the key in the ignition, Cady's intrusion both recalls Sam's disrupting his sexual attack in Baltimore and envisions how he begins to disrupt Sam's life, not to mention who holds the keys in their relationship for the majority of the film.

With the camera cutting outside the car to the first reverse shot, Cady continues: "Becoming any clearer now, Counselor?"

"Cady," Sam remembers. "Max Cady."

"Good," Cady says. "I wouldn't want to think you'd forgotten me."

"What do you want?" Sam tries to get to the point.

But Cady is in no hurry. He wants to make sure that Sam understands who he is and what he has in mind to do, all but referring to himself as his repressed (unconscious) Other. "You didn't remember me right off, did you? Well, I guess I've changed a little. Where I've been, if you don't change, they're real disappointed. You haven't changed a bit. And you know something? That's just the way I wanted it. I wanted you to be just the way you were the last time I saw you."

In the second reverse-shot, Sam is all business. "All right, you've seen me. What's the rest?"

"No rest," Cady, speaking in double entendre, hints at what he has in mind for Sam. "Just wanted to give you the word. Just wanted you to get the picture."

Having heard enough, though not enough to get the picture, Sam demands his keys back. "Why not?" Cady says, handing them over, knowing that the counselor can go back home, but that his life and family will never be the same. "No rest" indeed. Set free, Cady has come to shadow and harass Sam until he confronts him in his own game and acknowledges him as his wronged Other. That's the picture he wants Sam to get. And that's the picture Thompson wants us to get. His *Cape Fear*, after all, is about what happens when we try to keep the unconscious Other at bay, repressed from consciousness. As Edward C. Whitmont notes, "When we refuse to face the shadow or try to fight it with willpower alone ... we merely relegate this energy to the unconscious, and from there it exerts its power in a negative, compulsive, projected form. Then our projections will transform our surrounding world into a setting which shows us our own faces, though we do not recognize them as our own."[2]

With his keys returned, the second sequence of twin pairs of shot-reverse shots begin, this time with a closer shot of Sam from outside the car. "Now let me get this straight," Sam says. "You're not still blaming me for what you did?"

Cady's first reaction is an ominous snigger. Shown alone the only time in this four-shot sequence, Sam is envisioned as dissociated from his Other. In contrast, the subsequent three shots, showing the two together, seem to envision the Other coming into Sam's life. In the first one, the closer reverse shot from inside the car, Cady is overbearing and unrelenting. "You still don't get the picture, do you, Counselor?" Cutting back to the second shot outside the car, Sam merely looks inquisitively at Cady. In the second reverse shot inside the car, Cady speaks in a language Sam still doesn't understand. "Well, I can see this is gonna take a little time. A lot of time." Of course, as his unconscious Other, Cady's wanting Sam "to get the picture" is his way of saying that the Other "usually contains values that are needed by consciousness, but that exist in a form that makes it difficult to integrate them into one's life."[3]

In the segment's third and final shot-reverse shot sequence, the first pair envisions how each one sees their relationship. The first shot, from the backseat of Sam's car, shows a young woman crossing the street. As the camera follows her, Sam and Cady come into the picture, one after the other. While Sam looks straight ahead, Cady can't take his eyes off the woman. "Hey, look at that, would ya? Look at that wiggle." But Sam doesn't look. He's not like Cady, or doesn't allow himself to be, as suggested by the subsequent reverse shot from outside the car that once again shows him by himself, dissociated from his Other. Only Cady doesn't relent, reminding Sam when speaking *for* and *of* the two of them. "Maybe she thinks we don't know that's on purpose, but we've seen a thing or two, haven't we, Counselor?"

Whereas up to this point Cady merely suggested what he has in mind to do, the sight of the young woman gets him speaking an altogether different language. Shown by himself as Sam backs his car out, he reminds him, "You ought to be an expert on such things, Counselor. I hear you got your good-lookin' wife and got a daughter gonna be just like her." As Sam begins to drive away, Cady gives him a glimpse of things to come. "Give my love to the family, Counselor. I'll be seein' you."

Getting the Picture

Cady's mentioning Sam's daughter (Lori Martin) becoming "just like" his wife is taken up next, when the two are shown together, as Sam hugs his "little woman," who rushes to greet him when he comes home. Her reminding him he's ten minutes late not only alludes to the meeting that made him so (and to Cady's "I can see this is gonna take a little time. A lot of time."), his cynical response ("It's a mistake to teach women how to tell time. They always use it against you.") doubles for Cady's lewd remark about the young woman, as if Sam has already begun speaking "just like" his Other. His including his teenage daughter, Nancy, among the "women" in his very first words to her gives the impression that he sees his "little woman" just as Cady was pictured eyeing the young woman who appeared through his car's front window.

Before he enters the house, which doubles for Cady entering the courtroom, and his daughter again speaks of time ("Please don't be long, Dad. I asked Betty to bowl with us."), Sam may well be speaking of his Other when he shoots back, "Betty? Isn't that 'rancid little thing' that you detest with every fiber of your being?" This notion is reinforced by his wife, Peggy (Polly Bergen), who's shown in the segment's second shot, inside the home, descending the staircase to greet Sam "just like her" daughter before her. Answering for her just as Cady spoke for Sam while alluding to the Other, she informs him, "That was last week. This week they're inseparable."

Much like the "inseparable" projector and his Other, Cady's presence is represented by the hat and coat hanging on the wall between Sam and his wife, which is seen as the camera follows her walking toward him. The hat and coat (which Sam is never shown wearing, as if they don't belong to him) are taken up later in the movie when, coming down the same staircase at night looking for both Sam and Nancy (who are not in their beds), Peggy imagines the hat and coat are the shadowy Cady, who has his eyes on Nancy. As Marie-Louise von Franz notes, "One hangs a projection as one hangs a coat on a coat hook."[4]

Much as Nancy had invited Betty bowling, Cady's appearance at the bowling alley may well be Sam's unconscious invitation. Particularly as he's shown watching Nancy bowl and as his presence works on Sam's bowling as it had worked on the woman carrying the books in the courthouse. Where she had dropped one book, now Sam, who was earlier shown bowling a strike and "wiping" his hands clean, fails to "drop" the one remaining pin in the frame's second try. "Nice shot," Cady says, coming from behind Sam, who turns around to face him, both of them knowing why he blew his shot. Then, as if hinting that what's good for the counselor is good for the gander, Cady adds forebodingly, "Don't mind me, Counselor. I'm just getting a gander at the rest of your family."

After two harassments in one day, Sam uses his connections with the law to try and get Cady out of his life. But even when he meets with the police chief for his assistance, and tells his side of the story, his drinking beer associates him with the beer Cady ordered at the bowling alley. In fact, when the former "chief witness" reveals their connection to Chief Dutton (Martin Balsam), Sam seems to be talking about Cady as his unconscious Other:

> I was up in Baltimore about eight years ago, on a case. One night I was walking back to my hotel quite late. I heard a kind of commotion in the rear of a dark parking lot. It sounded like someone whimpering. I ran over. A girl was being attacked. I grappled with the man, she suddenly got her breath back and started screaming at the top of her voice. When he saw the police, he went completely berserk. Put the girl in the hospital for over a month. And that was Max Cady. Later on, I had to go back up and testify against him as a witness.

Considering all that's been suggested up to now, in witnessing Cady attacking a "girl," Sam witnessed his unconscious Other doing what he himself desires. Unable to acknowledge this illicit desire, he represses this traumatic event, thinking he had put it behind him for good. But now his repressed Other has returned, and with a vengeance. He has come to re-enact, or finish off, what Sam had interrupted, and this time on Sam's own turf.

That Sam is beginning to "get the picture" is revealed by what he shares with Dutton. "I thought it was strange when he showed up here this afternoon, but I wasn't really worried until I saw him at the bowling center. It was the way he looked at my family." It "really worried" Sam because it mirrored the way he himself looks at his family, especially his daughter.

What Sam saw in Cady's look is revealed by his savage attack on the young woman, Diane Taylor (Barrie Chase), whom he first spots at the Boar's Head nightspot, looking at her with undeniable sexual hunger. That Cady's incident with the promiscuous woman doubles for his interrupted attack on the "girl" in Baltimore is suggested by the two policemen interrupting his planned "pickup" by picking him up for questioning at Sam's behest. But Cady, having studied law in prison, thus becoming more like Sam, knows his rights within the law and doesn't provide the police with the excuse to throw him out of town. In fact, as he informs Sam when he arrives at the police station (laughing off his warning to "Stay off my property. Day or night."), "You're gonna be old and gray before I ever leave this town."

Like the return of the repressed, within a "couple of hours" of his release Cady goes directly against Sam's warning by poisoning his daughter's "best friend." Described by Sam as all bark and no bite, at this stage of his dealing with his Other the dog mirrors Sam, who merely warns his wife and daughter about Cady, all but calling him the Other. "Just be careful. He's a big man. He has dark hair. He smokes cigars and usually wears a Panama hat." That Cady is getting Sam to change is pointed out during his second visit to the police station, this time accompanied by his lawyer to protest his "persecution" by the law, who points out to Sam how he interprets the law when it comes to his client. "Sam, you know, if anyone had told me a week ago that you were capable of a remark like that..."

The change in Sam is mirrored in the *before* and *after* of Cady's unseen "assault" on Diane Taylor, who's shown immediately after the police station scene, riding with Cady in the front seat of his car. Before the assault, as if giving expression to Sam's mind, she speaks to Cady with a condescending tone of contempt that portrays him as an unconscious creature. "You're just an animal: coarse, lustful, barbaric," she says, snuggling to his side. "Max Cady, what I like about you is you're rock bottom. I wouldn't expect you to understand this, but it's a great comfort for a girl to know that she could not possibly sink any lower."

After the assault, which seems to recall the attack witnessed by Sam in Baltimore, this same woman will not utter a single word about the unmentionable things Cady had done to her, let alone file a complaint against him. When Sam's hired detective informs her while she packs to leave town on the first bus, "Cady has threatened his wife and daughter," she replies, "You believe that I could ever, ever in my whole life step up and repeat to another living soul what the man, what he did?" Bringing home "what he did," Sam later speaks similar words when explaining to his wife why they cannot file a complaint against Cady if he attacks Nancy.

Where up to now Sam has refused to take the law into his hands, he literally does so when Cady pushes his buttons at the marina by once again giving expression to his sexual appetite for his daughter (and wife). Sam issues a second warning: "Look, Cady, maybe you can get away with dog poisoning, beating up on a little drifter like Diane Taylor. Don't push your luck with me." Which is precisely what Cady does, motioning to Nancy, "She's getting' to be almost as juicy as your wife, ain't she?" Becoming more and more like his Other, Sam loses control, throwing two ineffective punches at Cady, who counters by saying, "You're not gonna push me into anything, Counselor." Taking a rain check instead, he gives Sam another piece of the picture. "Now you just had your innings. I'll make my stroke later."

Sam's overreaction at the marina illustrates how much Cady mirrors his own unconscious desire for his daughter. But what was merely suggested at the marina is more apparent the next time Nancy sees Cady, in the subsequent school scene, in which he wears precisely the same clothes he wore when confronting Sam in his car.

Now, sitting alone in the same car's front seat, waiting for her mother, Nancy spots Cady up ahead, leisurely striding in her direction. The fact that he plays in her mind more than in reality reinforces the notion that he's an unconscious figure of her psyche, mirroring what she dares not imagine about her father. It's not for nothing that she's momentarily knocked unconscious when she runs into an oncoming car after running away from Cady, whom she runs into when running away from the *imagined* Cady, which doubles for her running to hug her father after he first met his Other. Her repeating, "He's here!" while crying hysterically in her mother's arms seems to speak of Cady's uncanny presence in her mind.

This is the last straw for Sam, who rushes home to his daughter. That it mirrors his psyche is suggested by Peggy's "Are you out of your mind?" when she tries to stop her reactionary husband as he gets out his gun. "But he didn't do anything to her!" she reminds him. "He didn't hurt her!" Failing to change Sam's mind, perhaps because in the unconscious it doesn't matter if "he didn't do anything" or if he did, as he walks out the door with the gun, Peggy warns him just as he had twice warned Cady: "If you get into that car, I'll call the police." Her call, which doubles for Sam's call to Dutton after Cady's appearance at the bowling alley, is yet another suggestion that the two's roles have changed. But before Peggy gets through to Chief Dutton, Sam, having cooled off enough to think straight, returns and takes the phone from his wife, informing the chief, "It's a false alarm," which recalls his daughter's imagining his Other.

The Unconscious Against the Conscious

Like the return of the repressed, Cady returns to the Boar's Head, a name that can easily stand in for the unconscious Other. As he enters the nightspot, the scene's opening shot is of a young woman in the foreground, on the right side of the screen, sitting by the bar in the same place where his first "pickup" formerly sat. Only now, armed with his usual cigar and hat, he casually walks by her as the camera follows him striding toward the back of the room. There, in an enclave on a lower level, sits Sam. Having initiated the meeting, this time he has truly (consciously) invited his Other. This rather long confrontation between the two, packed with allusions to the unconscious and the conscious, marks both Sam's sinking to a lower (unconscious) level and taking the initiative in dealing with his unconscious Other.

Drawing a picture of what this meeting is fundamentally about, Cady orders two doubles. To drive home the point, he asks the waiter for salted peanuts, specifying "salted in the shell," if only to remind ("teach") Sam that they're two pea(nut)s in a pod, which is why he responds to their not having them, "I see I'm gonna have to educate this town." This is precisely what Cady wants to do to Sam, to "educate" his "rich cousin," as he calls him, of their being two sides of the same person. In fact, Cady, sitting across the table from Sam, compares the two right off the bat: "You're sweatin' a little, eh, Counselor? I know how it is. I sweat, too. For eight solid years I sweat."

Still not getting the picture, Sam is all business. "How much do you want, Cady?" But Cady, who has Sam playing his game, is in no hurry to stop his sweating, at least not until he finishes educating him by completing the picture he wants him to see. When Sam impatiently demands "an answer," Cady replies, "That takes a little figurin', Counselor. What do you reckon eight lost years is worth? You reckon a court could fix a value on that?... Like the value of eight years, the value of a family. Interesting calculations, wouldn't you say, Counselor?"

After Cady orders a second double, Sam, sinking lower, makes his offer of twenty thousand dollars, which doubles for the twenty dollar bill with which Cady taunted the waitress at the bowling alley. "Ten thousand dollars now and another ten thousand over the next two years, providing you keep outside the state." But Cady enjoys having Sam where he wants him, all the while showing him how similar they are. "Now, just for fun, let's go back to talkin' about values, the value of a family. You probably didn't even know I had a family, did you? One wife and one kid, that's what I had when you sent me up. She dumped me. Never even visited... It was the prison rap that she couldn't take. She couldn't stand the disgrace. And that was your doing, Counselor, not my doing!"

As Cady tells his side of the story of how he repaid his wife upon his release from prison, Sam, who has clearly heard enough, finally asks, "Why tell me all this?"

"Because," Cady speaks contemptuously, "I want to tell you all this!" He wants him to sweat about his own "wife and kid," especially the kid. When Sam brings up his daughter, Cady points with his cigar, as if putting his signature on the picture he drew for Sam to see, that he's his unconscious Other when it comes to his daughter: "Now that's your train of thought, Counselor, not mine."

Having seen enough, Sam gets up to leave, but not before adding, "Well, I've seen the worst, the dregs. But you ... you are the lowest." These words, which double for Diane Taylor's words to Cady in the car "that she could not possibly sink any lower," give expression to the low (unconscious) level to which Sam has sunk. To cap it off, in his parting words he admits his association with Cady in the only way he knows: "It makes me sick to breathe the same air."

Along with Cady's drawing a picture for Sam, Thompson draws us a picture of the two as representing the unconscious and conscious through the two pictures that hang on the wall behind Sam, the Confederate soldier on the left and the Union soldier on the right. Fittingly enough, the two are shown together on two occasions: on Cady's arrival and Sam's departure; significantly enough, between the showings of these two pictured rivals from the war between the North and the South, each time Sam is shown in a frontal shot the picture of the Confederate soldier is shown behind him, to his left. When he delivers his parting words, however, all the while standing above the seated Cady, whose hat hides the Confederate soldier, the picture of the dark Union soldier is shown behind him. As the two pictures illustrate, where up to this point Sam repeatedly shared the screen with the lighter Confederate soldier who fought for secession, just as he did all he could to disassociate himself from Cady, now he shares the screen with the darker Union soldier, which foreshadows the union, the integration, of the unconscious Other in his consciousness, in his "train of thought."

Sam may well allude to the psychological war between the unconscious South and the conscious North when, that same night, he gives Peggy the lowdown: "This is no war of nerves. He won't be bought off. It's Nancy he's after. And he'll get to her sooner or later, unless I change his mind." Having gotten the picture, he understands that, rather than a "war of nerves," it's a war of minds, the unconscious against the conscious.

As part of his union with his Other, Sam puts himself in Cady's mind when explaining to Peggy how he can "attack" Nancy and get away with it. He knows that Cady, who had studied law in prison, knows how far he can go. Cady knows that they will not press charges if he attacks their daughter, if only because they will not put her through the probing "clinical" questions that testifying against him would entail. "He knows that we'd never put her through an ordeal like that."

To protect his daughter (and wife), Sam decides to take the law into his own hands, something he wouldn't have considered a week before when his hired detective, who doubles for Cady's hired lawyer, suggested he could "change his mind" by roughing him up. Of course, as a lawyer, Sam "can't consider that." On the other hand, as the detective reminds him, "It's your family, not mine." Leaving no doubt what Sam is up against, he adds, "A type like that is an animal, so you got to fight him like an animal."

Just as Sam had enough after two confrontations with Cady and turned to the chief of police, after Sam's two attempts to get Cady to leave town, by paying him off and getting others to attack him at the waterfront, Cady has had enough. Doubling for Sam's calling Chief Dutton from the bowling alley, he calls Sam from a public phone booth. While the two talk, Sam is repeatedly shown in a shot similar to the one showing Cady. Only where Cady holds a black receiver and has the "one" of the "ph*one*" next to his face, Sam holds a white receiver, with a dark picture on the wall doubling for Cady's "one." As suggested by his threat, Cady is the wronged one of the two. "You're wrong, man," he says threateningly. "I'm gonna show you what it's like to be wrong." Sam, of course, is mostly wrong about wanting to disassociate himself from his unconscious Other by driving him out of town. Getting the message, the picture, he understands that the only way he can do it is by confronting him in a fight to the finish, by outplaying him in his own game, in the realm of the unconscious.

That Sam has crossed a crucial threshold in his dealing with his Other is made clear by Peggy's response to her husband's plan: "I can't believe we're standing here talking about — about killing a man." She even accepts Sam's plan to use their daughter (and herself) as bait, a scheme that mirrors the unconscious desire he projects on his Other. Objectionable as this notion may seem, particularly with the wholesome Gregory Peck playing the upright family man, it's repeatedly suggested in the course of the movie, starting with Cady throwing a look at the two young women when entering the courthouse and his reminding Sam how much they're alike when commenting about the young woman crossing the street in front of Sam's car. As Cady reminds Sam of his being "an expert on such things" in connection with his "good-lookin' wife" and his daughter "just like her," Sam is no less lecherous. He only represses this desire, projecting it on the convenient Cady, who, as the unconscious Other, never misses a chance to give it expression.

The clearest picture of Sam's unconscious desire for his daughter, no doubt, is drawn in the marina segment. Just as was suggested by the "shared" beers, when eyeing Nancy at the marina, Cady holds a can of Budweiser (identical to the one Sam shared with Chief Dutton), which now doubles for the can of thinner in Sam's hands when he spots him there, a can he went to buy while leaving his daughter alone, available for his Other's lecherous gaze. What the two cans merely suggest, Cady gives expression to when pointing out to Sam how his daughter is "getting to be almost as juicy as your wife." That Cady's words give expression to Sam's unconscious desire for his daughter is reinforced by Sam's overreaction in his uncharacteristic attack. In William Miller's words, "Any time our response to another person involves excessive emotion or overreaction, we can be sure that something unconscious has been prodded and is being activated.... What we decry in the 'enemy' may be nothing less than a shadow projection of our own darkness."[5]

All this comes to a head in the climactic scene when Sam lures Cady into giving full expression to his own unconscious lust for his daughter in the primeval jungle-like setting of the Cape Fear River, in the houseboat representing the unconscious just as his home represents the conscious. Recalling his finding the attacked "girl" in Baltimore in his first contact with his unconscious desire, Sam finding his wife "whimpering" after she's attacked by Cady on the houseboat and her screaming hysterically, "It's Nancy! It's Nancy," says it loud and clear. Her words are doubled by Nancy, who repeats to herself when seeing him through the window of the cabin's door, "He's here. He's Here," her very same words when she *imagined* Cady was coming after her when school let out. Now, with Cady standing bare-chested before her, just as he had confronted Diane before attacking her, the full meaning of his telling her after the beating, "Consider this only a sample," become clear. It's "only a sample" of what Sam would unconsciously like to do.

In the violent and wordless struggle that erupts between the two adversaries, Sam finally gets the upper hand when he retrieves his gun and shoots Cady. "Go ahead," Cady urges Sam when he cocks his gun to keep him down. "Go ahead. I don't give a damn." But his projector does. "No. No. That would be letting you off too easy, too fast," he addresses Cady as he had addressed him in their first encounter in the car. "Your words, do you remember? Well, *I* do!" His remembering, of course, is much more than his taking up Cady's words. Together with the turn of the tables, it signals and signifies his becoming conscious of his unconscious Other.

Unlike most films dealing with the Other, those in which the projector kills his Other after a violent struggle, symbolizing his integrating his unconscious Other in his consciousness, Sam refrains from pulling the trigger a second time. Despite Cady's encouragement, he doesn't take the second shot, and not only because he's a lawyer. In effect, Sam doesn't go through with what von Franz calls "the much more difficult problem where most people have great trouble: they know what their shadow is, but they cannot express it much or integrate it into their lives."[6] Rather than integrating his unconscious Other in his conscious life, Sam represses it once again in his psychic prison, thinking it will remain there "for life." "You're gonna live a long life, in a cage," he addresses his Other. "That's where you belong. And that's where you're going. And this time for life!"

Explaining Sam's relegating his projected Other to the unconscious, von Franz writes in her book, *Projection and Re-Collection in Jungian Psychology*:

> Unconscious contents can scarcely be integrated into the subject in their entirety. The process appears to be more like that of peeling an onion — one or more layers of an unconscious complex can, indeed, be integrated by the conscious personality but not the core itself. However, the core falls back into the unconscious in a condition of latency and is no longer an immediate problem.[7]

That Sam hasn't entirely integrated his Other is envisioned in the movie's two closing shots of the three family members, bunched together in the back of the boat, heading back to civilization on the Cape Fear River. The first shot shows Sam gazing straight ahead, as he did when Cady reminded him how similar they were in their sexual desire for the young woman. Sitting still, as if in shock or in deep thought, he's clearly disassociated from his wife and daughter. With Nancy between her parents, Peggy hugs her as if taking her, or keeping her away, from Sam, who had invited his unconscious Other into their lives. The troubled look on her face as she briefly gazes at Sam, and then at Nancy, seems to connect the two in her mind. Still in the same shot, both mother and daughter gaze toward the primeval mangrove trees on the shore of the Cape Fear River, where they experienced, and got a good picture of, Sam's unconscious Other. The solemn look on Sam's face may well mirror the dark guilt he feels for what has surfaced with Cady's arrival, for what he has put his family through.

That Cady hasn't gone away, that he's still part of Sam, though now more part of his consciousness than before his emergence, is envisioned by the epilogue's second, and the movie's final shot, which shows the white boat heading up the Cape Fear River. With the closing credits over this shot, it doubles for the opening shots of Cady, dressed in white, heading toward the courthouse and into Sam's life.

5

Cape Fear (1991): The Other Wronged

> *Somebody finally got to you.*
> — *Leigh Bowden to her husband, Sam Bowden*

The Other Movie

The "other" *Cape Fear*, Martin Scorsese's 1991 remake of J. Lee Thompson's movie, offers a rare opportunity to see how the two filmmakers use the same story to convey the subtext of the projector and his unconscious Other.

Basing his version on James R. Webb's original screenplay for the 1962 movie, Scorsese acknowledges and pays tribute to Thompson's movie by casting Gregory Peck, Robert Mitchum, and Martin Balsam in cameo roles. He also uses Bernard Herrmann's original musical score and his unused score for Hitchcock's *Torn Curtain*, which adds to the Hitchcock touch that so typifies Thompson's movie. As Andrew J. Rausch points out in his book, *The Films of Martin Scorsese and Robert De Niro*:

> Both Scorsese and De Niro agreed that they wanted their version of *Cape Fear* to be a conscious homage to Hitchcock. De Niro explains, "We spent a lot less time reconsidering the *Cape Fear* film from 1962 than we did watching many of the old Hitchcock classics, which were truly our inspiration here."[1]

Aside from Hitchcock, Scorsese's *Cape Fear* is both like and unlike the original. He uses most of the events from Thompson's movie, but under different circumstances. Or as Ellis Cashmore puts it in his book, *Martin Scorsese's America*: "Scorsese's *Cape Fear* strains to be as different from its original in as many ways as it can without shattering the nucleus of the plot."[2] The same can also be said of the film's subplot, its subtext of the projector and his unconscious Other. Just as "the nucleus of the plot" in both movies is Sam Bowden's (Nick Nolte) doing what he must to protect his family from the relentless Max Cady (Robert De Niro), the "nucleus" of the subplot is Sam's dealing with his projected Other, who gives expression to his unconscious desires.

While Scorsese presents a modern family with typical problems of the times, he has his own way of envisioning the "psychological thriller," as he called his *Cape Fear*. For instance, whereas in Thompson's movie Sam was merely a witness in Cady's trial, in Scorsese's remake he was his defense lawyer, who didn't do all he could to best serve his client. Or, rather than have Cady attack Diane Taylor, as he does in the original, he attacks Sam's young co-worker Lori Davis (Illeana Douglas), thus bringing his psychopathic violence closer to Sam. While Thompson has Nancy imagine Cady is after her when school lets out, suggesting he's a figure of her imagination, her unconscious, Scorsese has Sam's daughter, Danielle (Juliette Lewis), actually meet Cady in the school's theater, where his claiming he comes from "the black forest" points to his role as a creature from the unconscious.

Having been wronged by Sam in Scorsese's version may give Cady a more justified motive for seeking revenge, but he's no less Sam's projected Other. Where Robert Mitchum's Cady can be seen as the return of the repressed, Robert De Niro's Cady is more the return of the wronged Other. It's not for nothing that he calls himself "the Do-right Man." Besides, it's written all over him. Or as Mitchum's character in the movie, Lieutenant Elgart, comments upon seeing the tattooed torso of the "other" Cady, "I don't know whether to look at him or read him."

Of course, one way to look at and read Cady, as the movie suggests from start to finish, is his being Sam's unconscious Other. Seen through this psychological prism, rendered mostly through metaphorical images and double entendres, Scorsese's *Cape Fear* becomes, in the best tradition of Hitchcock, a modern masterpiece of the projector and his unconscious Other.

Title Sequence

Cape Fear's mysterious title sequence, to paraphrase Mitchum's character, is Hitchcock "all over the place." Along with Bernard Herrmann's musical score, the sequence itself was designed by Saul Bass (and his wife, Elaine

Bass), who had designed the title sequences for three of Hitchcock's most revered masterpieces, *Vertigo*, *North by Northwest* and *Psycho*, each containing a Herrmann musical score. While Herrmann's score introduces the movie's emotional mood, Bass's sequence, like many of his other title sequences, conveys their underlying story. As Bass himself had noted, the title sequence is meant "to set mood and the prime underlying core of the film's story, to express the story in some metaphorical way."[3]

In their own "metaphorical way," the various shapes and colors of the rippling water that dominate *Cape Fear*'s title sequence set the mood for both the river that gives the movie its title and the unconscious it signifies. The rippling water dazzles our vision so that we cannot really tell what takes place below the shimmering surface, though several distorted images come into view. In contrast to the dark water and images, the movie's titles are white, their disjointed lettering seeming to envision the split between the conscious and the unconscious, between the projector and his Other.

The first clear image is of an eagle (or hawk) swooping toward the water, opening its claws as if to catch unseen prey. As he flies out of the frame, the name "Robert De Niro" appears in its place on the left side of the screen, the juxtaposition associating his character with the bird of prey. Then, as the tip of its shadowy wing is briefly shown taking off, "Nick Nolte" appears at the center. His name is replaced by "Jessica Lange" on the right side of the screen, which is divided into two distinct sides of blue and gray, the colors of the Civil War's North and South, the conscious and the unconscious.

Next, as the background changes, various parts of a face are shown, such as eyes, mouth, and teeth, then the whole face itself, all seeming to envision the face of the Other. They're followed by an image of a shadowy figure's torso and arms, another image of the shadowy Other. Then, just before the last credit appears, "Directed by Martin Scorsese," which recalls Hitchcock's signature title, "Directed by Alfred Hitchcock," there's a close-up of a drop of water at the center of the screen, which drips from top to bottom in slow motion, with the screen turning red, the color the movie associates with Max Cady, the movie's Other.

With the end of the credits, the screen remains red as an extreme close-up of a pair of eyes appear in what seems like a dark room's red light — used to make black-and-white prints. In fact, the eyes change to a black and white negative. With a girl's voice announcing, "My Reminiscence," the eyes fade to "real-life" black and white, gradually fading into color together with the camera pulling away to reveal the young girl talking to the camera in front of a blackboard that's divided into two parts. Recalling the indistinct images and rippling water of the title sequence, the white writing on the blackboard is partially erased so that it cannot be read, and what seems like streaming water is superimposed on the whole screen behind the girl, whose words all but describe the eruption of the unconscious Other. "I always thought that for such a lovely river," the girl recites, "the name was mystifying: 'Cape Fear.' When the only thing to fear on those enchanted summer nights was that the magic would end, and real life would come crashing in."

"Heeere's Cady"

Announced by the same ominous four-note brass motif that opened Thompson's *Cape Fear*, real life comes crashing in as the camera cuts to Cady's prison cell, revealing a set of pictures taped to the wall, whose significance is underscored by the way the camera surveys them from top to bottom, from North to South. The first shown set consists of two black-and-white pictures of military men on either side of the sepia-toned picture of a martyred woman impaled by two spears. With Scorsese retelling Thompson's movie, the two pictures of the uniformed soldiers may double for the original's two pictures of the rivaling Civil War soldiers that hang on the wall behind Sam when he confronts Cady at the Boar's Head's backroom. In Scorsese's version, the unconscious South and the conscious North are evoked by Kersek (Joe Don Baker), Sam's hired detective, as the two anxiously await Cady inside the Bowden home. Dressed in black, Kersek speaks of the South's fear of the Other, linking it to the movie's name: "The South evolved in fear; fear of the Indian, fear of the slave, fear of the damn Union." On the other hand, the three pictures seem to foreshadow the three members of the Bowden family, who are first shown together in the movie theater, sitting behind Cady, rearranged with Sam between his wife and daughter.

As the camera tilts downward, the second set of shown pictures is much like the first, only transposed. Now, at the center, are two pictures of military men, Joseph Stalin and General Lee, while to one side is a picture titled, "Entrance of Alexander into Babylon," and, on the other, two colored pictures of two superheroes. General Lee, of course, alludes to the Confederacy, the South that this lower set of pictures signifies. Alexander's entrance into Babylon brings to mind that the girl's "real life would come crashing in"; the two superheroes foreshadow the movie's two super rivals, the projector and his unconscious Other.

With the camera continuing its descent, foreshadowing the movie's descent to the unconscious, the evocative pictures are replaced by equally telling books. Among the many law books, on top of which is a copy of the Bible that plays an important role in Cady's revenge, two pairs of "other" books stand out. One pair consists of two volumes by Nietzsche, *The Will to*

Power and *Thus Spake Zarathustra*, both of which are part of Cady's "mission ... to become more than human" during his "fourteen years in an eight-by-nine cell." While these two books explain the two superheroes on Cady's cell wall, the other two, Dante's *The Inferno* and *The Cell Within*, may well allude to the infernal Other incarcerated within Sam's unconscious.

As the camera starts pulling away from the pictures and books, Cady's head and tattooed back are seen as he does pushups. The tattooed cross on his back, which takes up the whole screen and rhymes with the picture of the female martyr, seems to suggest Cady's identifying with her, particularly as later he informs Sam that in prison he got in touch with his "feminine side." With a dish hanging from both arms of the cross, it's also a scale of justice. One dish holds a Bible on the side of truth; the other a sword on the side of justice. Like the telling pictures and books, this image implies that, at least in Cady's mind, justice was not served.

Still in the same opening shot, the two motif continues as two doors are opened for Cady, one of his cell (accompanied by the prison guard's, "Ok, Cady, the moment you've been waiting for."), the other of his cell block. With the closing of the second door, the camera cuts to the opening of the prison gate door, as Cady, now in civilian clothing, is shown strolling outside the prison in a two-shot sequence.

"What about your books?" inquires the prison guard carting his books behind Cady.

"Already read 'em," Cady replies tersely. With these words, the second shot shows him from a distance, walking directly toward the stationary camera as if nothing can stop him, while behind him looms an ominous thunderstorm, with lightning bolts like the two sets of three bolts tattooed on his chest.

The three prison shots that introduce Cady are doubled in the subsequent three shots, but in reverse order, with both the feminine replacing the masculine, and the Bowden home, shown in the establishing shot, replacing the prison that it later becomes. The second shot shows a pair of white shoes, as the camera tilts up to show the maid, Graciela (Zully Montero), getting out of a car and walking toward the camera, much as Cady did in the prison shot. The third shot shows Danielle coming out of the house (to dispose of trash) and greeting Graciela: "*Es ropa limpia?*" she asks concerning the two laundry bags the maid is carrying, one white, the other light blue.

"No, no," Graciela corrects her as the camera follows them walking toward the main entrance. "That means clean. These are dirty."

Bearing in mind that Sam is first shown wearing a light blue suit as he comes out of the courthouse together with his partner, who's also dressed in a light suit, the dirty laundry mistaken for clean may well represent his two sides, the clean that is visible and the dirty which is not, or the conscious and the unconscious. Perhaps that's why Danielle takes the light blue laundry bag from Graciela just before they enter the house, or why (as the two are shown entering) her mother is heard saying before the camera cuts to her, "The idea is to resolve the tension."

Whereas in Thompson's original, Sam was the first family member introduced, and then with his daughter before his wife, in Scorsese's remake his daughter is not only the first member shown, and paired with the maid, she's next paired with her mother, while Sam, as if disassociated from the family, is subsequently paired with his law partner. Underscoring that Danielle favors Graciela over her mother (as initially suggested by her trying to speak to her in her native language), she rolls her eyes when paired with her mother, Leigh, who tries to engage her in her search for "a motif that's about movement" to balance the "stability" in the logo she is trying to create. "Like an arrow, maybe," Danielle suggests, recalling the two spears in the picture of the martyred woman in Cady's cell. Not to be outdone, Leigh seems to talk about the kind of balance that recalls the scales of justice tattooed on Cady's back, or "maybe" about the balance between the projector and his Other, when explaining to her uninterested daughter of how to "balance those ideas in a way that's pleasing to the eye."

Cady himself first appears before the three members of the Bowden family with his back silhouetted against the background of the movie they're watching, *Problem Child*, a story of a young boy who becomes a monster as a result of repeated abandonment. Significantly, Cady deliberately sits down in front of Sam, who sits with his wife and daughter "balanced" on either side, precisely after the child's foster father breaks through his bedroom door, announcing, "Heeere's Daddy!" Sending a similar message, Cady lights his phallic cigar with a lighter in the shape of a woman in red bikini, whose nipples flicker in red light as he lights his huge cigar. All but announcing "Heeere's Cady," Cady puffs and roars nonstop, his demonic-like smoke and uproarious laughter chasing the Bowdens to other seats.

In the subsequent ice-cream parlor scene, Cady once again calls attention to himself by paying for the Bowdens' ice cream. Seeing him sitting in his red Mustang puffing his fat cigar, staring intently in their direction, Sam goes to his two "girls," as he calls them. "Girls, girls. Come on, let's sit inside." As he escorts the two inside, when he looks back Cady is no longer there. Considering Sam is the only one who sees him, it's another suggestion that he's his projected Other. Or, as Scorsese puts it, "He works on the conflicts that already exist in the family."[4]

Sandwiched between Cady's two disturbing appearances, "the conflicts" between the three Bowdens are revealed as they seem to give expression to their feelings about Sam and his unconscious Other. "Dad, you should've just punched him out," Danielle says, turning to her father.

"What?" Sam replies, clearly not getting the message. "Just punched him out? What do you mean?"

Her reply, "Yeah, you box," may well refer to his "shadow boxing" with his Other; shoving her father, she drives the point home: "You could've shoved him around, shut him out."

"Yeah, I can take you," Sam says, playfully putting her in a choke hold. "That's who I can take."

"Yeah, you know how to fight dirty," Leigh, who's been shut out of what seems to be a switch of roles between wife and daughter, joins in, foretelling what Sam will have to do to keep them alive. "You do that for a living."

However subtle, another tip-off as to what's really going on between father and daughter is revealed by what each one ordered. While Sam and Leigh ordered milkshakes, and Danielle a bowl of ice cream (shown in a close-up that opens the scene), the flavors (colors) tell another story. Leigh has a white shake, Sam a pink one, just like the color of his daughter's ice cream, a color achieved by mixing white with red, the color of Cady's Mustang and his lighter's nipples.

Invasion of the Other

After imposing himself on the Bowdens in two public places, Cady starts invading Sam's private space when he reaches into his car and takes out his keys from the ignition, just as he did in the 1962 original. Envisioning the two as opposite doubles, we first see a close-up of Sam's horizontal hand putting the key in, followed by an identical close-up of Cady's vertical hand taking it out. As in the original, this "key" scene is the men's first face-to-face confrontation. Whereas in the theater Cady appeared as a shadow, he now appears in a black shirt. Linking the two, when Cady asks, "Could it be you don't remember me?" Sam replies, "Sure, I remember you. You were at the movie house." At this point in their relationship, Sam doesn't recognize him as his unconscious Other.

Only after Sam asks for the keys does Cady reveal his name; and only after Sam remembers his case, "Atlanta, '77," does Cady return the keys. During the encounter, Cady merely wants Sam to remember him, the first step in acknowledging him as his unconscious Other. Letting Sam know what he has in mind, spews out from the side of his mouth as he walks away, "You're gonna learn about loss." Sam's "What?" as if hearing but not believing, recalls his "What?" to Danielle's telling him he "should've punched him out."

That Cady's words have disturbed Sam is suggested by the very next shot, which shows him at home, noodling the black piano keys. The shot envisions the projector and his unconscious Other not only by the black and white keys, but also by Sam's two hands, one horizontal, the other vertical, which recall the two "key" shots in the car, and by their being reflected in the wooden piano's shiny veneer. Mirroring Cady's disturbing words, Sam's playing disturbs Danielle, who's trying to read ("learn") her assigned book.

"What are you working on?" Sam asks Danielle while continuing to fiddle with the piano keys.

"*Look Homeward, Angel*," she replies, adding "which is a kind of reminiscence,"

Sam, more fatherly correct than genuinely engaged, asks listlessly, "What's it about, your reminiscence?"

"The houseboat," Danielle replies, seeming to reminisce about "those enchanted summer nights," before her father's unconscious Other came "crashing in."

Her words are accentuated by Sam echoing reminiscently, "Oh, the houseboat," while fiddling with the black keys again, now shown inside the piano, the felt hammers hitting the strings as if the words had struck a raw nerve.

Showing the keys "within" and the "reminiscing" way both Danielle and Sam say "houseboat" seems to suggest an unmentionable incident between the two, particularly when considering the sexual tension between them throughout the movie. It seems significant that Danielle's age is twice compared to the age of the girl raped by Cady, the crime for which he was imprisoned, which signifies Sam's repression of his Other, his relegating him to the unconscious.

The houseboat and Sam's crime are taken up in the subsequent bedroom scene with Sam and Leigh, which opens with an establishing shot showing the bedroom window from outside, reflecting the town's exploding Fourth of July fireworks, making it seem as if they're going off inside (a shot that recalls the kissing scene between Grace Kelly and Cary Grant in Hitchcock's *To Catch a Thief*). In the other establishing shot, inside the bedroom, Sam, preoccupied with Cady's words, suggests to Leigh that she "take two weeks off" and go "down to the houseboat." Only as Leigh informs him, he literally missed the boat. As he learns the hard way, once returned from the repressed, there's no escaping the unconscious Other, even at the houseboat.

Recalling the shot-reverse shot sequence in Thompson's original (when Cady first confronts Sam in his car), the first of the two bedroom segments envisions the projector and his Other by its shot-reverse shot sequence. Sam and Leigh occupy opposite sides of the screen; the reverse shots show the two as doubles by their reflections in one of the mirrors. In one reverse shot, Leigh's reflected image mirrors Sam's unconscious when she makes a wish about Cady and her daughter: "Maybe this drama teacher from the college will get her excited about something." To which Sam, the projector not reflected in the mirror, replies about his Other, "Yeah, about him, probably."

In another revealing reverse shot, when Sam, reflected in the mirror, comments on how marijuana use (for which Danielle was expelled from school) is still "forbidden," and Leigh adds somewhat cryptically, "Right up there with incest and necrophilia and bestiality," he spits out his toothpaste precisely after she utters "incest." Not only that, seeming to "get excited" by Leigh's words more than by her baring her shoulder, which he sees reflected in the mirror he's facing, Sam's "Honey, honey, honey" turns from denial to arousal. "Do that again," he entreats Leigh.

"What?" she asks, using the same word he used with both Cady and his daughter.

"Do that again," he persists, as they both seem amused by this sudden arousal. As Kirsten Moana Thompson notes, "The film displaces his [Sam's] unconscious incestuous desires for his child by projecting them onto Max Cady as the external sadistic threat to his family.... As a monster and as a doppelgänger of Samuel Bowden, Cady becomes the displaced external figure of the dread for a family already fractured by conflicts engendered by the father's ethical lapses."[5]

The bedroom segment's second part opens with a shot of two legs, one belonging to Leigh, the other to Sam, as they consummate their momentary arousal in bed, accompanied by the colorful glare of the exploding fireworks. With the camera closing in on Leigh's face, her eyes closed, she seems far away, as if wishing for someone to really "get her excited." Then, as the camera closes in on their entwined hands, the image of the hands fades to black and white, followed by a negative shot that recalls how Danielle was first shown, perhaps suggesting the incest that aroused Sam. When Leigh opens her eyes, the black and white fades into color before the whole screen fades into bright yellow. As it fades back into color, she's shown getting out of bed as if in a dreamlike trance.

Once again using the mirror to reveal the unconscious, the next shot shows Leigh sitting down at her vanity to examine her face, reflected thrice in the triptych's mirrors. Gently massaging around her eyes, she seems to conjure the image of the man who "can get her excited," particularly as it's followed by the screen fading into red, the color associated with Cady. As screenwriter Wesley Strick commented about this scene, Leigh is "unconsciously preparing for her first date with Max Cady."[6] The notion of excitement is envisioned by the subsequent shot, which shows Leigh sensually caressing her lips with a pink phallic lipstick, the color identified with her daughter, the same color shared by Sam and Danielle at the ice-cream parlor.

With the screen turning red again, Leigh goes to the shuttered windows as if drawn to what's outside. There, doubling for the three mirrors in which she saw her face, she sees Cady through the three wooden shutters, one after the other, sitting on their property wall with the orgasmic fireworks going off behind him. In each of her three sightings, the camera zooms in for a close-up of her eyes between the slats, which recall the close-up of Danielle's eyes in the opening credits, linking mother and daughter in their attraction to Sam's unconscious Other.

Awakened by Leigh's "Somebody's out there," Sam's ineffectual "I want you off my property," after Cady is already gone, is underscored by his inability to get Leigh's dog, Benjamin, off the kitchen table, which occurs immediately after Leigh asks, "So, who is he, and where did he come from?" The dog is associated with Cady again the following morning, when Sam asks Leigh, "What's he gonna do, lick him to death?" Leigh, having seen Cady, is clearly sexually excited when saying goodbye to Sam at the door, perhaps even wishing out loud, "What about a weapon? In case things get exciting around here."

Benjamin is linked yet again to Cady in the exchange between Sam and Leigh, following his poisoning. When Sam reprimands her, "I told you not to let him out!" Leigh, seeming to speak of his unconscious Other more than the dog, attacks him, screaming, "I didn't let him out! I didn't let him out!" Reinforcing the notion of "letting out" the Other, this scene is sandwiched between Sam's two encounters with Cady. The first one is in the street, when Cady drives up to Sam, revealing that he had learned to read in prison and acted as his own lawyer in his appeal, thus letting Sam know that he knows he had wronged him by burying helpful evidence. The second encounter takes place at the police station, where Sam, accompanied by the police lieutenant, played by Robert Mitchum, watches Cady unseen through a one-way mirror as he's subjected to "a full-body strip search," the words tattooed on his body revealing the revenge he has in mind. One extended arm reads "Vengeance is mine," the other "My time is at hand." This scene is shot in such a way as to show Sam's reflection in the glass superimposed on Cady, envisioning the two as opposite sides of the same mirror, one conscious, the other unconscious.

The one-way mirror changes sides when Sam spots Cady at the Independence Day street parade, looking intently in their direction through his mirrored sunglasses from the other side of the street. "Sooner or later he's gonna screw up," Sam explains to Leigh (and Danielle) in the scene's opening shot. "I mean, the sheriff assured me that they always do." But the one who screws up is Sam himself, and much sooner than later. Believing Cady is staring at Leigh, or worse yet, Danielle, he crosses the street and confronts him: "What the hell are you doing?" Cady's response, "Hot as a firecracker on the Fourth of July," drives Sam to do exactly what Danielle had said he should have done—punch him out. Cady's "What are you getting so upset about?" goes unanswered, but it's a clear case of the projector overreacting to his projected Other. Projection, after all, as Ken Wilber points out, "is very easily identified: if a person or thing in the environment *informs* us, we probably aren't projecting; on the other hand, if it *affects* us, chances are that we are a victim of our own projections."[7]

Cady continues to affect Sam by picking up and attacking Lori, Sam's current object of desire (whose age falls between Leigh's and Danielle's), in a scene that ends with a shot showing his silhouette through the bedroom window, which doubles for the shot of the window that preceded Sam and Leigh's lovemaking. Where the couple's window is *preceded* by the shot of the felt hammers and strings inside the piano, Lori's window is *followed* by an identical shot. Only in the second shot one string is missing, later used by Cady to strangle both Graciela and Detective Kerske, whom Sam, growing desperate, hires to deal with Cady. As he confesses to Leigh after they have it out about his "gravitating" to Lori and other women, "I'm scared. I keep feeling there's some animal out there, stalking us. I think he wants to hurt us in the worst way. And that's got me frightened to death." Leigh, turning to face Sam, whom she feels is finally being straight with her, speaks with unfamiliar empathy: "You really are scared, aren't you?" When Sam finally comes clean, "Oh, yeah," she replies with a certain sense of satisfaction. "Somebody finally got to you."

Having "got to" Sam through Lori, Cady proceeds to get to him through his two "girls." First, under the pretense of returning the dog collar, he drives up in his red Mustang when Leigh comes out to the mailbox, letting her know who he is by hinting that he had poisoned Benjamin and that he's been watching her sketching. "Oh, you're Max Cady aren't you?" Leigh says, putting two and two together. Despite her expressed revulsion, their brief exchange is replete with double meanings and sexual innuendoes. As Rausch notes, "The two of them spar verbally, but there's a strange and unmistakable sexual tension present between them."[8] Just when Cady remarks, "We might have been happy, Leigh," Danielle comes out to call her mother to the phone. Whether to keep her daughter from seeing Cady, or Cady from seeing Danielle, Leigh hollers, "Danny, don't come out here!" Cady, who perks up when seeing Danielle, starts driving away, all but answering Leigh's earlier question by saying, "You satisfied now that you've seen it?"

But Cady is far from satisfied. That evening, when Sam comes home, announcing "I'm home," and Leigh says the same about his Other when whispering in his ear, "He was here today," the camera cuts to a close-up of the ringing pink phone in Danielle's bedroom. On the other end of the line is Cady, pretending to be Danielle's "new drama teacher," all but making Leigh's wish come true.

While they talk on the phone, toward the end of the first shot that shows Danielle in her bedroom, Cady voice is heard: "You know, Danielle — all that negativity, you can use that." When she asks, "What do you mean?" the camera cuts to Cady's room, slowly surveying it until finally coming to rest on his hanging upside down, in a red shirt no less. Rather than give his name, he introduces himself as "the kind of teacher that takes a personal interest in his kids." His "personal interest," as his subsequent words reveal, is far from innocent. Siding with Danielle against her parents, he talks about her "sexuality" and "the anger that you feel that your mom and dad won't let you just grow up and be a woman." When Cady's face is finally shown, hanging upside down from a chin-up bar across his doorframe, he speaks about Danielle's anger like an unrepressed Other. "Don't suppress or deny it. Use it in your life and your work."

Not unlike her mother, Cady's words excite Danielle enough to make her take the braces out of her mouth. Just as he tells her that the class has "been changed to the theater," the camera turns upside down to show him as if he were right-side up to go along with his turning Danielle's world on its head, on its *other* side. "And remember, Danielle," he inadvertently alludes to her reminiscing about Cape Fear, "you can use all those fears to draw upon and learn." With Cady's "'Night now," Danielle, returning to being her parents' daughter, returns the braces to her mouth, which recalls her mother wiping off the lipstick after first seeing Cady.

Staging Sam's Unconscious Desire

Next morning, like Little Red Riding Hood's mother before her daughter ventures out alone into the unconscious forest, Leigh is worried as she drops Danielle at school. "Honey," she says, "I think maybe I should walk you in."

But Danielle has other ideas. "No, it's okay, Mom," she replies. "There's a lot of people here." Little does she know that "downstairs" in the theater she will be "alone now," as Cady sings to her, giving her the green light to smoke the joint he offers her from inside the witch's candy-covered cabin that's part of the stage's fairy tale *mise-en-scène*. Sharing the joint not only puts Cady on her side against her parents, it "eases inhibition," he explains.

With the marijuana smoke setting the stage, and as suggested by the fairy-tale setting and surrounding forest, the meeting between the two is a dramatization of Sam's unconscious desire for his daughter. Cady even alludes to this netherworld drama when he asks Danielle, "You down here for drama?" Underscoring its significance, this dramatization, this re-enactment, not only takes place midpoint in the story, it's by far its longest single scene, without any of the film's characteristically dramatic music, as if the drama on stage is enough.

Cady first connects with Danielle through "the book you have, Thomas Wolfe," referring to both the book's hero and Sam when commenting, "You can't escape your demons just by leaving home." Then, after connecting through other books known for their explicit sexual content, Danielle becomes suspicious when the "drama teacher" speaks knowingly of her relationship with her disapproving parents, all the while suggesting they project their denied feelings on her, and perhaps even alluding to Sam's unconscious crime, when speaking of their "deflecting their guilt and anger onto you for a crime that's not even a crime." Growing suspicious that he's "not the drama teacher," she asks him, just as her mother had twice asked her father about him, "Where are you from?" Cady all but depicts himself as a sexual creature from the unconscious when replying, "I'm from a black forest," and "Maybe I'm the big bad wolf."

In this unconscious staging, as in "Little Red Riding Hood," "the big bad wolf" personifies Sam's unconscious desire for Danielle. Connecting the two, Danielle asks Cady, "Why do you hate my father?" But Cady, speaking like her father's denied Other who's returned from the repressed to make Sam own up and acknowledge him, claims that he's "here to help him. I mean, we all make mistakes, Danielle. You and I have. At least we try to admit it. But your daddy, he don't." Having said that, Cady seems to demonstrate what Sam doesn't admit or allow himself (or perhaps what he had already done at the houseboat) when he asks Danielle, "Do you mind if I put my arms around you?" When Danielle says she doesn't mind, Cady, being the Other that he is, goes much further. He puts his arm around her, but then also inserts his thumb into her mouth, twice, and kisses her passionately on the mouth. Then, with the staging of the unconscious desire over, Cady promptly walks off the stage in the direction of "the black forest," back to the unconscious from which he came.

That Danielle's meeting with Cady is a staging of Sam's unconscious desire for her is reinforced by how he reacts when suspecting that there was more to their meeting than words, which is envisioned by his shadow projected on the open white door of her bedroom. Doubling for his overreacting to Cady's staring at Leigh at the street parade, Sam's imagination gets the best of him when confronting his daughter about their "connection." His ordering her to "put some clothes on," even though she's alone in her bedroom, is clearly to protect her from himself. As he says himself, "You're not a little kid anymore."

Getting her father's drift, Daniel informs him, "Dad, he didn't force himself on me, you know. I know you'd like to think he did, but I think he was just trying to make a connection with me."

Closing the door behind him and sitting down on Danielle's bed, Sam waves his finger before her face, his overreaction once again revealing what Cady represents for him. "There will never be a connection between you and Max Cady. You understand that?" Then, seeing Danielle's "reminiscing" and her rubbing her lips with her thumb, much as did her mother with her lipstick after seeing Cady, Sam asks what he already seems to knows. "Did he touch you?"

"*What?*" Danielle giggles, recalling her father's very same responses when she suggested he "should've just punched him out," and when Cady left him with, "You're gonna learn about loss."

"What are you laughing about? Why are you smilin'? I'm asking you a question. Did he touch you?" Danielle smiles again. "Wipe that smile off your face!" he explodes, putting his hand over her mouth and pushing her back against the bed's headboard. "Did he touch you?" he yells.

Danielle, looking away from her father, yells back when he tries to apologize for his outburst. "Get out of here! Get out of here!" she screams, horrified at what she had glimpsed of her father's unconscious Other.

Significantly, Sam's outburst, his overreaction, is sandwiched between two encounters with Cady. In the first one he warns him what will happen "if you don't leave my family alone and get out of here," to which Cady informs his "old colleague," as he calls Sam, "You could say I'm here to save you." In the second encounter, just as he projects his illicit desire on his Other, Sam lets other people do his dirty work in dealing with Cady. Whereas merely two days earlier he had refused such an offer, saying "I can't operate outside the law," he now agrees to this "hospital job" after learning that Cady, as he puts it, "came at my daughter at school."

Re-enacting Sam's Crime

Ultimately, like everything else in his dealing with his projected Other, in going against the law, just as he had done in Cady's trial, Sam once again turns the tables on himself. Only this time his profession and family are in danger. And as fits the *two* motif that informs the movie, in his last two dealings with his Other, Sam repeats what he had done in his first two encounters, but in reverse order and with much higher stakes. At first, he locks his "girls" inside their home just as he had taken them inside when spotting Cady parked in his red Mustang outside the ice-cream parlor. When that fails, he tries to escape Cady by leaving home and driving to their houseboat just as Cady's obnoxious laughter and noxious cigar smoke had driven them to change seats in the movie theater.

On the first night inside their home, when Sam looks for answers in the Book of Job that Cady advised him to read, Leigh reveals that she also wants some answers about their dealing with Cady. "I'd like to know how strong we are, or how weak," she says. "But I guess the only way we're gonna find out is just by going through this." With this, the camera cuts to Danielle, who wakes up suddenly in fright, as if from a bad dream. Come morning, suggesting that it was more than a dream, she finds the book Cady talked about in their meeting at the theater, Henry Miller's *Sexus*, hidden beneath a large tin can at the entrance.

The notion that Cady is more than a dream is suggested once more on the second night, when Sam, sitting up in bed like his daughter the night before, envisions him in his bedroom, dressed as he is in reality, gazing at him while smoking his cigar. Rubbing his eyes in disbelief when seeing him as a photographic negative, as the negative Other, he dissolves to positive before Sam's eyes, perhaps suggesting that Cady has indeed returned to "help him" assimilate his Other. When Sam rubs his eyes again, Cady is gone.

Much like the book that Cady had left for Danielle on the first night, he now leaves a double message for Sam by killing Graciela and Kerske, the two "best friends" of Danielle and Sam, the two family members linked to Sam's unconscious crime. With Sam's slipping in the puddle of Kerske's blood when reaching for his gun, he's baptized in the red associated with Cady, another sign that he's becoming more and more like his unconscious Other.

The double murder drives the Bowdens to flee their home and seek refuge in their houseboat, which recalls Cady's words to Danielle, "You can't escape your demons just by leaving home." But like everything in Sam's dealing with his demonic Other, it only makes things worse. In another reminder that he's Sam's inescapable Other, Cady straps himself to the underside of their Jeep, an image that envisions the unconscious Other, unseen beneath the vehicle driven by his projector.

Likewise, underscoring the realm of the unconscious that the Cape Fear River represents, the Bowdens' arrival at their houseboat and their sailing up the river is envisioned in a wordless sequence that emphasizes the river itself and the surrounding primeval woods. The sequence's last shot, before Sam heaves the anchor into the water, shows the houseboat sailing up the river, while in the distance a thunderstorm plays havoc in the evening sky, the same kind of storm shown behind Cady upon his release from prison. Now, before he sets out for his final act of the revenge of the repressed, Cady is shown reflected in a broken mirror, ceremoniously combing his hair for his *night* in court with his projector and his "girls."

No sooner do the Bowdens sit down for their first meal on the houseboat than the storm erupts, foreshadowing the eruption of the unconscious Other. When Sam decides to "go check the anchor," Danielle, as if once again sensing the shadowing Other, pleads with him, "Wait, Dad. Don't go out." Outside, Sam also seems to sense the Other as he gazes at the heavy rain falling on the river's rippling water, shown in a rather long close-up to underscore its significance as the unconscious. But rather than emerge from below, Cady hooks Sam by the neck from above, hauling him up to the houseboat's roof, where he chokes him until he passes out, tying him up and cutting loose the houseboat from its anchor. Then, replacing Sam, he jumps down through the door. "Good evenin', ladies," he says in greeting.

Making no secret of who he is, Cady turns to Danielle and states, "Danielle, I told you, you can't escape your demons just by leaving home." Once again, as in the theater of the unconscious, he connects with her through the book he had left her for "homework." That Danielle "knows" Cady is demonstrated by her saying while crying in fear, "I knew you'd follow me here," and by Cady's "You know me pretty well, don't you, darlin?'" Coming after he strangled Graciela, Danielle's words, "Yeah, I do," are not without horrific irony. When Cady takes it a step further, however, saying, "You gonna get to know me a whole lot better," she grabs a pot of boiling water and hurls it on his face. But Cady is hardly fazed. "Are you offering me somethin' hot?" he says, laughing it off.

Demonstrating both his sexual intentions and his imperviousness to pain, his becoming "more than human," Cady lights a phallic red flare and lets its hot liquid substance, erupting like an ejaculation, melt over his unflinching hand. But when Cady is about "to depict and dramatize both the heights and the depths of a mama's true love for her daughter," as he calls his intentions to rape Danielle before her witnessing parents, Danielle fights fire with fire by squirting lighter fluid on his lit cigar. Proving he's human after all, the burning Cady jumps into the river, followed by a shot that shows him sinking to the bottom. This shot is doubled by the one that shows him rising to the surface, followed by a shot of his bloody hand emerging from the turbulent water and catching hold of the frayed anchor rope he had cut minutes before.

When Sam, thinking they had left Cady behind them in the river, goes outside the houseboat to check the anchor's rope, Cady, proving once again that there's no escaping the Other, appears suddenly, holding Sam's gun to his head, announcing "The people call Samuel G. Bowden." With his burned face making him look ever more monstrous, he commences, as he puts it, to "depict and dramatize both" Sam's crime against himself and his crime against his Other, forcing him to admit before the jury of his "girls" what he had "buried" when acting as his defense attorney. Finding Sam guilty and sentencing him "to the Ninth Circle of Hell," Cady rests his case with his kept promise, "Now you will learn about loss! Loss of freedom! Loss of humanity! Now you and I will truly be the same, Counselor."

Just as Cady is about to teach Leigh and Danielle "to be an animal, to live like one and die like one," he's suddenly thrown off his feet when the houseboat almost capsizes in the turbulent water. With Cady down, Leigh and Danielle jump into the water, but when Sam is about to follow them, Cady catches him by the ankle, proving once and for all that they're together in the same proverbial boat. In the life-and-death struggle that erupts between the two, while Cady, getting hold of Sam's gun, is looking to shoot him, Sam, crawling on the floor, ties the other end of the handcuffs to Cady's ankle, for once succeeding to turn the tables on his Other.

The foot-cuffed Cady takes two wild shots at Sam, missing both times, just as the houseboat hits a rock and his gun flies out of his hand through the window and into the river. With the boat slowly breaking apart, Sam is shown jumping into the river at the very last moment, a jump shown twice, and in two different ways, underscoring his freeing himself from his unconscious Other.

With Cady's one foot handcuffed to a railing of the beached part of the houseboat, the two confront each other on the river shore like two primeval creatures in an archetypical struggle, trading blows with bigger and bigger rocks. "I'm gonna kill you," Sam howls at Cady, who counters, "You already sacrificed me, Counselor." Unmoved, Sam picks up a gigantic rock, raising it above his head to smash it on Cady's face. But when the rock comes down, in a brief sequence of quick shots, Cady, like several times before, is no longer there. The horrified Sam watches from the shore as the river's current draws the remaining part of the houseboat, together with the shackled Cady. For a moment, before Cady sinks underwater, in a double two-shot sequence that envisions them as linked to one another, the two stare squarely at each other, with Cady's knowing look seeming to say that it's all been the revenge of the wronged Other. Following an underwater shot that shows Cady's two black shoes, recalling Graciella's white pair, he's shown looking at Sam one last time as he slowly sinks underwater, back down to the unconscious from which he had returned.

Following a close-up of Sam's two bloody and shaking hands, when he washes them in the rushing water, he suddenly jumps in fright, as if there's really no escaping his Other. But seeing his hands are clean, washed of the red blood associated with Cady, he seems to look at them for what they've done in his fight with his Other. With his seeming to acknowledge his taking the law of survival into his own hands, the camera begins to rise up, distancing itself from Sam, crouched like an ape on the bank of the unconscious river.

In the subsequent two-shot sequence, the first shot, which Scorsese shot backwards to emphasize its primordial otherness, shows Leigh slowly rising up from the mud. The second shot shows the shaken and sobbing Danielle making her way to her mother, clinging to her in a fetal position as if returning to being her mother's daughter now that Sam's unconscious Other is out of their life.

In the movie's final shot, Sam is shown trudging in the shallow water towards his "girls." Reaching them, his placing his arm on Leigh's shoulder recalls the final shot of Thompson's *Cape Fear*, both shots showing mother and daughter huddled close together, keeping their distance from Sam.

However, unlike the 1962 movie, which showed the boat heading home on the Cape Fear River, in Scorsese's remake the camera continues its inward movement, coming in and resting on Danielle's eyes, thus ending the movie as it began. Only now the subsequent black-and-white positive, negative and red are in reversed order, a cinematic bookend to the opening. As Kirsten Thompson points out, "It is apt that Danielle is this film's narrator, as she is the focus of sexuality, both in her own nascent desires and in the unconscious and overt sexual attention that she receives from her father and Max Cady."[9]

Considering what the movie has suggested about Sam and Cady from start to finish, Danielle's closing words can be read as *Cape Fear*'s last reference to the unconscious Other:

> We never spoke of what had happened. At least not to each other. Fear, I suppose, that to remember his name, or what he did, would mean letting him into our dreams. And me, I hardly dream about him any more. Still, things won't ever be the way they were before he came.

By the end of the movie, Sam does much more than what Danielle said he should have done in their very first encounter with his Other: "punch him out." He "fight[s] dirty" just as Leigh said he knew "how to." His becoming like his Other is not unlike Gilgamesh's becoming like Enkidu, which signified his assimilating the unconscious wild man in his life. This, after all, is what Cady wanted from Sam all along, to acknowledge and assimilate him as his wronged Other.

6

In the Line of Fire:
The Knowing Other

> *I know something about people.*
> — Frank Horrigan (Clint Eastwood)

Older and Older

The unconscious Other is no stranger to Clint Eastwood's movies. Whether he's merely acting, as in *Tight Rope* or *In the Line of Fire*, or directing as well, as in *Unforgiven* and *Blood Work*, the Other is a subject Eastwood returns to in his films again and again. It's already in the first entry of his Dirty Harry series, in 1971. Harry Callahan's "pursuit of Scorpio is so intense," Laurence F. Knapp notes, "it becomes an aberration in itself, a sickness as profound as Scorpio's. Scorpio is Harry's Doppelgänger."[1] Paul Smith also sees this *Doppelgänger* "at the center" of *Magnum Force* (1973), the second of the five Dirty Harry movies: "The narrative device of marking the similarities between the hunter and the hunted (which, in her review, Pauline Kael calls the doppelgänger device) is a common one, of course, even in Eastwood movies; it could be said to be at the center of *Magnum Force*, for instance."[2] In Eastwood's 1992 *Unforgiven*, Sheriff Little Bill Daggett (Gene Hackman) shares with William Munny (Eastwood) more than the same first name. As David Cremean notes, "That Daggett shares his first name with Munny suggests he is at once a type of doppelgänger to the outlaw (their shared pasts are very similar), and also the aging killer's ultimate moral inferior, as Munny at least never lived under false pretenses. In effect, Munny also slays his lesser self by killing Daggett."[3]

Eastwood's more obvious movies of the *Doppelgänger*, as critics have noted, are *Tightrope* (1984), *In the Line of Fire* (1993), and *Blood Work* (2002). The *Tightrope* title itself comes from what a criminal psychologist says to the Eastwood character about his dark side: "There's a darkness in all of us. You, me, and the man down the street. Some of us have it under control, some act it out. The rest of us try to walk a tightrope between the two." In each of the movies the Eastwood character is a lawman, though with each successive movie his age increasingly affects his job and life. Where in *In the Line of Fire* he retires by the story's end; in the later *Blood Work*, made when Eastwood was 72, he's retired after the brief exposition. In both films his age is clearly acknowledged, mostly using self-deprecating humor. In *Blood Work*, he even has a heart transplant after a career-ending heart attack.

On the other hand, the Eastwood character's aging in *In the Line of Fire* and *Blood Work* shows him in a more human light. As Dennis Bingham notes in his book, *Acting Male*,

> Eastwood's slow movement toward naturalistic acting and three-dimensional characterization that nonetheless reflects on his star persona reaches a new stage in *In the Line of Fire*.... [It] shows Eastwood's evolution into full humanity, rather than attempting to work variations on or break off from the monolithic "masculinity" of his persona.[4]

A big part of this "evolution into full humanity" is Eastwood's dealing with his unconscious Other. The "new stage," the new age, is a time to take stock of one's life and deal with unresolved issues. Perhaps that's why in all three movies, along with the Other, there's a female character representing what Jung calls the *anima*, the feminine part of man's psyche. In effect, the closer the Eastwood character gets to his Other in these movies, the more intimate he gets with his *anima*.

Agent Lilly Raines (Rene Russo), *In the Line of Fire*'s anima, reminds the arrogant Frank Horrigan (Eastwood), "And field agents get older and older," when firing back to his remark that "secretaries get prettier and prettier around here." Just as the anima generally follows the shadow in the process of what Jung calls "individuation," the process of becoming a more whole individual by integrating the unconscious shadow and anima in one's consciousness, this initial meeting between the two comes after Frank receives the first call from Mitch Leary (John Malkovich), his unconscious Other.

Twos and Pairs

Much like other movies of the Other, Wolfgang Petersen's *In the Line of Fire* is replete with *twos* and *pairs*, which keep reminding us of the film's binary opposites. The most obvious example of these tropes, no doubt, is Leary's killing (with his two-bullet gun) two pairs, two females and two males, each killing following a pair of phone calls to Frank.

The twos and pairs are apparent in the establishing shots of Washington, D.C., where the story begins and ends. Like the two primary pairs, the first two shots show a pair of three familiar sites of the nation's capital. One shows the Supreme Court in the foreground, the Capitol building behind it, and the Washington Monument in the distant background; the other shot shows the White House in the foreground, the Washington Monument behind it, and the Jefferson Memorial in the distant background. In contrast, the second pair of shots shows one site each, the Jefferson Memorial and the White House. These four shots are doubled in the subsequent four shots by the four "verbal pairs" of Frank's Secret Service partner, Al (Dylan McDermott), who fears the consequence for being late to pick him up.

Following an establishing shot that shows his car speeding in a Washington, D.C., street, the second shot shows Al in his car, nervously talking to himself in pairs, "Oh, my God. Oh, my God." The third shot assumes his point of view from inside the car as he spots Frank up ahead, reading a newspaper on the street corner. "Oh, Frank, thank God, thank God. I'm dead. I'm dead," he mutters to himself in fear as he pulls up. "I'm dead. I'm dead," he repeats to himself in the fourth shot, which shows him inside the car from the passenger's side just before Frank opens the car door and sits next to him. As things turn out, Al's two pairs of "I'm Dead" foreshadow his "two deaths": a near-death in the subsequent counterfeit scene, and a real one when Leary kills him with two shots after Frank declines to shoot his Other and thus saves his own life.

In a movie in which Frank's age is an obvious factor, Al may well represent Frank as a young man. His age not only matches Frank's when he was protecting President Kennedy in 1963, he has a wife and child, just as Frank had a wife and child before she left him sometime after the shooting in Dallas. Al's trauma in nearly being shot by Frank in the opening scene may well mirror Frank's trauma in Dallas, which now resurfaces with the appearance of his Other. Significantly, it's Al who initiates Frank's investigation of his Other by giving him the message from the office "to check out some wacko." When Al proposes to accompany him, Frank seems to see himself in his young partner when saying, "No. You go home and hug your wife and kid." Going alone, Frank's "check out" leads to Leary's appearance in his life and ultimately initiates his transfer from pursuing counterfeiters to protecting the president, this time from his unconscious Other.

First Call: Closer Than Imagined

As if his unconscious Other is sending him a smoke signal, Frank is called to Leary's apartment because, as the landlady, a threshold guardian of sorts, informs him, "smoke alarm was going off. I get scared. I get more scared when I see what's inside." Behind two sliding doors, a photo of the younger Frank in Dallas is already pinned on the wall among many other pictures and headlines. As suggested by the camera zeroing on the picture from Dallas with the clipped newspaper heading "ASSASSIN NAMED" right above it, Frank sees himself in the picture taken on the day of Kennedy's assassination, which, like the return of the repressed, reminds him of the past he'd like to forget, the painful trauma he harbors "inside."

Seeming to sense his Other's presence, Frank looks out through the apartment window. And sure enough, as if awakened in Frank's imagination, his seeing himself in the picture is doubled by Leary's watching him through his pair of binoculars. Tying it all together, the camera cuts from the close-up of Leary's eyes looking at Frank to Frank subsequently looking at the computer screen for the results of the search for the tenant's name. His suspicion grows when discovering that the name he goes under is of *another* person, who had "died over thirty years ago," in 1961, *two* years before Kennedy's assassination.

Following up on what he knows, Frank's second visit to Leary's apartment, this time with Al, leaves no doubt that his Other has targeted Frank. For the only thing they find behind the double doors is the picture Frank saw on his first visit. As emphasized by the camera coming closer to Frank's young face, circled in red, his Other has him marked.

The picture from Dallas, of course, is merely the beginning. When Frank returns to his own apartment, Leary is shown shadowing him. Just as Frank is about to unwind with music and drink, the phone rings. Picking it up (after two rings), he learns that the call is from the very same man he's pursuing. Though never shown on the other end of the line, after confirming (in two questions) that he's speaking to "Frank Horrigan ... the Secret Service agent," Leary, as if already beginning to replace Al as Frank's other partner, all but repeats his words when seeing Frank's picture on the wall: "My God, it's really you." He then identifies himself as Booth, because "Booth had flair, panache." When Frank asks, "Where are you?" he replies as his knowing Other, "Closer than you might imagine," adding, "It's very exciting to talk to you. I feel like I know you."

Seeming to once again sense his Other's presence, Frank turns to the window, which reflects him like a mirror. "Why don't we get together for a drink?" he suggests.

"Oh, I'd love to," Leary replies, "but the less you know about me, the better." Nonetheless, despite himself, Leary informs him that he not only intends "to kill the president," but also that going against him "raises the game to a much higher level." The "much higher level," of course, is the "game" between the projector and his unconscious Other. Or, as Leary puts it, "Fate has brought us together, Frank. I just can't get over the irony."

"What irony?" Frank wants to *know.*

"You being intimately involved with the assassination of two presidents."

Just then, hearing in the receiver the same siren coming from outside his apartment, Frank realizes that Leary is down below. He tries to keep him on the line while he races outside, only to find the receiver swinging by its line and his Other nowhere in sight. Not without significance, up to receiving his first phone call from Leary, Frank is portrayed as if he's still like the two invincible icons that made Eastwood famous, the Man with No Name and Dirty Harry.

Second Call: I Know Things About People

Announcing a new chapter in Frank's life with a pair of twos, just before he and Al enter the Secret Service conference room, Sam (John Mahoney), the director and Frank's friend, is heard saying, "Two months before election, panic is what you get on a good day." When he comments to Frank that "it's been a long time since anyone's seen you in this part of the building," Frank replies, "Well, I hear the new director isn't much fun." Sam then reminds him that "I've been director for almost two years."

This scene, doubling for the opening with Al, initiates the pairing of Frank and Lilly, the pair whose growing intimacy parallels Frank's growing relationship with Leary. As with the Other, so with the *anima.* It's part of Frank's "evolution into full humanity." Frank even repeats his earlier assurance to Al, "I know things about people," when answering Lilly's question of how he knows Booth is dangerous. When she asks, "What makes you think he'll call again?" Frank uses Leary's own word, "He's got 'panache.'"

All goes well in the meeting until the "agent-in-charge" of protecting the president, Bill Watts (Gary Cole), who grills Frank for not taking "appropriate steps to know more that first night," reminds him, like Leary, of his "reputation for undercover work." Frank, losing his cool, interrupts him in mid-sentence, "What reputation are you talking about?" Being reminded by his Other is one thing; having someone who reminds him of himself insinuate it is another. "You know, Bill," Frank shoots back, "there was a time around here when I was almost as arrogant as you." When Watts leaves in frustration,

Sam himself reminds Frank by echoing his Other, "By the way, Frank, Watts is nowhere near as arrogant as you were when you had Kennedy's ear."

Later that evening, over a drink with Sam at the Old Ebbitt Grill (a name that evokes Lilly's "older and older" comment and Watts's grilling), Frank is still troubled by Watts's words. "Just what reputation was Watts referring to?" he wants to know.

"You know damn well," Sam says, and leaves it at that. But for Frank, there's no getting away from his age, or from his Other. When he asks to be assigned to the president, Sam echoes Leary's question on the phone about what had kept him in the game after all these years. "Christ, you're a dinosaur," Sam says bluntly.

But Frank counters, "This guy's gonna make a try, and I gotta be there." Sam agrees only after Frank repeats his reason, "I've got to come back, Sam."

"You *really* want to stand post again, Frank, at your age?" he asks.

Frank replies, "I've got at least one pair of good shoes in the back of the closet somewhere."

With a "pair of good shoes" or not, Frank's age clearly shows when he's subsequently shown running post at the president's motorcade, which is made to look much like Kennedy's motorcade in Dallas, as if relived in Frank's psyche. Shadowing Frank once again, Leary is shown looking at him through a pair of binoculars and smiling to himself as he sees Frank panting for breath. In Leary's mind, he's got Frank back right where he wants him.

That Leary is beginning to replace Al as Frank's other partner is doubly suggested by a subsequent pair of sequences that start when Al drives Frank home. Asking Al to pull over by a book store, Frank hunts for the *New Age Modeler* magazine he saw in Booth's apartment on his first visit. But rather than showing him getting back to Al's car, the camera cuts to Leary's other apartment, showing the same magazine on the table on which he's making preparations for his "day in the sun." The camera then cuts to a close-up of Frank leafing through the same magazine in his apartment while talking to Al on the phone about the "weird subculture" depicted in the magazine. Ironically, when receiving another call, Frank tells Al, "Hang on, I got the other line."

On the other line, naturally, is his Other, making his second call. Mirroring Frank's line about knowing something about people, Leary speaks knowingly about "the adversary I'd hoped for." At first Frank keeps him on the line so that they can trace his call, which Leary, the knowing Other, is on to. But the longer he talks, the more personal the call becomes for Frank. "By the way, I'm watching your movie," Leary informs him, proceeding to question the deeply disturbed Frank about fulfilling his role in the line of fire. The movie he's watching is shown with the young Frank superimposed on the older one listening to Leary's words in such a way as if it's playing in his mind. "Late at night, when the demons come, do you see that rifle coming out of the window or do you see Kennedy's head blown apart? If you'd reacted to that first shot, could you have gotten there in time to stop the big bullet? And if you had, that could have been your head being blown apart. Do you wish you'd succeeded, Frank, or is life too precious?"

Frank dismisses Leary's words by saying, "What's done is done." But Leary manages to get under his skin when referring to the *Esquire* magazine article he's shown holding on his lap. "So sad how your wife left you and took your little daughter," he says tauntingly. "And you were so forthright about your drinking problem and the fact that you weren't easy to live with. I was so moved by your honesty." When Leary, his head shown from the back, cuts the call short with, "I'll talk to you again soon," adding, "Nice to have a friend" before hanging up, Frank is shown slamming down his receiver, so enraged he almost forgets the tracing of the call.

Frank's overreaction, of course, is a clear sign that Leary is his projected Other. Or as the White House Chief of Staff asks Frank, who insists on drastic measures to combat his adversary after playing Leary's second call in the White House conference room, "Isn't it possible that this guy has pushed some buttons in you? And now you're overreacting just a little?" "Whenever we strongly react to any person with attraction or repulsion, projection is at work.... An invisible part of us has become highly visible in someone else."[5]

Third Call: So Much in Common

That Frank and Leary are opposite sides of the other is underscored in Leary's third call, this time to the Secret Service office to which Frank has been transferred. Like the first call, in which only Frank was shown in his apartment, now only Frank and the other agents are shown, particularly Lilly, who listens to the conversation and looks intently at Frank's reaction.

"Frank, I hope you don't mind me calling you at the office. I was in the neighborhood," Leary talks as if he and Frank had become friends. "We've got so much in common."

"We *do*?" Frank asks while other agents listen in. "Like *what*?"

"We are both willing to trade our lives for the president. We're both honest and capable men who were betrayed by people we trusted." When Frank claims he "wasn't betrayed," Leary, insisting "Sure you were, Frank," points out the other side of the Warren Commission's report on the assassination. The more information Leary presents, the more irritated Frank becomes. Finally, having finished explaining his side of things, he asks, "But what do *you* think, Frank?"

Frank pitches it right back: "What about you, Booth? Who betrayed you?"

Once again suggesting they're one and the same, Leary replies, "Some of the same people." Then he adds, "But I'm gonna get even. I'll have my day in the sun. The question is: Will you have yours?"

Having heard more than he can stomach, the angry Frank puts his hand over the mouthpiece and asks his colleagues, "How much of this shit do I have to listen to?" Just then the call is traced to a pay phone outside the building.

As Frank reaches the pay phone, once again he's too late; and when he looks around for Leary, once again he's shown through his pair of binoculars. Underscoring that the two adversaries are getting closer to each other, Leary's face is revealed for the first time in the movie, albeit under disguise, as he stands on the other side of the street taunting Frank, who sees his Other for the first time. Calling to his partner, "That's him! Al, that's him!" Frank both pairs his words like Al and echoes the ones he used when identifying him in the picture ("That's you"). The two start chasing after Leary, with Frank in the lead, but when Leary runs behind the other side of a passing bus, once the bus is out of the way, he has vanished. All he leaves for Frank are his fingerprints and some unanswered questions from "that day."

Fourth Call: Same as Me

Frank's growing relationship with Leary is depicted in two political rallies. In the first one, looking but not seeing, he unknowingly looks directly at Leary, who once again looks at him through his binoculars. In the second political rally, in Chicago, his "hunch" that Leary is there is proven correct by Leary himself. Unseen at first, he makes his presence known by popping a balloon with an election button's pin, which puts the feverish and disoriented Frank "on the wrong side of a judgment call," as he calls his mistaking it for a gunshot, embarrassing both the president and himself.

Later, on Air Force One, Frank's calling the "false alarm" and speaking frankly before the angry chief of staff gets him fired from the protective detail. But hooked by his Other, he asks Sam, in their second meeting over drinks, to let him "stay on the Booth case." This time, when Sam reminds him of his age ("Face it, Frank. You're too old for this shit."), Frank nods his head in quiet resignation. He even raises a glass in a humble touché. This new attitude is another signal of the change he's undergoing in his growing relationship with his Other. Now, rather than protecting the president, he's after Leary.

Just as Frank is hooked by Leary, Leary, shown watching Frank playing piano to himself in his bar (this time through a window), cannot seem to keep his eyes off the man. Though Frank doesn't notice him, the two nonetheless share the screen for the first time in the movie. This pairing is rhymed by the subsequent shot showing Frank putting two Alka-Seltzer tablets in a glass of water, shown in a close-up, just before the phone rings in his apartment with Leary on the line, making his fourth call, letting Frank know that he's been shadowing him.

"What happened in the Windy City, Frank?" Leary asks tauntingly. "The balloon gave you a little panic?"

"You were there?" Frank asks. (He may have been wrong about the balloon, but he was right in his "hunch" about his being there.) Envisioning their correspondence from opposite sides, the two are shown talking from their beds and occupy equal time on the screen.

"I'm on offense; you're on defense," Leary reminds Frank. "You're the same as me, Frank."

Having made his point, Leary hangs up, as Frank is heard on his receiver: "Wait. Wait, Leary." In his frustration, Frank yanks the phone line from the wall socket, never even bothering to drink his two Alka-Seltzers, as the subsequent close-up of the glass reveals, thus ending the fourth call sequence as it had started and with the same headache caused by Leary.

Fifth Call: I Know Who You Are

As if doing his part as Frank's partner in the investigative work that leads to learning Leary's name and now vacating the stage for the drama's two key players, Al, after seeing pictures of what Leary does to his "friends," informs Frank that he's decided to quit the force. But Frank's emphasizing that he needs him (something he wouldn't have said when we first met them, or before Leary had wormed his way into his psyche) dissuades him from doing so. "Okay, Frank. Okay," he once again pairs his words. Ironically, Al's last words to Frank in the car, "You kill me, Frank," which echo his first words, "I'm dead," come true after Leary's fifth call, which immediately follows this brief scene in the car.

Whereas up to this call Leary has always called the shots, in his second call to Frank at the office the tables are turned. Calling himself (and speaking as) Frank's other friend, Leary loses his usual composure and control in the following exchange about "monsters" and "demons":

> *Frank*: I know who you are, Leary.
>
> *Leary* (after a moment of silence): I'm glad, Frank. Friends should be able to call each other by name.

6. The Line of Fire

Frank: We're not friends.

Leary: Sure we are.

Frank: I've seen what you do to friends.... I saw a picture of your friend lying on the floor with his throat cut.

Leary (raising his voice): But you didn't see, Frank, what you couldn't possibly know is that they sent my best friend, my comrade in arms, to my home to kill me!

Frank: Your voice is shaking

Leary (screaming): I never lied to you, Frank, and I never will!... Frank, you of all people, I want *you* to understand. Because we both used to think that this country was a very special place.

Frank: You don't know what *I* used to think.

Leary: But you know about *me*? Do you have any idea what I've done for God and country? Some pretty fucking horrible things! I don't even remember who I was before they sunk their claws into me.

Frank: They made you into a real monster.

Leary: That's right. And now they want to destroy me because we can't have monsters roaming the quiet countryside, now, can we?

Frank (asking the same question Leary had asked him in his second call): What do *you* see when you're in the dark and the demons come?

Leary: I see *you*, Frank. I see you standing over the grave of another dead president.... That president is coming home from California in a fucking box.

Frank: *Where* in California?

Leary: Oh, you want the *address*? Come on, Frank. I'll keep you in the game, but I'm not going to throw it for you.... I have a rendezvous with death. And so does the president. And so do you, Frank, if you get too close to me.... You're alive because I have allowed you to live. So you show me (screaming) *some goddamn respect*!

Before he slams down the receiver, Leary has already given the agents enough time to trace his call, thus going against himself in refusing to give Frank "the address." What angers him most is Frank's refusing to acknowledge him, as when he responds to his having "a rendezvous with death," "You have a rendezvous with my ass, motherfucker!" All Leary wants is for Frank to acknowledge him as his unconscious Other, to *know* the side of himself he had buried with Kennedy. As Leary says so himself, he wants his "friend" to "know about me." He wants Frank, "of all people," to "understand" what made him "into a real monster," into his Other.

As Frank and Al race to Leary's traced address, Al spots him walking away in the street. In the *Vertigo*-inspired roof chase that ensues, there is a key deviation from Hitchcock's famous sequence. Both the James Stewart character and Frank hang helplessly from the top of a roof after coming up short in one of their jumps from roof to roof, but while we never find out how the Stewart character is saved, Frank is saved by Leary, who extends his hand to him, saying "Take my hand, Frank. Take it. If you don't, you'll die." When Frank does give him his hand and Leary grabs it with both hands, causing his sunglasses to fall, Frank sees his eyes in their first physical contact. In this bizarre face-to-face encounter, with his life literally in Leary's hands, Frank nonetheless draws his gun on him with his other hand. "You'll shoot me, Frank, after I saved your life?" Leary asks, taunting him as he had on his second call (when asking, "Do you wish you'd succeeded, Frank, or is life too precious?"), even using the same words, "The only way to save the president is to shoot me. Are you willing to do this, to trade your life for his? Or is life too precious?" Raising the stakes, Leary literally puts Frank's gun where his mouth is, before heaving him to safety to a nearby fire escape landing.

With Frank safe, Al, who's been following it all from the other roof with a drawn gun, aims it at Leary, warning him, "Don't fucking move!" But as he takes his eyes off him for a second to gleefully announce, "Frank, I got him," the more experienced Leary shoots him dead with two shots.

As the roof chase makes clear to Frank, he's alive because Leary, as he had put it over the phone, has allowed him to live. Not only that, he has put him in a position where he's forced to answer Leary's crucial question about his willingness to trade his life for the president. On the other hand, just as he needed Al, Frank needs Leary alive so that he will go through his plan to attempt to assassinate the president, thus giving him a chance to redeem himself. He wants him alive just as Leary, despite himself, wants to be found out by his projector and acknowledged as his unconscious Other, which is underscored by his inadvertently (unconsciously) leaving a coded message in his room (shown next), which ultimately helps Frank identify him at the very last moment.

Sixth Call: Unconscious Message

Once again in his bar, Frank is shown looking at a photocopy of the "message" found under the bed in Leary's room, shown in a close-up between a glass and a bottle just as it's written "Skellum" is sandwiched between two pairs of capital initials, SW and LA. His studying Leary's "message" is interrupted by the messenger himself, making his sixth call. He begins by apologizing for killing his partner: "I'm sorry. It was in self-defense."

Ignoring the disingenuous statement, Frank says, "Tell me about Skellum." But Leary only reveals that he's "barking up the wrong tree" and that

"Skellum's worthless." Significantly, whereas Leary addresses Frank by his first name from his very first call, Frank starts addressing him (twice) by the more personal Mitch only after their face-to-face encounter on the roof.

When Frank acknowledges that he wants to kill him, Leary, reminding Frank of their relationship, points to their being binary opposites: "The same government that trained me to kill, trained you to protect. Yet now you wanna kill me, while, up on the roof, I protected you…. You could have taken me out, but you chose to save your ass. Don't cry about it now. Ok? You know, it does make me wonder about Dallas, though. Did you *really* do all you could have or did you me a choice there, too? Do you *really* have the guts to take the bullet, Frank?"

"I'll be thinking about that when I'm pissing on your grave," Frank says before slamming down the receiver. But as demonstrated by Leary's last two calls, in which each one pushes the other's buttons enough to make him slam down the receiver, the two are now equals. Their new relationship is pointed out (once again) by the chief of staff in the conference after the sixth call, when he answers Frank's "I don't think he'd lie to me" with "Have you become that close, have you?" The chief's words, of course, echo Leary's words on his first call, when saying to Frank that he's closer than he might imagine.

Frank's closeness and overreacting to Leary is underscored when, following the conference, as he approaches Lilly with a request to talk to Watts about his being on the advance team, she replies, "He thinks you'll overreact," adding, "I think maybe you're too close to all this." This closeness, Frank claims, is precisely "why I've got to be there. I can spot him. I can anticipate him." Reminding Lilly that "that son of a bitch killed my partner, my friend," she echoes Leary's apology, "I know. I'm sorry." She only takes his request seriously when, like Leary himself, he brings up his failure in Dallas. "You're looking at a living legend: the only active agent who ever lost a president. Please."

His request granted, Frank's arrival in Los Angeles with the advance team is introduced by a symmetric establishing shot showing a landing jet from inside the terminal, which once again envisions the symmetry between the two adversaries and introduces the rather long sequence that alternates between Leary preparing to kill the president and the Secret Service doing all they can to protect him. In one of these attempts, as Watts had feared, Frank overreacts when suspecting a bellboy for Leary, which, ironically enough, is followed by a shot of the fundraiser's host coming from behind the disguised Leary, putting his hand on his shoulder. "Finally we meet," he greets him by his other name, his alias "James Carney," all but calling him an unconscious Other. "I was starting to wonder if you really existed or maybe you were an angel sent down to help the party."

"I'm very much human," Leary assures him. Given an invitation to the fundraiser and informed he has "a great seat ... just a stone throw away from the president himself," the stage is set for Frank's worst nightmare.

While Leary gets ever closer to the president, Frank, as Lilly informs him in the vacant presidential suite, is dismissed from the protection detail by the president himself, because "he beat up a bellboy on television." Reminding him, "It's not just you against Leary," Frank reflects back to what *really* happened to him "that day" in Dallas:

> You know something? For years I've been listening to all those idiots on bar stools with all their pet theories on Dallas.... None of that has meant too much to me. But Leary, he questioned whether I had the guts to take that fatal bullet.... The first shot sounded like a firecracker. I looked over and saw him. I could tell he was hit. I don't know why I didn't react. I should have reacted. I should have been running flat-out. I just couldn't believe it. If only I reacted, I could have taken that shot. That would have been all right with me.

When the clearly moved Lilly reaches for Frank's hand, he's also visibly moved. The last shot of the two ends this segment as it had started, in another symmetric shot, showing them standing before the suite's panoramic windows, holding hands and gazing out. Once again, the closer Frank gets to his Other, the closer he gets to his anima.

Frank's Call: Decoding the Other's Message

Thick with irony, to paraphrase Leary, Frank's break in catching Leary not only comes after he gives expression to (and answers Leary's crucial question) what really happened "that day" in Dallas, as fits their primary means of communication, it's linked to a telephone number. "What's the number of the San Diego office?" Frank asks the driver who drives him to the airport.

"Six-nineteen Ukulele," the driver says. "That's how I remember it: seven numbers, seven letters. You just push u-k-u-l-e-l-e."

When subsequently shown pushing the lettered buttons in a pay phone, the same kind of phone from which Leary had made his first call, Frank finally puts two and two together. "Wait a second," he says to himself just as his flight to San Diego is announced on the public address. Realizing Leary's "Skellum" has seven letters (the same number of calls he makes to Frank), he makes his first and only phone call in the movie, the call that leads him to Leary.

Shown returning to the president's fundraiser detail from which he was fired, Frank matches Leary's "other" name with the sitting arrangement, spotting him covering something underneath his napkin just as the president approaches his table to shake hands. "Gun!" he calls out, racing towards Leary. As Leary takes aim and pulls the trigger Frank jumps in the line of fire, taking the bullet for the president. Leary, of course, has a second bullet. And from what's shown, he seems to have enough time to take a second shot at the momentarily exposed president. But the film does not dwell on this option. As emphasized by showing Frank falling to the ground in slow motion after taking the bullet, the scene is more concerned with Frank and Leary than with the president. There's no need for another bullet. At least not to shoot the president, who's rushed out to his car by the Secret Service. When the camera cuts to Leary rushing to Frank lying on the floor, he does take a second shot, but at an agent who calls out to him to "put the gun down."

In the pandemonium that erupts, Leary, using Frank's gun, holds him hostage and leads him into a glass elevator. Stopping halfway up, midpoint between the conscious and the unconscious that the two represent, Leary takes off his disguise and faces Frank as he is. Sharing the same elevator allows the two men to exchange last words as binary friends. While to Leary it's all a game, Frank refuses to acknowledge the friendship that Leary so desperately wants.

"So, you had the guts," Leary seems pleased. "You took the bullet."

When Frank, who wears a bulletproof vest, confesses, "I broke my damn ribs," Leary once again apologizes, as he did for shooting Al: "Sorry. I wasn't aiming at *you*." As Leary sees it, Frank's wearing the bulletproof vest is "a bit of a cheat. Otherwise you played a good game."

"It's no game, Leary," Frank fires back. "I was doing my job."

But Leary, who doesn't "want to leave this miserable world alone," wants the two to go as friends in a "double suicide" of the projector and his Other. "It's better to die with a friend, don't you think, Frank?"

"We're not friends," Frank says, denying his adversary. "You're a damn killer, you sick bastard." "Don't talk to me like that," Leary says, genuinely hurt. "I saved your life. You owe me."

"I don't owe you shit," Frank shoots back.

Leary reminds Frank, "I was always honest and fair with you."

Once again playing dishonestly with Leary, Frank presses Lilly over the wireless to shoot him. "What are you waiting for?"

The usually sharp Leary, who so desperately wants Frank's respect and acknowledgement, misses this tactic: he thinks Frank is talking to *him*. "I'm waiting for you to show me some goddamn gratitude. Without me, you'd still just be another sad-eyed, piano-playing drunk. I brought you into this game. I let you keep up with me. I made you a goddamn hero today.... I redeemed your pathetic, shitty life."

Before Leary, who catches onto Frank's "double" talk to "aim high," can get off a clean shot, the police sharpshooters' shots shatter the elevator's glass panels, saving Frank's life at the very last moment. In the struggle that ensues between the two adversaries, Leary, receiving one of Frank's blows to his face, tumbles out through the window, catching hold of a metal bar at the very last second. Doubling for the rooftop scene, but with the tables now turned, Frank extends his hand, echoing Leary's words, "Take my hand. If you don't, you'll die."

"You wanna save me, Frank?" Leary, hanging by his two hands, wants to know.

"To be honest and fair with you, no. But it's my job."

With Frank being "honest and fair with" him at last, Leary lets go of his hold and falls to his death.

Like Frank doing his job when offering his hand, Leary has done his part in drawing Frank to reenact his traumatic role in the line of fire, this time doing his job. All the same, his letting go and falling to his death, as Drucilla Cornell notes, is a "significant twist on the traditional end of the doppelgänger film, in which the hero is freed by destroying the symbol of his own darkness. Here Leary takes responsibility for his own death, freeing Horrigan not by an act of vengeance but by accepting the retribution due to him, which is death."[6]

Leary's Last Call: The Other's Goodbye

Fittingly enough, Frank's hero's return to Washington is shown in a pair of brief one-shot scenes, the public and the private. The first shot shows him arriving at the Washington airport, paired with Lilly and, for the first time in the film, dressed in casual civilian clothing. When a reporter asks him why he's retiring from the Secret Service, Frank points to their "plastering my picture everywhere," a big change from the picture of him with Kennedy in Dallas that Leary had left for him in his apartment.

The second shot shows Frank returning to his apartment with Lilly. Whereas in the first such return, before Leary's first call, he put on jazz music, now, having gotten used to Leary's calls, he presses the answering machine. While he goes to another room to change shirts, Lilly is shown hearing Leary's recorded message in his last call to Frank: "Hello, Frank. By the time you hear this, it'll be over. The president is most likely dead, and so am I." The camera, together with Lilly, turns from the answering machine toward Frank, who appears in the doorway with a fresh shirt, as Leary is heard asking, "I wonder, Frank, did you kill me? Who won the game?" Leary's voice continues as Frank walks toward Lilly, his eyes turning to her from the source of Leary's voice. "Not that it matters. For among friends like you and me, it's not whether you win or lose, but how you play the game. Now the game is done and it's time to get on with your life." Without a word, Frank leads his new partner in life out the door as Leary continues, "But I worry that you have no life to get on with. You're a good man. And good men like you and me are destined to travel the lonely road." Closing the door behind him, Frank doesn't wait to hear his parting words: "Goodbye. And good luck."

Frank's discernible indifference to Leary's recorded message underscores his release from his unconscious Other, whose call is a virtual call from a ghost. As Frank had proposed to Lilly in one of their intimate exchanges, "What were to happen if I gave up my job for you?" he has given up his job for the new partner in his life. His "redemption," as Leary called it, is illustrated by the final stationary shot, showing the two from behind, sitting on the steps of the Lincoln Memorial with the Washington Monument in the background up ahead, a shot that doubles for the earlier one that showed them sharing ice cream on the same spot. Where in the first shot the Washington Monument was reflected in the pool, seeming to come between the two, now they're embracing each other.

Recalling the four opening shots and Al's four verbal pairs, this symmetrical shot contains four pairs of its own: Two monuments, Frank and Lilly, two joined busses that cross the street below, and the two pigeons that may well remind Frank of his link to Leary. "I'll bet you that brown pigeon down there flies off before the white one," Frank says, calling attention to the two.

"How do you know?" Lilly asks.

"I know things about pigeons," Frank says simply.

This twist on his motto, "I know things about people," may well mean he knows things about the brown and the white, about the knowing Other and himself.

7

Blood Work: Double Feature

> *You know, two for the price of one.*
> —*Graciella Rivers to Terry McCaleb*

Two for One

"The script seemed like an interesting detective story with a certain vulnerability, both physically and psychologically, for the guy to overcome," Clint Eastwood has explained his reason for making *Blood Work*. "At this particular stage in my maturity, I felt that it was time to take on some roles that maybe had a different obstacle than I would, say, if I was a young man in my thirties or forties doing this kind of job."[1]

Where the Eastwood character's growing "physically" older was barely an "obstacle" in the earlier *In the Line of Fire*, in *Blood Work*, made nine years later, his "certain vulnerability" is his advanced age and failing heart, which puts him out of commission early in the movie. The psychological "obstacle," on the other hand, is his unconscious Other, or double, as spelled out on two occasions early in the 2002 movie.

The first double is *Double Down*, the name of the houseboat adjacent to Terry McCaleb's (Eastwood) own houseboat, *The Following Sea*. Unlike the name of McCaleb's boat, which is mentioned twice in the course of the movie, the name *Double Down* is never mentioned, only shown each time its owner, Buddy Noone (Jeff Daniels), is on his boat. Appropriately enough, the second "double" comes up on McCaleb's boat, when he wants to return Graciella Rivers (Wanda De Jesus) the photo of her dead sister (the donor of his heart), in which she's pictured with her son. "I have a double," she says. "You know, two for the price of one."

Graciella's "double," or "two for the price of one," is precisely what both the Eastwood character and the audience get in *Blood Work*: a double feature. On the one hand, with a new heart that gives him a new life but renders him physically vulnerable, McCaleb gets a second chance to deal with his psychological obstacle; on the other hand, along with "an interesting detective story," in which McCaleb tries to track down his donor's killer, we get a subterranean subplot of the projector and his unconscious Other, the two that are one.

Exposition

Much like *In the Line of Fire*, *Blood Work*'s subtext of binary opposites is continuously envisioned and suggested by the countless twos, pairs, and doubles that crop up in the course of the movie. Like the unconscious which communicates "indirectly" through symbols and metaphors, what Edward C. Whitmont calls "the symbolic language of the psyche,"[2] the movie's unconscious Other is given expression indirectly through these tropes and double entendres. And once again, nothing illustrates this "symbolic language" better than the movie's exposition.

Blood Work envisions the two that are one right from the start, in the opening aerial shot (taken from a helicopter that hovers above the opening crime scene) of two identical well-lit parts of a building, one on top of the other like the conscious and the unconscious, as a second helicopter comes into view. While the first helicopter keeps flying over the crime scene, the camera cuts to a second aerial shot from the second helicopter, which follows McCaleb's car's twin red rear lights, passing by two well-lit tennis courts. In one of the two courts, two figures are playing against each other from either side of the net, not unlike the movie's two adversaries, the projector and his Other.

Following two aerial shots from each helicopter, a pair of transitional shots — one an aerial shot from inside the first helicopter, showing the crime scene — the other from inside McCaleb's car, show his arriving at the crime scene, the only time he drives in the course of the movie. With the camera cutting to a pair of detectives waiting for McCaleb at the crime scene, the darker of the two, the Spanish-American Arrango (Paul Rodriguez), turns to his partner as McCaleb's car arrives. "McCaleb," he shakes his head in disapproval. "Whatever happens, it'll be his face on the front page." Functioning mostly as a nagging voice of the Other, Arrango clearly has a score to settle with McCaleb. As the darker "*Other*" of the two detectives, his suggesting to his partner that McCaleb doesn't often find himself on the back page alludes to the neglected part of the psyche, the unconscious, where the Other dwells.

In contrast, the other detective, Waller (Dylan Walsh), is all business, informing McCaleb of the two victims and that, like the return of the repressed, the "Code Killer strikes again." While Waller gives McCaleb the information he has, Arrango aggravates him at every opportunity. "You're sick, you know that, Arrango?" McCaleb finally responds to his cynical and obnoxious remarks, calling him the same "sick son of a bitch" he calls his Other when confronting him after figuring out his identity.

When the three reach the second floor, where the second victim lies dead, and they see the writing on the wall, "McCaleb catch me," written in the victim's blood, Arrango turns to McCaleb and says, "Another love note. Maybe the two of you out to get a room someplace." Below the three words, the "Code Killer" leaves a second message, a coded message of three sets of three numbers, "903 472 568."

Of course, as suggested by these two messages, another coded message by numbers is the movie's ubiquitous number two that represents the binary opposites of the projector and his Other. Like all disowned (repressed) parts of ourselves that communicate in coded symbols, the unconscious Other, who dares McCaleb to catch him, seeks to be found out and acknowledged. All McCaleb needs to do is figure it out. All he needs is to make the unconscious conscious.

Outside the two-story building, with Arrango once again grumbling to his partner about McCaleb's "love" for the front page, the reporters are all over him, asking questions that repeatedly suggest the relationship between the projector and his unconscious Other:

"Why is he singling you out?"
"What does the message say?"
"Why does he focus on you?"
"What does he want?"
"You got a motive?"

These nagging questions, which McCaleb obviously doesn't "love," go unanswered at this point, and not only because McCaleb spots the pair of bloody sneakers, which recall the twin tennis courts in the movie's opening. As demonstrated by McCaleb's repeating the "Chuck Taylor" name Arrango gives to the owner of the Converse sneakers (that left bloody footprints on the stairs leading to the second floor), the Latino detective, despite himself, helps him identify the killer.

"Chuck," McCaleb says to himself, weaving through the reporters and starting to chase the sneakers' owner, who takes off when realizing he's been identified. But after a rather long chase, in which the two's "pairness" is envisioned by the pair of identical shots that the show each of their shoes, just when McCaleb gets close enough to grab one of the killer's sneakers, as he climbs over a doubled fenced gate, he succumbs to a heart attack and is unable to continue his pursuit. Somewhat like the prince in *Cinderella*, he's left with one of his Other's sneakers.

Seeing McCaleb's condition, the killer, who continually remains in the shadows, comes back for a closer look from the other side of the gate, as if both relieved and disappointed that McCaleb is unable to continue the chase. But before McCaleb succumbs to his failing heart and loses consciousness, he gets off several shots, one of which hits the killer in the back. Ultimately, this shot helps McCaleb, prince of the press to Arrango, find the killer much as the slipper helps the prince find Cinderella.

Significantly, like his Other's coded message communicated in blood, in failing when in pursuit of his Other, McCaleb's body sends him a message that there's a neglected part of himself that needs tending. Like the psyche's Other, the body, as John P. Conger points out, "*is* the shadow insofar as it contains the tragic history of how the spontaneous surging of life energy is murdered and rejected in a hundred ways until the body becomes a deadened object.... For those who can read the body, it holds the record of our rejected side, revealing what we dare not speak, expressing our current and past fears."[3]

Connecting with McCaleb through the body, his shadowy Other sees to it that he gets the kind of heart his body will not reject. And though he's unaware (unconscious) of this "gift" at the time, McCaleb's new heart is behind his decision to take up his search for his Other. In the process, as he says on two occasions to his two agents of transformation, Buddy and Graciella, he feels his life energy is "coming back." This is McCaleb's message to himself. Like his new heart, the bodily organ most associated with love, he needs to accept and assimilate this "rejected side." This he does in the parallel course of tracking down his Other and through his growing relationship with Graciella, just as the prince does with Cinderella.

Two Years Later

Considering the last time McCaleb is shown he's falling unconscious as the helicopter above him shines its search light on him, with this closing shot of the search light shot from below dissolving into an identical shot of an operating room lights, the events that transpire "Two years later" (as a subtitle) may well take place in his unconscious, particularly as he now lives on the water of the unconscious sea. What McCaleb's doctor, Bonnie Fox (Angelica Huston), twice calls "blood work," another term for blood test, is the physical counterpart to the movie's "*shadow-work*," what Connie Zweig and Jeremiah Abrams call (in their book, *Meeting the Shadow*): "The conscious and intentional process of admitting to that which we have chosen to ignore or repress."[4] This "shadow-work" is precisely what McCaleb is called to undertake by both his shadowy double and his female counterpart when we first meet them.

As if picking up where his failing heart stopped him from scaling the fenced gate, in the second scene of "two years later," McCaleb is shown passing through his marina's fenced gate just as a woman goes out, literally opening the gate for him. On the other side of the fenced gate, as two years before, is his unconscious double, whose identity is spelled out in another coded message by the name of his boat, *Double Down*, situated right above his head, though barely shown at this early stage of McCaleb's awareness.

"Morning, Terry," Buddy Noone, who lounges on his boat and plays harmonica to himself, greets McCaleb.

"*Morning?*" McCaleb replies, checking his watch. "It's two in the afternoon, Buddy." But for Buddy, as for the unconscious, time doesn't exist.

"As long as my old man keeps sending them checks," he explains, "it's whatever time I say it is."

On his own boat, *The Following Sea*, McCaleb encounters the dark-skinned Graciella Rivers, his other agent of transformation. When he refuses her appeal for help, Graciella tells him, "I think you could help me," adding knowingly (intuitively), "Maybe even help yourself." She backs up her words by showing him the picture of her sister and her son. Unaware how he's linked to the picture, just as he's unconscious as to how he's linked to his Other, McCaleb rejects her appeal. "Just look at it again, please," she implores. "Just one more time, then I'll leave you alone. Just tell me if you perceive and feel anything." As suggested by her telling him she has "a double" when he offers to return the picture, adding, "You know, two for the price of one," McCaleb can help himself by helping her because her sister's killer is the same Code Killer he was trying to catch two years earlier. It was his Other then; it's his Other now. "You'll want to keep that one," she advises him.

"Why is that?" he asks.

Graciella replies by sliding her hand over the left side of his chest, adding, "Your heart, Mr. McCaleb. It was my sister's."

In Graciella the prince of the press gets his Hispanic Cinderella. Only in this version, rather than look for the princess, the good sister of his donor comes looking for the prince, touching his heart where he's most sensitive and calling him to start looking for his Other, who two years before had left him his bloody sneaker. Informing McCaleb he has the same blood type as her sister, and that he was "operated on the same day she died," she tells him as she leaves, like the killer leaving him the message in coded numbers, "My number's on the back, if you change your mind."

Come night, that realm of the unconscious, McCaleb is sleepless as he ponders Graciella's words. In two succeeding shots, he's shown shining his flashlight on the picture of his donor and her son, turning it over (to the *other* side) to see Graciella's phone number; then, having changed his mind, he's shown calling her from a pay phone outside the marina, saying he's "going to the police tomorrow to see what's going on." These two brief shots, as suggested by the flashlight and the telephone, signal McCaleb's beginning to shine a light on his unconscious and communicating with his feminine counterpart, which ultimately leads him to his Other.

Come morning, McCaleb starts looking into his Other's two killings, carried out two weeks apart. Though he doesn't know it at the time, the first victim he researches, Gloria Torres, is actually the second. In fact, the two killings and his investigation are depicted as doubles. And considering he investigates the two in the same day, it's another case of two in one. Like his Other's needing two killings to get him a new heart, in his new investigation McCaleb gets a second chance to catch him.

McCaleb's saying that "a fresh pair of eyes won't hurt" in trying to convince Arrango to let him see the video of Gloria's killing, on second viewing he notices the killer winking into the surveillance camera as he walks out of the store following the shooting. From the taped evidence, he concludes that "this guy's done it before," though not imagining it goes as far back as two years and more. In his visit to the crime scene, when the store owner's widow remarks that "the only way to keep evil out is not unlock the door," she may well be referring to the repressed Other, who presently shadows McCaleb in a black car parked on the other side of the street, which he notices briefly when its engine is started. Suggesting it's his projection, when he looks again the black car is gone.

After learning that there were actually two killings by a killer wearing a ski mask, McCaleb watches the video of the first shooting and notices that the shooter is speaking directly into the surveillance camera. Echoing his own "fresh pair of eyes," the policewoman who gave him the video, Detective Jaye Winston (Tina Lifford), whom he had once helped crack open a murder case and perhaps, as suggested several times, even had an affair with, speaks in double entendre when saying to him, "I think we're going to need fresh blood to solve this one." Then, after talking to the man who found the first victim at the ATM and called 911, when McCaleb once again checks out the crime scene, his Other, wearing a disguise, as well as two items taken from the two victims (a Crucifix earring and sunglasses), comes from behind him (like *The Following Sea*) and puts his arm on McCaleb's shoulder. "You done?" he asks the startled McCaleb, who stares at him intently, almost as if he knows him.

Connecting the Numbers

In the subsequent scene, signaling that one chapter is "done" and another begins, in McCaleb's second passing by his double on his way to his boat, this time the *Double Down* is most prominent in each shot that shows Buddy, whom McCaleb asks to be his driver so that he can continue his investigation. Unaware of his neighbor's real identity, when Buddy, who wants to get as close as possible to his projector, starts asking questions about an investigation, McCaleb sets him straight: "Look, I just need a driver, not a partner."

Unconscious of his double as he may be in daylight, come night McCaleb sends himself a coded message in the nightmare in which, to his horror, he's repeatedly shot by a masked man in a store like the one in the second killing. Bearing in mind "that dreams do not hide but reveal, that they invariably point to something yet unknown which they express in the vocabulary of the known,"[5] McCaleb's dream seems to suggest that the shootings are meant for him, to give him a new heart, which is precisely what he comes to realize in his investigation. Apparently, that's what the dream's storekeeper means when he speaks to him with double meanings, "You don't deserve it." As the dream's coded message tells him, to deserve it he must find the man behind the mask, his unconscious Other.

This revealing dream, which signals McCaleb's getting in touch with his unconscious, gives expression to his unconscious fear of his double. That his dream is an unconscious message is reinforced the following morning by McCaleb calling himself "the Lone Ranger," the masked man, when confronting Bolotov (Igor Jijikine), the ex-con he calls "a two-time loser" and falsely suspects of being the shooter. That McCaleb projects on Bolotov his unconscious Other is suggested by his overt aggression and by the two's "split" faces of dark and light sides mirroring one another. Not buying McCaleb's projections, Bolotov confronts him with a doubled question that may well ask about the projector and his Other: "Who are you? You're not a cop. Cops goes in twos. Who are you?" In effect, with Buddy wanting to accompany him to interrogate Bolotov as "good cop, bad cop," or as "Starsky and Putz," as he calls themselves, McCaleb has his Tonto, his sidekick Other in the driver's seat.

McCaleb's growing partnership with his double is subsequently underscored at the sheriff's office, when Detective Winston, echoing Bolotov's question to McCaleb, turns to Buddy as he walks in with a drink for McCaleb and asks, "Who the hell are you?"

All but speaking as McCaleb's Other, he replies, "Buddy, Terry's partner." Turning to McCaleb, who doesn't like what he hears, he adds, "Sort of." But as suggested by McCaleb's doubling his "Sort of" (in the subsequent scene, when Graciella, coming to his boat with Raymond, asks him about their dinner date, "You forgot, didn't you?"), the two are more like partners than he imagines.

In keeping with the number two that informs the movie's unconscious subtext, Buddy accompanies McCaleb on two consecutive days. Ironically, the two outings provide Buddy with the information he needs for his next killings, which are all coded messages for McCaleb, and which provide him with the information he needs to crack open the case, making the unconscious conscious.

On the second day, as Buddy drives McCaleb to the home of the shooter's first victim, he turns to him, trying to connect in a more personal way: "I gotta ask, Terry. How did it feel? Back in the day, back when you were going up against all those sickos?"

"Connected," McCaleb replies. "That's what it was when I was at the top of my game. I felt connected to just about everything. The victim, the killer, the crime scene. Everything. Just felt it was all part of me. It's beginning to feel that way again."

Illustrating their growing partnership, when the first victim's widow asks McCaleb about Buddy sitting in the car, "Is that your partner?" he concurs, "Yeah," even if only to make it appear so. Like Graciella before her, who told McCaleb her sister's crucifix earring was missing, she informs him that her husband's sunglasses, which he usually kept in his car, are gone. McCaleb shares this new information with Buddy in the car, as if they've become partners. "You know, I saw the killer, Buddy. At the bank, at the ATM. Where Cordell was killed." But when Buddy wants to know more, such as how "it fits the profile," as McCaleb calls it, he is again reminded that he's merely the driver: "Just take me to the L.A. County Sheriff's Office." From there he's called to the murder scene of Bolotov, who's found with a bullet slug in his mouth, another coded message to McCaleb from his double.

Curiously enough, considering Buddy could have only known that McCaleb knows about the two "trophy items" when he was with McCaleb, and that he was constantly with him, when could he have put them with the slain Bolotov? The night before? It doesn't seem likely, at least not in the "real" events of the story. On the other hand, bearing in mind that the movie is about the unconscious Other, it stands to reason that this inconsistency is the expression of the unconscious, where time and "real events" don't exist. The same can be said of the second such incident, when Buddy, who's supposed to be babysitting Raymond, shadows McCaleb from his car during his second visit to the store where Gloria was shot to match the times of the second shooting and the call to 911.

At the end of their two days together, McCaleb wants to pay Buddy (two hundred dollars) and asks if he'll "take a check" and "Who do I make it out to — Buddy?"

"No. Jasper. Jasper Noone. N-O-O-N-E," he corrects him as McCaleb had first corrected him about the time, spelling out in letters the message he had left him in numbers.

"Yeah," McCaleb replies, not without irony, "I know the Noone part. But *Jasper*?" Then, hinting that he's not who he seems, that he's his unconscious double rather than Buddy, as hinted once again when he's shown with the *Double Down* above his head, Buddy shoots back, "I look more like Buddy than a Jasper, huh?"

McCaleb may "know the Noone part," as he puts it, but he doesn't connect the name with his coded message. The "fresh eyes" he needs for the "code I was supposed to break, but I never could do it," as he tells Raymond (Mason Lucero) about the killer's coded numbers, McCaleb gets from the young boy.

"There's no one," he informs him. "Nine-zero-three-four-seven-two-five-six-eight; it's all the numbers, but no one."

Still, McCaleb doesn't make the connection. "How about that?" he says, missing (and dismissing) Raymond's insight, "No one's."

Only after he physically (sexually) connects with Graciella, on the night she and Raymond sleep over on his boat, does McCaleb start connecting the two, though not without the help from his Other, who taunts him with each killing, seeking to be found out. Interrupted by Arrango and his partner while in bed with Graciella, McCaleb is called to the scene of the killer's next victim, the man who called 911 in the first shooting, who is found sitting up with a bullet in his forehead, leaning against the same fenced gate where McCaleb almost died from a heart attack two years before. As was then, the coded killer has left him another pair of messages. Only this time McCaleb is beginning to understand what the killer wants from him. Shooting at a pile of nearby newspapers and taking out the slug, he tells the accompanying Arrango and his partner, "Ballistics will match up this slug with the one in Bolotov's mouth. It was the Code Killer for all of it. Torres, Cordell, Bolotov, all of them. I shot the guy right here two years ago. The slug in Bolotov's mouth is the one I hit him with." All but calling him his unconscious Other, he adds, "Now I'm back, so is he."

With the "Happy Valentine's Day" decoded, McCaleb still has to figure out the second message. Even when speaking unknowingly (unconsciously) of his Other in answering the police captain as to why "this Code Killer likes to impress" him ("I guess he missed the matchup, me and him, being on the news every night."), McCaleb doesn't realize the connection between the "no one" and the killer. He knows *why* the Code Killer shot Cordell and Gloria Torres, but he doesn't know *who* did it. "Cordell, Gloria Torres — he did it for me. He missed the action. Me and him. In order to get it back, I needed a new heart, so Happy Valentine's Day."

McCaleb figures out the killer's identity only after returning to his houseboat, when he hears Buddy's harmonica and looks at his boat. Buddy himself isn't shown, but the name of his boat is. Whether McCaleb notices the "Double Down" isn't made clear. He only recognizes it when, looking at the check he wrote out to him the night before, he notices the name Noone and finally connects it with the coded "no one."

When McCaleb confronts Buddy on his boat, he's delighted to play along. "I'm the following sea, man," he plays on the name of McCaleb's boat, which refers to a wave direction that matches the heading of the boat, hinting to his being his double like the name of *his* boat. Adding, "I'm the one you need to watch out for," Buddy doubles McCaleb's words to Raymond about the meaning of his boat's name: "That's the one that you have to watch for, that's the one that's right behind you." With Buddy sitting with his *back* against a big mirror, he's envisioned as a "double," rhyming with McCaleb's looking at his scarred *chest* in the mirror the night before, underscoring their being mirrored opposites. Sure of his power over McCaleb, mostly because he holds Graciella and Raymond hostage, when McCaleb cocks his gun and aims it at his head, Buddy smiles, speaking once again like his Other: "Come one, man. You're mine forever. Every breath you take, every beat of that stolen heart is the echo of my voice in your head.... It's us. We were meant to be. We're Cain and Abel. Kennedy and Oswald."

With Buddy thinking he has McCaleb where he wants him, when he inform him, "I have to leave now. And you're not gonna follow me," McCaleb remains silent, staring squarely into his face as the two are envisioned as binary opposites, facing each other from opposite sides of the screen. With Buddy shown reflected in the mirror, McCaleb is envisioned looking squarely at his double. And as if transfixed by the vision of his monstrous Other, he stares in horror as Buddy starts walking away, saying, "You'll sit by that pay phone and you're gonna wait for me to call you from time to time, and when I'm relocated and ready, I'll let Graciella and Raymond go. Then you and me, we can start all over again." But when he says in parting, driving home their being doubles, "I hope you think of me as often as I think of you," McCaleb, waking from his momentary spell, shoots him in the arm, wounding him enough so that he agrees to take him to Graciella and Raymond before he "bleeds to death." Now, with McCaleb conscious of what was formerly unconscious, Buddy no longer has power over him.

On the way to the abandoned ship on which Graciella and Raymond are held captive, Buddy aggravates McCaleb much as Arrango does throughout the movie. At one point he even does a Mexican accent. Once aboard the ship, the corridors they walk through look much like a labyrinth, another classic symbol of the unconscious. This realm of the unconscious, after all, is where the projector and his unconscious Other usually fight it out to the finish in a violent struggle. And *Blood Work* is no different. Only in this movie, in which the hero has a woman's heart, it's the woman, Graciella Rivers, who carries out the final act of killing the killer. And rightly so, for she's the outer expression of her sister's heart in McCaleb's body just as Buddy is an outer expression of his unconscious Other. In the end, with McCaleb's double down and out, the heart wins over the psyche.

New Life

As a former FBI profiler whose job included profiling criminals, McCaleb may have been all head and no heart. But now, after a heart transplant, he finds himself in a new and unfamiliar situation. As Walter Metz notes, "*Blood Work*, instead of hiding Eastwood's age, thematizes it. Clint-as-Terry, after his heart attack, can no longer intimidate suspects ... No longer can Eastwood's character rely on masculine force to implement vigilantism; now he requires the help of his Latina lover, Graciella."[6] In fact, as fits the movie of countless twos, McCaleb requires the help of not one woman, but two. Significantly, the two, Graciella Rivers and Jaye Winston, are shown together in McCaleb's second visit to the store where Gloria was shot, when he figures out the shooter's motive.

Gloria's heart not only initiates McCaleb's investigation of his psyche, it also gives him a new life. As he tells Graciella at the hospital, when she wants to call off his investigation upon seeing what it's doing to his heart condition, "I got a new heart, but I didn't necessarily get a new life." When she says, "I don't know what you mean," he repeats what he had told Buddy in the car about feeling connected: "I lost a little something, but knowing you and working with you on this, I feel a little bit coming back." Hearing this, she clutches his hand and gently strokes his cheek.

That night, when sleeping over on his boat, Graciella comes to McCaleb while he stands before the bedroom mirror, before his mirrored double, looking at and feeling the scar that runs up and down his chest. "You don't have to hide it," she tells him before tenderly kissing the scar. Then, she invites him before kissing him on the mouth, "Show me your heart. Show me."

Ironically, in giving McCaleb the new heart he needs to live, Buddy brings about his own detection. His figuring out that both victims had the same blood type put McCaleb on the right track. It's also Buddy's blood, dripping on the boat's windshield, that tells Graciella that he's on the boat, causing her to ram it against the abandoned ship so that he's hurled forward onto its deck. There, standing above him with a drawn gun, McCaleb shoots him once in the "ten ring," his heart, when he reaches for his rifle. But it's Graciella who completes the job, pushing Buddy's face under a puddle of water, back to the unconscious from which he came. Significantly, she submerges his face immediately after he speaks his last words to McCaleb, "I saved you," which indeed he has, and in more ways than one. Either way, as his "double buddy" or "body double," Buddy doubly saves McCaleb, to use Eastwood's words, "both physically and psychologically."

When all is over, when Detective Winston asks McCaleb, "How are you planning to deal with all this?" he replies, looking at Graciella and Raymond, "Well, I got Gloria Torres's heart. I'll probably just let that guide me." In echoing Graciella's words, "You have Gloria's heart. She will guide you," he's already talking like his feminine Other and new partner in life. Having dealt with and assimilated his double, which Buddy's death signifies, McCaleb is ready for his *anima*, the next stage in Jung's process of individuation — becoming more of who you are.

In the movie's closing shot, of McCaleb sailing on his boat in the sunset, joined at the helm by Graciella and with Raymond at the stern, fishing in the unconscious sea, he's replaced the donor of his heart with his new family. As he tells Detective Winston, his former partner, he's "never felt better ... there's 'no one' anymore." With "a new heart," to paraphrase what he had told Graciella, McCaleb also gets "a new life." Or as Graciella had told him at their first meeting, "You know, two for the price of one."

8

Something Wild: The Other Half

What are you gonna do now that you've seen how the other half lives?
— *Lulu to Charlie Driggs*

Goes Around

Whereas in *Blood Work* a woman's new heart guides the Eastwood character to "a new life," as he calls it, in Jonathan Demme's *Something Wild*, Charlie Driggs, played by the same Jeff Daniels who plays the Other in Eastwood's movie, is taken for a wild ride to the other side of his life by the unpredictable and irresistible Lulu Hankel (Melanie Griffith). Wearing a black dress and a black pageboy wig to match, this free-spirited femme fatale takes him much further than merely the other side of the Hudson River.

Like most depictions of the Other, Demme's 1986 film employs the usual twos, pairs and doubles, and the opposite colors of black and white, to envision the protagonist and his other half. But unlike most of these movies, in which the Other appears quite early, at times even opening the movie (as in *Shadow of a Doubt* and Thompson's *Cape Fear*), in *Something Wild* he appears rather late, roughly halfway into the movie. Until then, though foreshadowed on countless occasions, we don't really know of his existence. But what he misses in the story's first half, he more than makes up for it in the second half. In fact, until his other half appears, the movie is primarily a comedy, albeit a dark one, of Charlie's relationship with his feminine half, Lulu. Afterward, the tone becomes sober, darker, and violent.

Being a self-conscious road movie of initiation, a rite of passage from one half of life to the other, *Something Wild*'s many double-meaning roadside signs point to the subterranean journey of transformation that Charlie (and, to a certain extent, Lulu/Audrey) undergoes. Some foreshadow future events, many point to the protagonist's other half. Ultimately, they all lead back to the beginning, but with Charlie now a changed man, a man who's discovered and experienced the other half of himself. As he himself says to his other half, "Goes around comes around."

That Charlie Driggs "goes around comes around," that he ends where he started, is already suggested in the opening credits, by the accompanying boat tour that encircles Manhattan, the "island in the bay" mentioned at the beginning of the accompanying song (David Byrne's "Loco de Amor").

The film's two halves and underlying subtext of the projector and his dark Other is indicated by the "opening" shot of the Twin Towers and by the boom box, with two speakers on either side, that comes into view as it's carried on the shoulder of a young Afro-American, who's listening to the song that accompanied the opening credits. Still in the same opening shot, as the young man crosses to the other side of the street, the camera pans to the left, coming to rest on a red-brick Hero Shop diner, situated on a street corner so that its two "Hero" signs are shown, each one sandwiched between two red and white Coca-Cola logos, symbolizing the hero's two sides, his two halves. The second shot, inside the diner, shows the hero sitting at a table by himself.

Two shots later, two middle-aged men — one black, the other white — are shown talking across a bar, as a black waitress (Sister Carol) crosses the screen wearing a beret with the tri colors of the Ethiopian flag — yellow, red, and green — and a silhouette of the Dark Continent on the front. As she exits the scene, the camera cuts to a white woman reading a book about Frida Kahlo, a Mexican painter known for her primitive art. This first shot of Lulu not only doubles for the one that came before, with each woman sandwiched between two men, Lulu herself doubles for the black waitress. The "primitive" aspects associated with the two women envisions Charlie's *anima*, what Jung called man's unconscious feminine side.

Clearly attracted to Charlie, Lulu first spots him when he calls for the check. Then, after he nervously debates what to do with it, to pay or not to pay, when he tucks it inside his coat pocket and walks out, she notices his shady deed and follows him outside. Liking the fact that he walked out without paying, she sees in him her male opposite, the *animus* she denies. Where he presents a clean-cut personality to the outside world, the kind that usually pays his checks, but breaks the law when he figures he can get away with it, Lulu presents herself as a dark free spirit when inside she's really the homely blonde Audrey.

Half of It Now

"Hey, you didn't pay for your lunch," Lulu calls Charlie on the street outside the diner.

"What?" Charlie answers, trying to look as if he doesn't know what she's talking about, denying his doings just as he denies his other half.

"You didn't pay your bill, big boy," she says, approaching him.

"Oh, sure I paid, didn't I?"

"The check's in your pocket," Lulu reminds him. When he tries to dismiss it by blaming his absentmindedness (his unconscious?), she doesn't let him off so easy. Like a street-smart therapist, she gets him to own up, to take responsibility for his deed, by threatening to call a cop. Charlie never comes out and admits it, but he doesn't have to. Seeing through him, Lulu takes another step toward him, saying, "Let me guess. Sometimes you don't pay for your lunch, or maybe you steal the occasional candy bar or newspaper." Charlie is somewhat amazed but likes what he hears coming from her red lips, especially when she slips in, "You're a closet rebel."

No sooner does Lulu give voice to Charlie's other half than his tele-pager calls him back to the office. Considering the wild ride she takes him on, her asking "Which way are you going?" may well be asking him to choose between the two voices, hers or the voice of "the office." But Lulu doesn't wait for his answer. "I'll give you a ride," she immediately offers as if knowing that in his present state of mind the decision needs to be made *for* him. She tells him she knows of a shortcut. As Charlie is surprised to learn, Lulu doesn't even work at the diner. The money never really mattered to her. She has something else on her devious mind, something wild.

"Are you coming?" Lulu asks Charlie, starting to cross the street toward her car. While she crosses easily with no thought of oncoming traffic, Charlie, a novice in crossing to the other side, is almost run over. Sitting down behind the driver's wheel and putting on her sunglasses, Lulu half-invites half-warns Charlie, "Ready or not, babe?" Charlie, looking in from the passenger window, finally steps inside and sits down in the seat beside her. "I'm Lulu," she extends her hand.

"Charles. Pleased to meet you," he says politely, shaking her hand.

Rather than take Charlie to "the office," the real "shortcut" Lulu meant is the road to the other half of himself. First, she throws the tele-pager out the window. Then, despite Charlie's protesting and his wanting to "go back," she drives through the Holland Tunnel to the other side of the river. "Hey, Charlie, relax," she urges him. "Take the afternoon off. You deserve it. Really."

But Charlie, unable to relax, threatens Lulu, "If you don't turn around and take me back, you're gonna make me do something that I don't wanna do."

"I can hardly wait, Charlie," she replies, turning on the primitive African music, that sets the mood for what she has in mind. The first shown road sign on the other side of the tunnel has a twofold message, WRONG WAY and GO BACK, giving expression to Charlie's desire to return to his safe and familiar state of mind. Only by now it's too late, as the very next sign reads: "Welcome to New Jersey."

While Charlie wants to know where they're going, particularly as they're getting farther and farther away from the office, Lulu wants to know if he's been married a long time. "Are you afraid of me, Charlie?" she asks when he refuses to show her his family picture. Proving he's not afraid, and that he is indeed married, he shows her his family picture and even agrees, at her urgings, to take a drink. In turn, proving she's just like him in not paying, when she stops at a liquor store "to get another bottle," she pays for four bottles of Scotch, but takes back much more when emptying the cash register while the stuffy salesman, the "Country Squire" of the store sign, isn't looking. Walking out the door, she disconnects the pay phone with which Charlie is talking to his secretary at the office, replacing the mouthpiece with a long sensual kiss from her lipstick-red lips. "Coming?" she asks Charlie suggestively.

Getting into the spirit of things, Charlie takes a belt of Scotch and says, "You were right. I *am* a rebel." When Lulu giggles, he insists, "I *am*! I just channel my rebellion into the mainstream." A minute later he even assures her, "I may look straight, you know. But right down in here, that's where it counts. Deep down inside, I got what it takes." "Do you?" Lulu asks, happy to hear it, wildly veering off the interstate to find out for herself.

At the first opportunity, when Lulu drives up to the motel, Charlie is far from the man of his words. "Maybe it's not such a good idea getting a room," he says cautiously. "I mean, don't you have some place we could go?"

Despite having plenty of cash on her, Lulu insists that Charlie pay for the room. It's part of his initiating rite.

"The rest," she tells him, "is free."

That Lulu is initiating Charlie to his other half is suggested by the primitive music she turns on and the two ceremonial objects she uses before shackling him to the bed with the emblematic handcuffs. Now, with Charlie hers to do with as she pleases, she rips open his white T-shirt before doing the same to her black undergarment. Then, she takes Charlie on a ceremonial rite of burning his bridges behind him by calling the office and forcing him to lie about why he won't be returning this afternoon. "Charlie, you're a really good liar when you wanna be," she commends him for his rebellious performance.

Afterward, as suggested by the shower he takes and his laughing over what he had said to his superior, Charlie feels like a new man.

"Sure you know what you're doing?" Lulu asks him when he decides to continue with her rather than go back.

"No," Charlie giggles happily. His one hand may be handcuffed, but he has never felt more free.

Now that Charlie chooses to go with Lulu, she puts him through another initiation rite. In fact, considering all that transpires in the movie's two halves, she takes him through the three phases of what's commonly called "Rite of Passage," a term first coined by Arnold van Gennep in 1909, a three-part ritual representing separation, transition, and incorporation.

Charlie's first separation is from "the office," when he calls off his meeting with his superior. His second one is from "Dad," at "Mom and Dad's Italian Restaurant." As part of the separation rite, Lulu, who knows that Charlie doesn't have much money left, offers to pay for the meal since, as she says, "You got the room." But rather than pay, on her way out she tells Dad that "the gentleman would pay for dinner," leaving Charlie with the check but unable to pay, since they don't accept "*any* credit card." Still wearing the handcuff, Charlie bolts for the door, diving head first into Lulu's waiting car. "What are you doing?" he asks incredulously. "I could've been killed."

"Come on, Charlie," she reminds him, "you don't like paying those things."

Celebrating Charlie's successful separation, and with his head in Lulu's lap, they sing along with the song on the radio, The Troggs' "Wild Thing." Its opening lyrics, "Wild thing, you make my heart sing," seem to give expression to Charlie's new state of mind as they cross the state line from New Jersey to Pennsylvania. When shown next, at night, with the two in a state of inebriation, Lulu drives the car off the road and into a sign that calls them to head back: "WHOA! YOU JUST PASSED THE BEST SCRAPPPLE IN PENNA BACK 500 YDS." Perhaps that's why she knocks it down. Now that they're in her home state, there's no turning back, not even 500 yards.

On the morning after, with Charlie having crossed into the state where he meets his other half, the man at the motel (the "motel philosopher," as the character is listed in the credits) gives him something for his hangover, saying, "Take half of it now, half of it later, and you'll feel a lot better." Then, offering some advice, he adds, "Remember, no matter what: It's better to be a live dog than a dead lion." That Charlie is the "live dog" of the equation is suggested next by Lulu's toasting with the whiskey bottle, "Hair of the dog that bit you, babe."

But having taken "half of it now," Charlie is a changed man. As he tells Lulu, "Last night was last night." He then insists that she, too, consume some of the "tried and true" remedy. Liking Charlie's first display of his new manhood, Lulu drinks willingly from a White Castle cup, which may well allude to her fairy tale fantasy of home and family, which doubles for the first motel, the Palace Motor Lodge. This fantasy is also suggested by the sign at their backs as they leave the motel, "FAMILY ATMOSPHERE AT FAMILY PRICES."

Another sign that things are changing is Lulu's abandoning her green car, which she claims is "still registered" under her ex's name, and then buying a red one. And this time, *she* pays, not Charlie. In another act of celebration, the two are shown riding in their "new" car, singing "Wild Thing" again, though this time together with the hitchhikers they picked up along the way, the whole ride is a collective celebration of Charlie's successful separation from two patriarchal figures, a notion underscored by Charlie (and Lulu) meeting up with the patriarchs' other halves, the maternal figures in the next two stops.

The first stop is a second-hand store called, of all things, Charley's Famous Shop. Inside, Lulu approaches the store's two elderly salesladies (Dorothy Demme and Emma Byrne), shown sitting by two old televisions. "Ladies, we need something for the gentleman here," she says. With Charlie shown standing before the mirror in a new outfit, a much more colorful one than his office wear, Lulu observes, "Oh, Charlie, it's *you*."

"Absolutely, with all certainty, no," he says, true to form.

Lulu turns to one of the salesladies and asks, "If you were *my* mother and I brought this guy home as my husband, what would you think?"

"Very nice," the saleslady replies, while the other one sees the other half: "But *I'd* get rid of those handcuffs if I were you."

Outside, Charley checks out the new "him" reflected in the store window, liking what he sees. But it's nothing compared to what he sees when Lulu comes out in a flowery white spring dress. "Don't look so surprised," she says when seeing the happy look on his face. "Get in the car." She shoves him lightly toward the car, throwing his old clothing into an incinerating drum, but picking up his wallet that had fallen out of one of his jacket pockets.

Transition

Signaling a *transition* between the *separation* and *incorporation*, and between the two maternal stations, an iris in/iris out transition (the only such cinematic transition used in the film) transports us from Lulu getting inside the car to their arriving, later that day, at her mother's home where she grew up.

"Where are we?" Charlie asks, as Lulu, taking the saleslady's advice, opens the handcuff latched onto his wrist. "What are you doing?" Charlie asks.

"I'm setting you free," Lulu replies.
"Maybe I don't *want* to be free."
"Maybe you're not."

Having changed into new clothing and freed from the handcuffs, Lulu's instructing Charlie "Don't call me Lulu, call me Audrey," marks a new beginning for the two. Whereas up to now he was Lulu's captive, doing what she drove him to do, now that she's Audrey, who introduces him to her mother as "just the kind of man you always said I should marry," Charlie is free from one woman but hitched to another.

That the whole home segment with the mother, Peaches (Dana Preu), is a *transition* between the *separation* and *incorporation* is signaled by the segment's other transition, the diagonal wipe that transports us from the "newlyweds" in Audrey's bedroom to Charlie lying on the bed in white shorts. He looks through her high school yearbook and stops at the picture of a young Audrey, bookmarked by newspaper articles about the "Quincy Gunman." Shown scanning two such items, Charlie is unknowingly introduced to Ray Sinclair (Ray Liotta), his other half, already referred to by Lulu/Audrey. Once, when saying that the green car she abandoned was registered in his name; the second time immediately before Charlie opens the yearbook, when she tells him, as Audrey, that her mother doesn't know she had married *him*. "No, I never told her," she explains. "She didn't like him anyway."

The home "transition" segment ends with Audrey's second transformation, when she walks through the kitchen's two white swinging doors. Her hair returned to its natural blonde, she is wearing a white dress, with a necklace and a small cross replacing her colorful ornaments and trinkets.

"Oh, my gosh," Charlie reacts, happily stunned once again.

"I had this dress in high school," she explains, suggesting she hasn't changed much since then. "My mama saves everything." Mama, seeming to know much more than she lets on, says confidentially, "I hope things work out for you, Charlie." Later, in the movie's other half, her parting words take on a whole other meaning.

Reunion

Recalling Lulu's "ready or not" before Charlie got into her car in New York, Audrey half warns him when they arrive at their next station, "Get ready, Charlie! It's my high school reunion." A hint of what this reunion holds for the two is envisioned by their greeting a black couple, their shadowy counterparts, when they enter the ballroom through a curtained threshold of red stripes. Once this brief meeting between the two couples is over, Audrey and Charlie are out of the picture as the camera follows the band playing on stage and the other dancing couples nearby, with the singer giving expression to Charlie's growing feelings for Audrey when singing of being unable to leave her.

The two are shown again only after a fellow worker from the office, Larry Dillman (Jack Gilpin), spots Charlie on the dance floor, saying to his pregnant wife, "I know this guy. That guy's in my office." Though Charlie may think he's the last person he wants to meet, especially after Audrey introduces herself as his "lover," as it soon turns out, he's merely the second to last. Impressed by what he sees, Dillman's parting words are "Driggs, I didn't think you had it in you." But Charlie, having been reminded of the office, suddenly gets cold feet when realizing he's missing his wallet and storms out of the ballroom with Audrey right behind.

"What's wrong?" she asks.

"If I don't get my wallet back, you know what? I'm fucked!"

"Charlie, I *got* it. I got your wallet. It's in the glove compartment."

Relieved, Charlie has second thoughts about the time he's having with his companion. "Lulu, look. God, you're a great girl. You got a few problems, but you're a great girl. And you're loaded with potential, but you're just too much for me. I can't handle this. Let me just get my wallet, and I'll catch a bus, and I'll go back to my boring and very safe life while I still got one."

But Lulu/Audrey doesn't let him go back without hearing the other side, "Look, tomorrow you're going to wake up. You're still going to be Charlie Driggs, you know? And this will all be over and done with. So why don't we enjoy it while we can? And then tomorrow, no more Lulu. Unless you really want to go, then go." Charlie's response is envisioned when they're shown dancing inside, coming into the picture just as the singer on stage gives expression to his feelings, once again singing about never leaving his girlfriend. The two stop dancing, embracing tenderly, as the singer sings repeatedly that he'll "be there," words that foreshadow things to come.

Presently, the transformation in Audrey, former consumer of Scotch, is underscored by her asking for a soda when Charlie asks, "What do you want ... from the bar." But before Charlie gets there, Irene (Margaret Colin), dressed in a black dress like the former Lulu, spots him, much as Lulu had first spotted him at the diner. While she squeezes herself next to him, trying to pick him up, the camera cuts to Audrey, shown sitting with the same black couple who function as their paired Other. Dillman, seeing Charlie at the bar with Irene, comes from behind Audrey, sharing with her his observation, "I had no idea Charles had such a way with the ladies!"

"Neither did he," she replies knowingly.

A bit later, reinforcing the notion that the black couple function as their other half, Charlie, shown dancing with Audrey, begins to copy the black man's dance moves, recalling John Travolta and his partner in *Saturday Night Fever*, particularly as it's actually Saturday night and as the black man is dressed like Travolta. Getting into the spirit of things, he even attempts Michael Jackson's signature moon walk. But all this merely foreshadows Charlie's actual dark half, who makes his appearance by the very next song.

"Hi, baby," the black-dressed Ray Sinclair, dancing with Irene, greets Audrey, "Surprise."

From her half of the symmetrical screen, Irene hisses like a snake, "Hi, Charlie." Knowing what this "surprise" means, Audrey, telling Charlie, "Let's go," heads to the door. But Dillman, a threshold guardian of sorts, detains the two long enough for Ray and Irene to catch up. Unaware of how Ray figures into Audrey's life, just as he's unconscious of his role in his own life, Charlie introduces himself.

"Well, Charlie," Ray says, "pleased to meet you. I'm Ray." "We have to go," Audrey insists, "See you all in ten years."

Only Ray doesn't intend to wait that long. With Irene by his side in his dark Cadillac, he drives up to Audrey and Charlie at the parking lot where their car won't start, greeting them with, "Hi, you all."

Charlie, surprised to see Ray so soon, wonders, "How'd he get out here so fast?"

But Ray, speaking more like his spirited other half than flesh and blood, merely replies, "Always keep 'em guessing, Charlie." Anxious to be alone with Audrey, he talks her into having one drink. Then, with Audrey and Charlie in the back seat, he stops by a store and asks Irene, "Why don't you and Charlie go in and get us a couple of six-packs?" But Audrey, knowing Ray, volunteers to go instead, leaving Charlie alone with Ray in the car, inadvertently giving him a chance to get acquainted with his other half.

At first, Charlie, unconscious of his other half, doesn't realize who Ray is and what he really wants. Having been informed by Dillman that Charlie's "wife takes the kids and runs off with the family dentist," Ray speaks as if he's on his side, asking about his married life with Audrey, the wife who had left *him*. While inside the store, when asking Irene, "When did he get out?" Audrey speaks of Ray as if he's the return of the repressed, outside in the car Ray hints that he's Charlie's other half when confiding about Audrey, "She looks like she can fuck you right in half."

"Ray, there's no call for that kind of talk," Charlie says seriously, looking Ray straight in the eyes.

Ray, who senses that Charlie is no pushover, especially when it concerns Audrey, pretends to agree and understand: "You're right. You're right."

Not having his way with Charlie, Ray walks inside the store "for smokes" and tells Irene, "Charlie's lonely out there. Give us a couple of minutes alone."

But Audrey, not wanting to be alone with him, starts walking out, telling Ray when he tries to stop her, "I got nothing to say to you, Ray." He presses her by asking, "What are you saying, that you don't love me anymore?" "Yeah," she says bluntly. "That's what I'm saying."

Only Ray, like the relentless Other that he is, doesn't give up so easily. Getting Irene to "run back in and get me some cigarettes," he drives off despite Audrey's protest, inviting Charlie to join him in the front seat. When Charlie invites Audrey, who refuses, Ray raises a toast with his bottle of beer, foreshadowing things to come, "It looks like it's you and me, pal."

Retracing Audrey's and Charlie's road trip of *initiation*, Ray's first stop at Don and Connie's, an all-night market whose name is a transposed "Mom and Dad's." Or "you and me." For just before Ray invites Charlie to come inside with him, the two are shown drinking from their beer bottles as doubles, particularly with Ray dressed in black and Charlie in a white shirt. Unseen by Charlie, who's still unconscious of his other half, Ray is shown tucking his gun inside his pants as he gets out of the car.

Inside the market, like Lulu before him at the liquor store, Ray empties the cash register. But he doesn't stop there. He brutally attacks the store worker and throws Charlie over the counter when he tries to intervene. After Audrey rushes in, screaming, "Ray, goddamn you," perhaps to underscore Charlie's new way of seeing Ray, the rest of the segment is shown on the small surveillance TV screen, which shows Ray beating up Charlie and shoving both Audrey and him into the front seat of their vehicle before driving off.

The retracing's next station is Ray's motel room, where he forces Audrey and Charlie to "play a little game of true confessions." While Audrey repeatedly confesses that she only "met him yesterday," Ray, who refuses to accept that Audrey had left him, gets Charlie to confess what Dillman had told him at the reunion, that his wife had left him "last September."

Surprised, Audrey repeats her line, "You're a really good liar, Charlie." Only this time he has lied to *her*, which completely changes the way she sees him, as if he took advantage of her more than she of him. Or as Ray puts it, "Who's shitting who here?" Changing sides, she tosses Charlie the keys to her car, as Ray chimes in, "Get the fuck out."

That one part of the rite of passage has ended and another has begun is suggested by another rare dissolve, from Audrey lying on the motel bed in her white dress to Charlie arriving at her car, parked outside the reunion pavilion. As Charlie gets inside, turns on the ignition and drives off, all in one shot, the screen fades to black, then, after a brief black screen, it fades in to white, marking a whole new chapter, a chapter that shows Charlie active rather than passive, initiating rather than being initiated, doing all he can to get back the woman he loves, now held captive by his other half. If Charlie's admitting that his wife had left him does something to Audrey, it also does something to Charlie. It frees him from what he's been keeping from her; it frees him to be his other half.

Half of It Later

Opening a new chapter on a new day (Sunday), Ray and Audrey are shown driving away from their motel, followed by their literally driving into the new chapter's first station, the gas *station*, where they stop to "fill her up." As the camera pans to the left, Charlie is shown driving into the gas station on the other side of the road, where the black attendant, Nelson (Steve Scales), doubles for the one that asked Ray if he wants to "fill her up?" Personifying his "bright shadow," he surprises Charlie by doubling his habit of calling people by name from their name tags when calling his name from his reunion tag. Inside the station's store, which doubles for the second-hand store where Lulu got Charlie to change clothes before meeting her mother, Nelson points to Charlie's bloody shirt, persuading him to buy a new one; then, on second thought, he suggests a whole new getup, one that is all white. As Charlie's helping shadow, who doubles for the "motel philosopher," he gives him advice for the perilous road ahead: "Hey, Charlie. Attempt to be cool." When Nelson gives him a second advice, to "see somebody about that nose," Charlie, beginning to incorporate his Other, repeats Ray's very words to him, "Broken nose ain't gonna kill you, Nelson."

In his new garb, Charlie follows Ray's car into Virginia, where he and Audrey stop at a roadside motel, similar to the one Charlie and Lulu had stopped at two days earlier. While the Union and Confederate flags on the front of the cap on Charlie's head suggests that he has crossed the "Mason-Dixon Line" that divides his two states of mind, the conscious and the unconscious, his white shirt with two red "love" hearts and "Virginia is for lovers" suggest that he's also in a new state of heart.

In her motel room with Ray, mirroring the change in Charlie, Audrey tells him she's "gonna go change" in the bathroom, but this is actually a ruse which will allow her to escape through the bathroom's narrow window. The ever-suspicious Ray, breaking down the door, chases after her as she runs away, dressed in white shirt and shorts, just like Charlie. Catching her, he drags her to the motel swimming pool. "You wanted to swim?" he taunts her. "You want to swim? Swim!" he says as he throws her into the water.

That Ray's throwing Audrey into the water mirrors Charlie's baptism is suggested by the subsequent showing him on the other side of the road, sleeping in her green car right in front of a small white church, with a cross on each of its front double doors. This "double" is taken up as Charlie is awakened up by a young black girl dressed in her Sunday best, who asks him, "Do you need any help?" while on the other side of the road, Ray is shown flirting with the young blonde salesgirl (Kristin Olsen), shown with a yellow bag behind her that reads "NEED HELP."

The doubling of the two continues at night, as Charlie, with the twin crosses always behind him, watches Audrey and Ray through a pair of binoculars from the car as they walk into an adjacent restaurant with a pair of big painted cacti on either side of its entrance. "Okay, fine. Here we go," Charlie says to himself before crossing the road and waiting outside the restaurant, which doubles for "Mom and Dad's." He only enters after he sees a black policeman enter the restaurant, whose presence "assists" him as did Nelson and the little girl. Protected by the lawman, Charlie sits down next to Audrey and opposite Ray, ordering "just a coffee" from the waitress before turning to Ray and saying, "You don't mind, do you, Ray?"

"Charlie, you got to be out of your mind," Audrey says warningly.

Ray, even more surprised than Audrey, says, "Charlie, you are one dumb son of a bitch. I'm almost starting to like you, Charlie."

But Charlie is far from dumb. As he tells Ray in no uncertain terms, "I want Lulu."

Ray turns to Audrey and asks, "Is that your name this week? *Lulu*?" Then, trying to set Charlie straight, he informs him, "You know, Charlie, she's not gonna be too happy driving around in a station wagon the rest of her life. You better think about that. You better ask yourself if you really want her."

Charlie, looking adoringly at Audrey/Lulu by his side, smiles as he speaks to her more than to Ray, "I really want her."

But Ray, speaking as his Other, informs him, "You got to fight for a woman like this."

"I don't have to fight you, Ray. I'm gonna take Lulu; we're gonna waltz right out of here, and there's not a damn thing you can do." Motioning to the nearby policeman, he knows he has the upper hand as he looks Ray straight in the eyes, counting off his list of recent crimes.

To make sure Ray doesn't follow them, Charlie exacts from him his car keys and wallet, with Ray warning him (twice) that he's "gonna regret this." Then, recalling what Lulu had done to him under different circumstances at "Mom and Dad's," he tells him while picking up the tab, "Look, Ray, just to show you that there's no hard feelings, this one's on me." But when the waitress delivers the check, she informs him, "The gentleman said you'd take care of this." Left alone and with no money, Ray nonetheless appreciates Charlie's audacity, which surely reminds him of himself.

As Charlie and Audrey ride off with her at the wheel, she soon stops the car before a railroad crossing, telling the stunned Charlie, "Okay, liar. Get out!" When Charlie refuses, she informs him that now they're even. "You saved me. I saved you. Now get out." The resigned Charlie, seeing she doesn't want him, as she had not wanted Ray, gets out. But after crossing the threshold of the tracks, Audrey, having second thoughts, stops the car again and drives back. "Goddamn you, Charlie," she yells angrily. "I saw your wedding ring. Shit. I saw the family pictures. I get myself involved with a married man who's not even married."

In his defense, Charlie comes clean, "Okay, I guess I still wear the ring because I hate to admit to myself that my family fell apart. I told you I was married to protect myself, and then I was afraid that if I said, 'Guess what? I'm not really married,' you'd take off."

"You're right," Audrey shoots back, but then agrees with him when he reminds her how similar they are. "You were lying a blue streak to me, too."

As the two are shown driving off together again, leaving behind the crossroad of their relationship, the camera cuts to Ray in the restaurant, unable to leave without paying. But like Charlie's break with the policeman, his lucky break comes when the blonde salesgirl, the one with the "need help" sign, taps on the other side of the booth's window. Promising her he'll "be back in a couple of days," Ray steals the first open car, a station wagon, and starts chasing after Audrey and Charlie. As Charlie had told Ray before leaving with Audrey, "Now it's *you* with something to lose," he not only turns things around with Ray, he turns around the direction of his journey from the unconscious South to the conscious North, heading back to New York (identified by the same Twin Towers that opened the movie).

Audrey, unable to go back to her old life, admits, "I just don't want to go to my apartment anymore."

"You can stay at my place," Charlie suggests, adding, "for tonight." But before the two reach Charlie's home, Ray, after getting Audrey's address from the reunion pamphlet, is shown breaking into Lulu's apartment and phoning information for Charlie's address. Meanwhile, Charlie and Audrey are shown driving into Charlie's driveway, with the station wagon Ray had mentioned parked outside. Inside, when Charlie tucks the exhausted Audrey into bed, she whispers to him, half-asleep, "What are you gonna do now that you've seen how the other half lives?"

"The other half?" he asks.

"The other half of *you*," she clarifies as she drifts off to sleep.

Just then Charlie's other half, announcing his arrival, hurls a lawn chair through the front windowpane and enters the house. "Let's see what you're made of now, Charlie!" Ray threatens as he throws Charlie around.

When Audrey comes in from the bedroom, screaming, "Ray, stop it! You'll kill him!" Ray shoots back, "I'm just warming up!" Manacling Charlie to the bathroom sink's drain pipes with Lulu's handcuffs, he goes after Audrey, repeatedly asking why she's doing this to him. Charlie, hearing her screaming to him from the bedroom, forcefully frees himself and comes behind Ray, strangling him with the very device with which he was shackled.

In the violent struggle that ensues, the classic fight to the finish between the projector and his Other, just before Ray can use the knife he draws from his black boot, Audrey knocks it out of his hand with a golf club. While Ray tries to take the club away from her, Charlie picks up the knife, which Ray, turning around to face him, walks right into, stopping in his tracks. Doubly stunned, the two face each other for the longest moment, as if each one recognizes himself in the other. "Shit, Charlie," is all Ray can say, as Charlie pulls out the bloody knife, which drops to the floor between them, shown in a shot that envisions the projector (in white socks) and his Other (in black boots). Then, as if checking to see that what he saw in Charlie's face is true, or the other way around, Ray drags himself to the bathroom mirror, staring at his reflected face and running back his bloody hand through his black hair.

In the subsequent segment outside the house, where the police question Charlie and Audrey about what transpired inside, one of the detectives asks Charlie, "Mr. Driggs, did you know him? Did you know the guy?" With the wounded and traumatized Charlie unable to say how he knew his other half, Audrey replies on his behalf, "He was my husband." Hearing this, the detective, needing "more information," escorts her to the back seat of a nearby police car, from which she looks at Charlie through the rear window, and he looks back at her with longing. As the car pulls away, she raises her hand in parting. He does the same. The screen goes black, signaling the end of the movie's "other half."

Comes Around

Like the transition between Charlie turning on the ignition of Lulu's car and starting to follow her ride south with Ray, the screen once again changes from black to white, only this time to the bright sky as seen from Charlie's office. Surveying the buildings outside, the camera tilts down to show a new high-rise building under construction, which seems to mirror Charlie's new state of mind, still under construction, particularly as he's shown next, gazing listlessly outside the window, his right arm in a sling, his face bruised and scarred. His present state of mind is emphasized by his brief exchange with Dillman, who comes around to let Charlie know that "we're all real sorry about your leaving." He then adds, "There's no way to get you to change your mind, is there?"

But Charlie's mind is made up. Dillman asks what's probably foremost on Charlie's mind, "How do you figure a guy like Ray Sinclair?" But the traumatized Charlie, who hasn't fully incorporated his other half, doesn't know what to say, just as he was unable to respond when the detective asked if he knew him. Shaking his head, the initiated Charlie can only repeat the advice he had received from the "motel philosopher" on the morning after his first night with Lulu, "It's better to be a live dog than a dead lion."

Charlie's new state of mind is best expressed by the opening line of the song that accompanies the movie's epilogue, "As I look out my window, I don't understand what I see." But considering how he's dressed, with a checkered shirt of black, gray, and white, and by his being without the physical signs of his clash with Ray, Charlie seems to have figured him out, or at least has made him part of his psyche. As his checkered shirt suggests, and as Ray's death signifies, he has incorporated his other half, the unconscious Other that he formerly repressed and projected onto Ray.

In this state of mind Charlie goes looking for the woman with the two names. He looks for her in her old apartment, only to be told that she had "moved out," just as he had left the office. Then, for a brief moment, he thinks he sees her in her old getup of black wig and dress, a fleeting vision of his dark *anima*. But when he runs after her and turns the corner, Lulu is nowhere to be seen, just as she's no longer an autonomous *anima* in his psyche.

In the movie's final scene, following an establishing shot of the diner that doubles for the one that opened the movie, Charlie, hoping to find Lulu where he had first met her, is shown sitting at the same table, as if nothing has changed. Except for Charlie, of course. No longer compelled to give expression his other half by not paying, this time he pays. That's why he's amazed when, just as Lulu had followed him outside and called him back for not paying, now the black waitress, Dottie, the same one depicted as Lulu's binary opposite, calls him back, all but repeating her first words to him, "Hey! You didn't pay for your food."

Puzzled and trying to explain that he did pay, this time telling the truth, Charlie only figures it out when he sees Audrey holding the five-dollar bill he had left on the table, smiling delicately in a black dress with white polka-dots, not to mention black shoes and a white hat that represent the unconscious and the conscious. Walking toward her, Charlie says, "You never said goodbye."

"I never wanted to say goodbye," she replies simply. Then, recalling their first meeting, she asks, "Want a ride?" motioning to the parked station wagon with wooden panels on the sides, the station wagon Ray claimed she'd never be happy driving for the rest of her life.

After a brief exchange of wordless looks, Charlie happily responds, "Sure, *Audrey*, why not?" Only this time, underscoring the change he had undergone, when Audrey starts heading to the driver's side, he reaches out to her, opening for her the other door, and walks to the driver's side. Having incorporated his other half, he's neither a dead lion nor a live dog, but a *whole* new man, a man with a *whole* new woman by his side.

9

Sea of Love:
The Feminine Other

> *You know, when it gets late sometimes I feel like a big cat in a small cage.*
> — *Frank Keller to Helen*

Keller as Killer

Unlike *Something Wild*, in which the Other appears halfway into the movie, in Harold Becker's *Sea of Love* he appears at the very end. Granted, he appears briefly on two earlier occasions, but more as a witness than as the Other. He also "appears" unseen on two paired occasions, in the first two killings and in his two visits to the protagonist's door. When he finally does appear as the Other, in his third visit, it comes as a complete surprise to both the protagonist and the audience. It comes as a surprise despite the movie's countless tip-offs that the two are one and the same, that the killer is the protagonist's unconscious Other.

The most obvious linking of the two, no doubt, is the protagonist's name, Frank Keller (Al Pacino), which recalls Joe Keller, the "killer" in Arthur Miller's *All My Sons*. Another linking is the two's inability to let go of their ex-wives. As the movie repeatedly suggests, rather than deal with his failed marriage directly with his ex-wife, who's never seen, Frank projects it onto Helen (Ellen Barkin), whom he suspects as the killer, with himself as her next victim. That his suspicion is dictated by his projection is underscored by the symmetry of Helen being to the killer what Frank's "ex-wife, Denise" is to him. In the course of his investigation, Frank re-enacts his troubled relationship with his ex-wife through his volatile relationship with Helen, but he only comes to terms with both women, and with himself, after killing the real killer, his unconscious Other.

Good News, Bad News

Opening with the same shot of the Twin Towers that open *Something Wild*, *Sea of Love* envisions the binary twins of the projector and his Other right from the start. Only where *Something Wild*'s director, Jonathan Demme, shows the towers in daylight and as the opening shot, Becker shows it at night and in its second shot, which follows the opening shot of a bluish body of water with dark projections protruding above the surface, as "Sea of Love" appears on the screen. These projections (from the unconscious sea) are again shown in the foreground of the second shot, with the Twin Towers in the background against a bluish night sky, reflected in the river's bluish water. Between the two is a horizontal bridge, which both connects the two sides of the river and divides the screen in two halves, the sky and the water, the conscious and the unconscious.

Linking Frank to the killer right from the start, he's introduced in two consecutive scenes, day and night, sandwiched between the two brief scenes of the first killing. Both scenes, the killing itself and its discovery the following night, are accompanied by Phil Phillip's "Sea of Love," spinning on a record player in the opening and closing of the killing scene. The 1959 song that gives the 1989 movie its title, the voice from the past that asks, "Do you remember when we met?" is not unlike the unconscious Other who suddenly erupts after years of repression. Frank may project his repressed Other on others, but as the movie demonstrates, "The refused and unacceptable characteristics do not go away; they only collect in the dark corners of our personality. When they have been hidden long enough, they take on a life of their own — the shadow life."[1]

When introduced, Frank is confident and in full control as a detective heading a team of policemen in tricking a group of wanted felons to turn themselves in by inviting them for brunch with the New York Yankees. This scheme underscore's Frank not being who he seems when initially shown pouring orange juice for two young felons.

"You a Yankee?" the one in the darker suit asks him.

"You don't recognize me?" Frank asks in return. While never saying he's "a Yankee," his "Holy cow!" (made famous by the former Yankee Phil Rizzuto, known as Scooter) leads the two to think he's the former shortstop, foreshadowing Frank's mistaking the killer for someone else.

"Do that again," the other felon asks him.

"Holy cow!" Frank obliges. "Yo, Phil," the other one asks, "how come you're pouring us juice?"

Frank only answers the "juice" question when shown next, addressing the invited men from the stage. "I got some good news, and I got some bad news," he begins. "Now, which do you wanna hear first?" The bad news is that "the Yanks can't make it" and that "you're all under arrest"; the good news, as he explains, is the vodka the police are shown pouring into the orange juice. Frank's own "bad news," what he calls his "mid–life crisis," is suggested when he's introduced by a colleague who joins him onstage, using the occasion to "propose a toast. To Detective Frank Keller, on today, his twentieth anniversary on the job."

Later, as he's getting into his car, a young black man comes running up to him with his small son, asking, "Hey, am I too late?" Informed by his colleague that the man is wanted for "grand theft auto, two counts," Frank, looking at the young man's son, informs him in double entendre, "We're all booked up." Repeating it when the man insists he "got an invite," he flashes his police badge. Catching on, the young man thanks Frank, who waives him off with another double entendre, "Catch you later."

Come nighttime, we see Frank's other side. Shown drinking and smoking in his apartment, he's a lonely and dejected man, a mere shadow of his daytime self. What makes him so is revealed when, later that night, he calls his ex-wife under the pretext that he thinks he's "got appendicitis," only to have her hang up on him. Apparently, his real reason for calling, as suggested by the closing line of "Sea of Love," heard next as the camera cuts to the apartment building where the killing took place, is to tell her he loves her. The song's repeated playing, which brings the victim's next-door neighbor to discover the body when knocking on the apartment's open door, continues throughout the movie, some of it playing in Frank's head.

Summoned by his Other, the following day Frank is shown arriving at the scene of the crime with Gruber (Richard Jenkins), his investigating partner. In the elevator, with his back to Gruber, Frank apologizes for the "that phone thing last night," chalking it up to his "having a mid–life crisis." But as suggested by the color of the two's clothes, the more darkly dressed Frank, who projects his anger and frustration on the man he blames for taking his wife, is unable to confront him face to face. Just as Gruber reminded Frank on the phone that his "wife" is now his "ex-wife," his presence is a constant reminder of her having left him.

That Frank enters the unconscious realm of the Other is suggested as soon as he gets out of the elevator, by the two lights in the hall and a pair of policemen, one black, one white, who walk out of the victim's apartment as Frank and Gruber walk in. Inside, in the living room, the elderly woman who discovered the body is talking to two other policemen, one blonde, the other dark-haired, telling them about Joe Louis. Her informing the two that "they called him The Brown Bomber," like the song "Sea of Love," is another "shadow" from the past. Louis is brought up, no doubt, for having fought Max Schmeling for the world heavyweight title in two historic matches, both held in Yankee Stadium. Like the projector and his Other, the two fights were perceived by Germans as matches between the *white* "Aryan" and the *black* American.

Both the projector and his Other and the two women who figure in Frank's life are illustrated by the large symmetric painting of two women, in two separate "frames," both in erotic poses, which hangs above the head of the bed on which lies the victim's body. As the two partners put on latex gloves before inspecting the body, Frank is doubly shown, reflected in a mirror though never looking at his reflection, just as he hadn't looked at Gruber in the elevator. Now, shown in a symmetric shot on either side of the bed, sandwiched between identical lamps on each side, Frank explains his late-night call while they try to determine the time of the victim's death.

Considering that the killing was done during the previous night, Gruber is correct in his determining 36 hours to Frank's 48, which may well mirror their viewpoints regarding the woman in their lives. Particularly after apologizing for the phone call, and the two shake their gloved hands over the dead body, Frank says, "We're in the same squad six years. We don't so much as even have a beer together. How the hell do you take my wife away?"

Gruber, letting go of Frank's hand and pulling away, shoots back, "I didn't take nobody nowhere. You understand? You didn't treat her right. She walked." But Frank, who blames Gruber for taking away his wife just as the killer blames the men who sleep with his ex-wife, doesn't understand. Before storming out of the room, Gruber all but advises Frank to deal with his Other when saying, "You want to kick somebody's ass about it, you kick your own."

The following day, on his return to the crime scene, the doorman (Manny Alfaro), a threshold guardian of sorts, sets Frank on the right trail by mentioning that there was "a cable TV repair guy here, I think." While Frank is shown reflected in the mirror when questioning the man, his "double" is rhymed in the subsequent scene in which the cable guy, Terry (Michael Rooker), is shown with his "double" (the man sitting next to him in an identical uniform), as he tells a dirty joke of double entendre to two colleagues. The punch line, "in the butt," links him to the victim's butt (actually shown in an earlier scene), but also to Frank being told by his partner to kick his own. The cable guy admits he was at the apartment building of the shooting but claims he didn't "see anybody over there, not looking right," only "a couple of ladies going to the laundry room," which recalls the two women pictured above the victim's bed. Unknowingly (unconsciously) linking the man to the killing, Frank evokes the song's "Do you remember when we met?" when giving the man his calling card, saying, "If you remember, you want to give me a call,"

The notion of unconsciously connecting with his Other through the song is underscored when Frank is subsequently shown in his apartment, putting a 45-rpm record of "Sea of Love" on the turntable as if trying to get in touch with him in the only way he can. As he pours himself a drink, the camera cuts to another apartment, where inside the bedroom, once again showing "the butt," the killer shoots a second man in the same way he killed the first one, shooting him from behind, in the back of the head, while forcing him to demonstrate how he "humped" her. Only this time, linking the two, the accompanying song is playing in Frank's apartment.

Double Doers

The "Sea of Love" song comes up again in the very next scene, in a party for newly promoted detectives, in which Frank meets Sherman Touhey (John Goodman), the detective investigating the second murder, who soon replaces Gruber as his new partner. We first see him as he watches Frank shadowboxing an Asian-American detective, who, recalling Joe Louis, functions as his shadowy Other in this imaginary fight. "Where the hell did you learn that?" he asks Frank. "That's like watching a movie." As the two start comparing the evidence from the two killings, Frank mentions they found "cigarette butts with lipstick on them," but it's Sherman who first suggests his "guy got done by a broad," which is all Frank needs to hear to suspect a woman. "Let's compare tomorrow," he suggests in return, ordering "double Dewars on the rocks" as if foreshadowing the double "doer," as Frank calls the killer, the real one and the one he projects. When the two sit down around a table with other detectives, Frank asks Sherman if they "found any records there," telling him of the "Sea of Love" record found at the scene of "his" killing, which starts the two singing the line, "Do you remember when we met?" After Sherman does a brief but most entertaining take on the song, Frank tells his colleagues sitting around the table, "I just met this guy."

Significantly, Frank first mentions that the killer is a woman as he and Sherman descend the stairs on their way out with Gruber, like a shadow, right behind him. Comparing the unknown woman to his ex-wife, he starts badgering Gruber about his "ex-wife, Denise." With Frank dishing out one too many jibes, Gruber suddenly grabs him by his jacket. Frank grabs his in return and starts beating him with his fists until Sherman pulls him off, thus ending the event as it had started, only this time the boxing is real. This assault on his partner is another intimation that Frank could be the killer. The two, still attached to their ex-wives, project their repressed rage on the men they blame for taking them away.

Later that night, still feeling victimized, Frank revisits the first victim's apartment. Inebriated and tired, he lies down on the "rippled" mattress, seeming to be floating on water as the camera closes in on him from above. But before he sinks any deeper, he's startled by the door's buzzer. Opening the door he sees a middle-aged woman with three floating balloons tied to each of her wrists. Mistaking Frank for the victim, she giggles embarrassedly when reciting her rhymes, "Silver balloons, a lifetime of Junes, old rock tunes."

"Who the hell are you?" Frank asks, slow to make the connection. "Oh, wait a minute," he finally catches on, asking the frightened woman his name. "Jim Mackey," she calls him by the victim's name, as if completing his immersion.

Inside the apartment, sitting opposite each other on the two couches, Frank confirms her story, "So you answered his ad in the *New York Weekly*?" When he suggests that "maybe you'd feel better if you took those balloons off," the woman, Gina (Christine Estabrook), whose balloons seem to represent the two sides of the projector and his Other, may well be speaking for Frank when replying, "They're the only things that's keeping me up," particularly as it comes after he was envisioned floating on the sea-like mattress.

The following day Frank finds his new partner waiting for him at his desk, as the two get the green light to join forces in investigating the two killings, or as Sherman calls it, "Me and you, a two-man task force." Underscoring this new partnership and his role in helping his partner integrate his unconscious Other, Sherman asks the divorced Frank, "Hey, you like weddings?" This notion continues at the wedding, as Frank, who briefly "plays" "Sea of Love" in his head while the female singer on stage sings "another one bites the dust," gets the idea to "how we catch her." As he explains to Sherman, "We know the broad is into rhyming ads, right? So we put a rhyming ad. Moon, June, spoon, sand dune. We set up dates with thirty, forty, fifty of the ladies who answer. We take them out, some restaurant, some bar, get their prints on a wine glass. Bingo! She's dropped."

At first Frank's boss doesn't go along with this "bullshit" plan, as Sherman calls it. He only agrees after the third man who placed the rhyming ads is murdered. Inspired and ingenious as this scheme to "catch her" may be, it's based on circumstantial projections and on Frank's feeling victimized. He's certain the killer is a woman just as he's certain his ex-wife stuck it to him, as he calls it.

The Feminine Other

While looking for the suspected woman by setting up a line of dates in a restaurant with the women who answered their rhymed ad, Frank meets Helen, the woman he's looking for, though not for the initial reasons. As Frank, wearing a wire, sings for sound check while waiting for his first date, "Do you remember when we met? That's the day I knew you were my pet," his words may well speak of both his ex-wife and Helen, the *anima* who replaces his "pet." This explains his saying to his first date, a woman older than he expected, old enough to be his mother, "We'll call you." The "we," which the unnamed woman picks up on, recalls the song's "when we met," reinforced by the overheard, "We need some more dinner plates, on the double," when Sherman, who acts as the pair's waiter, is shown in the kitchen, putting the woman's wine glass in a plastic bag for fingerprints. Seeing through Frank, through his "persona," the woman responds to his correcting himself, "I'll call you. Me," with "No, you won't."

The woman's seeing through Frank is taken up again with his second date, who speaks to him most frankly about his deliberate *persona*. "I get this very weird feeling you're not who you say you are." When Frank asks what she means, the unnamed woman may well be speaking in the voice of his ex-wife when calling his bluff before she gets up to leave. "You got cop's eyes.... When you look at me, I feel like I did something.... My ex-husband was a cop. What did you say? What are you, you're a printer? If you're a printer, I got a dick."

Having encountered two sides of his feminine Other, the mother and ex-wife (who sticks it to him with her imagined dick), Frank is shown taking a cigarette break with Sherman. But judging by his apparent fatigue when meeting the next woman, he needs more than a brief break. He may have succeeded in tricking the group of male felons into believing he was someone else, but once again he cannot do it with the instinctive woman facing him from the other side of the table, one who doesn't like what she sees. "You're a printer; I manage a shoe store. And I don't believe in wasting time on this stuff. You know what you know, and you go with it."

"You go with *what*?" Frank has no idea what this blonde in a red leather jacket is talking about.

"You're just not my type. I believe in animal attraction. I believe in love at first sight. I believe in this," she snaps her fingers before his eyes. "And I don't feel it with you." When Frank urges her to take a drink (so he can have her fingerprints), she gets up to leave, assuring Frank, "It's nothing personal."

Now that Frank has unknowingly met his ex-wife, the following morning the cable guy, Terry, is waiting for Frank at his office. Shaking Frank's hand, his telling him that he saw "a black kid" in the basement can be taken two ways, particularly when recalling that in their first meeting he was telling a double entendre joke and claimed he saw "a couple of ladies." On the one hand, as the real killer he tries to throw off the two in their investigation by projecting it on a convenient "black kid" from the market. On the other hand, as Frank's unconscious Other, who admits to "working down in the basement," his mentioning "your partner" and the "black kid" is his way of telling Frank that the killer is the shadowy Other of his psyche, especially as the "black kid" from the market is never seen and as his former boss asks, "What he do, kill somebody?"

Later that night, in another market, while Frank hums "Sea of Love" to himself, the woman who believes in animal attraction, enters the scene as if out of the blue, or the unconscious. "'Hell on wheels,' huh?" she says, confronting Frank with his own words to help him "remember when we met," particularly as she follows with "How quickly we forget" when he looks up with a stunned look on his face.

"No, I don't forget you," he remembers like the singer of the song. "You're the 'animal attraction.' 'Love at first sight.'" Only now, as she tells him what she liked, what changed her mind about Frank (the rhymed poem he put in the magazine), it's "like" at second sight.

Seeing through him once again, she confronts Frank with the truth: "You know that poem you wrote? You didn't write it. You see, I read this poem in the magazine and figured, this is either a very sensitive guy or else, maybe, he ripped off some lady's poem, or some girl's poem. You didn't write it, right?"

"Nope," Frank finally admits, starting on the right foot in his second chance with his feminine Other. Inadvertently giving expression to the one Frank suspects of the killings, she says, "Some lady did it, right?"

"My mother wrote it some fifty-odd years ago," he informs her. "That's why my father fell in love with her."

It's also why, as she tells Frank, she has fallen in "like" with him. "I like that. I like that you did that."

In using his mother's poem, Frank gives expression to the feminine voice, to his feminine Other, which this unnamed woman clearly represents. When he speaks admiringly of her behavior in their first meeting as "poetry in motion," she once again reminds him "when we met" when asking, "You still want to go have that 'happy hunting toast?'"

"What happened to the animal attraction?" Frank asks in return.

That this as-yet-unnamed woman replaces his ex-wife, as in "animal" for "pet," is suggested when, shown talking to Sherman from a public phone about her proposed "happy hunting toast," Frank uses Gruber's very word when reminding him that "this one *walked*." Sherman, on the other hand, reminds him, "She's a friggin' suspect, Frank. Just walk away." At first Frank agrees, saying to Sherman, "I'm walking," and saying to the woman, "Something came up." But he quickly changes his mind when, asking her, "What's your name again?"

"Helen," she replies.

With Frank repeating her name and changing his mind, the camera cuts to the two sharing a drink at his favorite watering hole. As Nancy Qualls-Corbett points out in her book *The Sacred Prostitute*, Helen, the sole name she's known by (in the movie and the credits) is not without significance.

> As man's consciousness widens, his attitude toward both his feminine side and women in general is altered. Jung describes four stages of anima development, analogous to historical images of the feminine personified by Eve, Helen of Troy, the Virgin Mary and Sophia.... As Helen, whose beauty and charm have been idealized as a prototype of erotic love through the ages, ... she is an individual in her own right, experienced as the feminine Other.[2]

The notion that Helen of Troy applies to Helen, that she's Frank's "feminine Other," is suggested by her coming from York, which Frank points out twice, when the two first meet and at the end of the movie. York, after all is practically Troy spelled backwards. Or as Frank puts it, "You know, it's interesting your coming from York, Pennsylvania, because, in a way, you went from York to New York."

Suggesting each one replaces the other's former spouse, both Helen and Frank talk about their failed marriages. When she says, "I found out I was pregnant, I walked," as did Frank's wife, he unknowingly (unconsciously) asks her about his Other. "You walked? What do you mean? The guy doesn't know about the kid?"

Helen, speaking as an ex-wife, assures him unknowingly, "He's out of the picture." Then, speaking as the intuitive feminine Other, she gives expression to his predicament when saying what she learned from her relationship. "There are very few mistakes in life that can't be corrected if you got the guts."

That Helen brings out the *anima* in Frank is suggested by what he shares with her at closing time. "You know, when it gets late sometimes I feel like a big cat in a small cage."

With the camera cutting to Frank's "small cage," the projector and his *anima* are envisioned by the close-up of their facing each other from either side of the screen. Both excited and afraid, Frank doesn't know if he's the hunter or the hunted. Particularly when, after some passionate kissing, he sees what he imagines is a gun in Helen's pocketbook, which she takes with her to the bathroom, from where she tells him to "Get in bed." Panicking, Frank reverts to his role as detective when he pushes Helen against the wall as soon as she comes out of the bathroom, frisking her and shoving her into a closet, an even smaller cage. Only when he compares her "gun" to his, which receives a close-up, does he realize it "ain't real." His mistaking her "starter's pistol" is surely not helped by his feeling victimized by his ex-wife. When things get intimate, he feels threatened.

Frank only succeeds in persuading Helen he "got scared" when, pinning her to the bed, he tells her, "Feel my heart." Getting up, she alludes to his unconscious Other, her ex-husband, when saying, "I'll tell you some stories about 'scared' sometime. You don't know." Significantly, Frank gets Helen to warm up to him when describing himself as "an animal."

Taking charge, Helen pins Frank against the wall, removing her bathrobe as she frisks him erotically, even climbing on him from behind like an animal, asking repeatedly, "What are you looking for?" Frank, of course, is looking for the gun, though it looks as if he's looking for the dick. Helen has neither, but when she climbs on top of him in bed for a second round of passionate lovemaking, Frank, mixing sex with murder, responds, "You're killing me," meant as double entendre to the woman he suspects of being the killer. But in the movie's subtext it also means she's killing the part of himself he unconsciously projects on her. At one point, he says, "We don't live for work, do we?" Speaking as "Wonder Woman," as she calls herself, the "icomic" figure "created as a distinctly feminist role model whose mission was to bring the Amazon ideals of love, peace and sexual equality to 'a world torn by the hatred of men,'"[3] Helen counters, "I like to think I live for love. I mean, what else is there?" With Frank having reached the age at which he can retire, and believing "There's nothing out there after this," her words must surely strike home.

Though never shown, and unbeknownst to Frank, shortly after Helen departs he's almost attacked by her ex-husband who comes to his door, which he tries to open when Frank, who's showering, doesn't hear the buzzer (which recalls the buzzer in the first victim's apartment). That on the other side of the door is his unseen (unconscious) Other is suggested by both the shower curtain's two musician-alligators, which are cinematically singled out as if playing rhythm to "Sea of Love," and by the picture of another pair hanging in the hall that Frank passes by on his way to the door, which recalls Picasso's famous sketch of Don Quixote and his sidekick, Sancho Panza. By the time Frank opens the door, however, the person on the other side is already in the elevator, going down as if returning to the unconscious "basement" where he said he was "working" the day of the first killing.

The pair motif is taken up next morning, when Frank visits Helen at the shoe store she manages, a place where things come in pairs. Back to being an undercover cop, even after his decision not to bring in her coffee cup for fingerprints, Frank starts asking her "about some of the people you've been seeing over the past month or so."

Helen replies frankly, "It's none of your business."

Before things get too sticky, however, a pair of young men, in gray suits like Helen and Frank, enter the store. Recalling the two felons who mistook Frank for "Scooter," the lighter of the two asks about a pair of boots he saw some six months ago. Frank, seeming to see his young Other in the arrogant young man, and not liking what he sees, stares at him, transfixed. The young man, noticing his glare, comes up to Frank, "Hey look, pal, can I help you with something, or *what*?" When Frank gets up to face him, he asks, "What's your problem?" Coming from his young Other, his two questions ask much more than Frank is able to answer. The young man only backs off when the darker one of the two half whispers to him, "The guy's a cop."

Frank unwittingly answers his young Other's questions by his overreaction to the other's revealing he's a cop. Where to Helen what really matters is that he lied to her, to Frank, ever the victim, it's his being a cop. Just as he blames his ex-wife for walking out on him, he tries to project his culpability on Helen by claiming that his "being a cop is just too much" for her. Only Helen doesn't buy it. Chasing after him when he storms out of the store, she sets him straight, "Don't try to turn this around on me. You lied to me." As she tells him when he tries to explain his lying, "So, you're a cop, huh?" she has no problem with that. Even so, he unwittingly evades her when saying, "I'm Frank. Ok? Just Frank." He means his name, but still suspecting her, he's far from being frank.

"Don't lie to me again, Frank," she warns. "I don't like it."

As the shoe-store segment shows, Frank's "problem" with his Other gets in the way of his relationship with his feminine Other. Perhaps that's why he attempts to reconnect with her by replaying their chance meeting (to double his pleasure?) when he calls Helen and entices her to come to another market, where they play out an erotic fantasy. Only this time they end up in *her* apartment, where all goes well until, unable to shake off his cop's suspicion and his fear of his feminine Other, Frank looks for "Sea of Love" among her collection of 45's. Finding it, despite Helen's telling him she's saving the records for her daughter, he's back to treating her as the killer when lifting her Social Security card. The song associated with the killer is another indication how the unconscious Other gets in the way.

Still another indication that the Other is on his mind comes when Helen shows him her sleeping daughter, and once again speaks as Wonder Woman when remarking, "I wonder what kind of father you would make."

Frank evades her question by asking a question, "She's got a father, doesn't she?" On his way out he repeats his question, unknowingly projecting it on his Other from whom they're both divorced. "He's not dead. You're divorced, right?"

Unseen but very much alive, as is the unconscious, Frank's shadowy Other, like the return of the repressed, comes to his door for another try at revenge. And once again Frank is saved, this time by stopping at his local bar for "double Dewars." By the time he gets home, his Other is gone, though not without leaving a sign of his darkness by putting out the light in the hallway, as if sending a message of what he'd like to do to the man sleeping with his ex-wife. Whereas on his first visit Frank was baffled, now he's clearly scared.

Though not physically present, the Other once again gets in the way at the restaurant to which Frank takes Helen by the violinist playing "Strangers in the Night," a song made famous by another Frank (Sinatra). As he told Sherman and the black detective at the restaurant where they continue their scheme to get more fingerprints, Frank intends to "ask her to move in with me." Despite being under the influence, as Helen points out, he's unable to say what he intends. When Helen asks, "So, what's this important thing you wanted to ask me?" he keeps harping about the poor service, which, bearing in mind he was last seen in the role of waiter, is probably another one of his projections. When Helen asks again, "What's the big question you wanted to ask?" he calls for the waiter and complains about the music, choosing to "walk." Considering how the word "walk" functions in Frank's psyche, his inability to commit himself to his feminine Other is envisioned by the red "Don't Walk" light changing to the white "Walk," which are singled out when Frank and Helen are next shown at a street crossing. This dilemma, this split, is the split between the projector and his Other. What Frank cannot say intentionally, he says unintentionally, letting his unconscious get the better of him, as when he says, "If you live with a cop."

Helen picks up on the phrase, repeating it.

"*What?*" Frank says, unaware of what he had just said.

"You said, 'If you live with a cop.' You mean, if *I* live with a cop. *Me*, right? Have you thought about it at all?"

Rather than using this opening to ask Helen what he intended to ask her in the first place, Frank is back to projecting. "I want to ask you something," he begins, but instead proceeds to ask about her dating: "How can you do that shit? I mean, you know, go out with guys like that. How can you do that?"

"What do you mean?" she says defensively. "*You* do it." She inadvertently recalls the words he sang from "Sea of Love" to test the wired mike when sitting down in the restaurant for his dates, "Did you forget how we met, Frank?" Frank himself refers to how they met in his response, all the while revealing more than he intends, his unconscious once again getting the better of him: "I was on a job. I mean, that was a job. I was wearing a wire.... I'd never do that for real. I'd never do that."

Stunned at what he has revealed, Helen asks, "That part about the wire. You want to run that by me again?" Not wanting to hear any more, she *walks*, parting with "Fuck you!"

As earlier in the story when Frank had called his ex-wife late at night, now, after drinking two "double Dewars" in his local bar, he's shown at Helen's apartment door. Helen's mother, who opens the door, informs Frank, "It's one o'clock in the morning." She lets him in despite the lateness of the hour.

In Helen's kitchen, Frank not only comes out with what he had in mind to ask her, he also understands and takes responsibility for his words: "I was just saying that to push you away from me because I was going to ask you to live with me. And I got scared, you know?" Though reverting back to the same excuse he used in their first night together, it's nonetheless a step forward in that, this time, it's about his admitting he's scared of his feminine Other. But Frank's fear is doubled when he spots the names of two victims circled in the newspaper ads attached to the refrigerator door, reverting back to his suspicion and his fear of being her next victim, as his circled name on the first page suggests. Seeing the names of the two victims under his own name almost takes him back to where he started. He even uses the same words he used at the start of the movie, "Catch you later," when Helen, perhaps sensing his change of heart, changes her mind, choosing not to wake up her mother to tell her she's going to his apartment.

Home to Roost

Frank's finding Sherman in his apartment, and with Gina, the woman with the balloons who came to the apartment of the first victim (whose name he just saw circled on Helen's refrigerator), foreshadows his repressed Other coming home to roost. In this situation, with Sherman and Gina taking his place in bed with Helen, Frank takes his Other's place by barging in on his partner in his own apartment. Sherman's "You scared the shit out of me" even recalls Frank's "I got scared."

No sooner does Frank see his partner to the elevator than he hears footsteps down the hallway. Looking back, he sees Helen emerging from the darkness in her red leather jacket, striding threatingly towards him. "'Catch you later?' Huh?" she once again echoes his words. "What's that supposed to mean? Is that some kind of brush-off, Frank?" Frank's words, of course, particularly as first used by him with the black father and son, have double meanings.

Once inside his apartment, Helen is all over Frank. "I got something for you," she says seductively. Frank, back to suspecting her of being the killer, is sure of it when she plays for him her record of "Sea of Love." But as her "you were looking at this like it rang some bells" suggests, Helen seems to play the song, which starts with an invitation to the sea of love, to get Frank in touch with the memories it brings from his own sea of love. This seems to be the "something special" she has for him. Only Frank never finds out. For him it can mean only one thing, a gun. Still the victim, Frank even presses Helen to "get it over with," while Helen, continuing her role as his feminine Other, intuitively suggests that he and the killer are one and the same when asking, "You've been following me around?" While Frank, insisting she's the killer, offers her his gun, Helen repeats her question, "How long have you been following me?"

Considering Frank's problem with his ex-wife, he may be unconsciously alluding to her having walked out on him when asking Helen, "Why'd you do it, Helen? Tell me why you did it. Tell me why you did it. Tell me why you did it. I want to know everything, all right? Come on. Talk to me." But now, neither the killer nor his ex-wife, Helen cannot comply with what he so desperately wants to hear. Finally, in telling her to "get out" he does to her what he unconsciously did to his ex-wife. But however he may force Helen "to get" out of his life, he cannot stop his real problem, the one who gets in the way in his relationship with his feminine Other, from forcing himself upon him like the return of the repressed.

No sooner is Helen gone than the door buzzer sounds. Thinking it's Helen, Frank opens the door and looks into the dark hallway. Suddenly, as if erupting from the unconscious darkness, his Other lunges at him with great force. "I know you," Frank says, recognizing Terry from their two encounters, though not as his Other.

In the violent struggle that ensues in his apartment, Terry, holding a gun and ordering Frank to "get down on the bed," mounts him from behind, demanding to know if he had "a good time with her last night." Not knowing who he means, just as he's unconscious of his Other, Frank can only deny, "I don't know who you're talking about." Only when Terry calls Helen his wife ("I'm talking about my wife. My wife, Helen."), as Frank called his "wife" over the phone to Gruber, does he realize that *he's* the killer. In his "You remember her, don't you?" Terry even recalls the words from "Sea of Love." Forced by his Other to reenact "what you did to her," Frank reenacts, or abreacts, what he did to his "ex-wife, Denise."

In the midst of acting out this unconscious drama of doer and victim, the tables are turned when Frank, reaching for the bowling trophy he had hidden from Helen underneath the bed, swings it at Terry's head to knock him off. But even though Frank gets the upper hand with the gun, it hardly stops the enraged Terry. As if asking Frank if he's going to repress him again when he goes to the phone, Terry asks, "What are you going to do? Lock me up and throw away the key?" Howling "It's not your wife. It's not your family," Terry leaps at the stunned Frank, who manages to get off a shot. But the wounded Terry, like the return of the repressed, is no less relentless. In the second violent struggle that erupts between the two, Frank inadvertently hurls him out the window, forever silencing the voice that keeps repeating, not unlike the repeated playing of "Sea of Love," "It's not your wife!"

The Complete Person

Appropriately enough, the change in Frank is revealed in the movie's epilogue's *two* scenes, one with Sherman, the other with Helen. Though in both encounters Frank doesn't necessarily refer to his Other as such, he clearly has integrated the part of himself from which he was divorced and unconscious.

Meeting Sherman at his local bar, Frank explains his questioning about drinking only "club soda and lime" (which replaces his "double Dewar"), "It's the new me." Sharing with Sherman what he learned about the killer, he all but calls him the Other: "The husband, Terry? Turns out he'd been shadowing her for eight months.... She always had that edge, you know. Like she smelled him, like she sensed him, or something. I must've sensed him, too.... She had that nutcase over one shoulder, me over the other." Sherman doesn't have to say a word about Frank's still wanting Helen when he declares he's "going to let it go," as, by now, he must have done with his ex-wife. He only has to sit back and give his big smile that says otherwise.

Frank doubles what he tells Sherman in the bar when, in the second and final scene, he follows Helen in the street as she locks up the shoe store, talking about "the complete person," the one no longer divorced from his unconscious Other, his other half. "You never really got to know me," he says. "Not a hundred percent. The person you got involved with, that was half of me. You owe it to yourself. Check out the complete person." Helen, who has had "enough" of his talking, nonetheless changes her mind, as she did after their first meeting, when Frank reveals he's "been on the wagon for seven weeks now."

Perhaps recalling better days, she asks him, "You still drink coffee?" "Like it's going out of style," Frank admits. With that, she invites him for a cup. It's not much, but with *her* ex-husband and *his* unconscious Other no longer around, their walking away side by side portends a new beginning, particularly with the new version of "Sea of Love," by Tom Waits, playing on the soundtrack.

10

Fight Club:
The Imagined Other

I'm free in all the ways that you are not.
—*Tyler Durden to the narrator*

False Starts and Subliminal Flickers

As movies of the Other go, David Fincher's *Fight Club* is an anomaly. It neither adheres to the *Gilgamesh* prototype nor to the *Jekyll and Hyde* exception. Rather, the 1999 movie, adapted from Chuck Palahniuk's novel, is both like and unlike the two, which is part of what makes it so fascinating and so challenging.

Fight Club is like *Jekyll and Hyde* in that the binary friends, the narrator (Edward Norton) and Tyler Durden (Brad Pitt), are expressly two sides of the same person. Making this point, when the narrator half admits to Marla Singer (Helena Bonham Carter), "I know that it got to seem like there's two sides to me," she shoots back, "Two sides? You're Dr. Jekyll and Mr. Jackass." Only unlike *Jekyll and Hyde*, in which we know from the beginning that the Dr. and Mr. are two sides of the same person, in *Fight Club* we (and the narrator) learn it only toward the end of the movie. In effect, the narrator already knows the story he's telling us. His getting to know his imaginary (projected) Other, we find out, is his story.

Fight Club also breaks from *Jekyll and Hyde* in how it ends with the Other's death. While Jekyll is killed simultaneously with Hyde when he's shot by the police inspector, in *Fight Club* only Tyler dies when the narrator shoots himself. This ending, despite the narrator's shooting himself, is closer to the *Gilgamesh* prototype in which the projector remains alive after killing his Other.

Even so, with Tyler not existing by his own right, *Fight Club* follows the exception of *Jekyll and Hyde*. He's a projection of the narrator's split personality that only *seems* real to his projector. Only *he* sees him. What others in the movie see is him *being* Tyler. We think they see Tyler as an autonomous person because we are the narrator's audience. We see through his eyes, what he narrates, what he projects. It's no accident that Tyler is a part-time projectionist, nor that the two, the projector and his Other, start drifting apart when Tyler initiates Project Mayhem. The real mayhem, after all, is in the narrator's psyche, a mayhem he unconsciously projects on Tyler Durden. Perhaps nothing better illustrates this psychic mayhem and its projection than the narrator accusing Tyler, "You're insane," and Tyler shooting back, "No! *You're* insane!"

This psychic mayhem is behind the narrator's (and our) seeing the imagined (*subjective*) Tyler as if he's a real (*objective*) person. Just as we think our unconscious projections on others are real, we think that what we see is what's really happening. We imagine the movie's subjective camera is objective. This ploy, this envisioning the subjective "objectively" almost until the end of the movie, makes *Fight Club* an illustration of how to perceive the projected Other in movies that adhere to the *Gilgamesh* prototype, movies in which the protagonist projects his unconscious Other on an autonomous (objective) person.

The discovery that Tyler has been the narrator's projected Other all along makes us more likely to examine how it's conveyed up to this revelation than in a story à la *Gilgamesh*, in which the Other is projected on a convenient person who "merely" signifies and mirrors the Other. This revelation is where the intrigue and the fun begin. As George M. Wilson and Sam Shpall point out in their revealing essay on the movie's confusing point of view, "Unraveling the Twists in *Fight Club*," just as the narrator, whom they call Jack, imagines Tyler:

> What we have to imagine, when we consider the film in retrospect, is that Jack does utter most of the things we hear him say and performs most of the actions that we observe. We are also meant to imagine that, on these occasions, Jack is simultaneously hallucinating Tyler's presence, his deeds, and speeches, and that Jack is responding to these fantasized occurrences.[1]

Much as Tyler challenges the narrator to see an*other* way, Fincher goads us into seeing how the movie suggests that Tyler and the narrator are actually one person, which we can only discover by repeated viewings. In a game of sorts, the trickster-like Fincher, whose previous project was *The Game* (1997), seems to say we could have figured it out long before Tyler's revelation. He certainly gives enough tip-offs in the course of the story. The most obvious one, certainly, is the narrator's voice-over that accompanies the seemingly objective point of view. In effect, both the movie and the narrator suggest right from the start that it's all subjective, that what we see is a projection of the narrator's troubled psyche. The opening, the title sequence, clearly takes place in the narrator's head, and his first words, "People are always asking me, did I know Tyler Durden?" suggest an intimate relationship between the two. Answering this question, the narrator ends his opening narration by alluding to their being one and the same: "I know this because Tyler knows this."

Warning us right from the start that things are not what they seem, Fincher hints that he's playing a game by the "false start" in *Fight Club*'s title sequence, when a tune is briefly heard from a scratchy record before the phonograph stylus is heard screeching over the record and the "real" music comes on, The Dust Brothers' "Stealing Fat." In case we missed it, Fincher repeats this false start with the coming out of the Tenth Anniversary Blu-ray Disc in 2009, inserting a fake menu of Drew Barrymore's *Never Been Kissed*, which most of us probably assume (at least at first) is a technical error. Only after some glitches appear and the sound screeches to a halt does the real *Fight Club*'s menu appear. Perhaps Fincher added a second false start to match the narrator's own pair of false starts: his beginning to narrate his story just before the actual end, with Tyler's gun inside his mouth, and his starting over while his face is buried in Bob's "bitch tits," explaining how he got there in the first place.

Another form of game playing, and another tip-off that Tyler is the narrator's unconscious projection, is Fincher's "splicing" frames of Tyler into the film, projecting on the movie screen what the narrator projects on his mind screen. Altogether, as many critics and fans of the film have noted, there are four single-framed flickers of Tyler, what Fincher calls "subliminal Tylerisms." They're all seen from the narrator's point of view and with Tyler looking directly at him. All take place at critical stations in his life, foreshadowing Tyler's "actual" appearance.

1. The first flicker comes immediately after the narrator's false start, when he backs up and starts narrating his story from the beginning. "For six months, I couldn't sleep," he informs us while lying awake in his bed. His voice-over continues while he's shown using a copying machine in his office. "With insomnia, nothing's real. Everything's far away." Then, in the middle of his line, "Everything is a copy of a copy of a copy," Tyler flickers on the screen, standing on the opposite side of the copying machine, suggesting that he first flickers in the narrator's psyche as a simulated Other, another side of himself, but a copy nonetheless.

2. The second flicker comes at the hospital, where the narrator is imploring a doctor to give him "something" for his insomnia. Advising him, "You need to lighten up" and "You need healthy, natural sleep," as the narrator follows the doctor to the hallway, saying, "Hey, come on. I'm in pain," the doctor replies, "You wanna see pain? Swing by First Methodist, Tuesday nights. See the guys with testicular cancer." Just as he emphasizes, "*That's* pain," Tyler flickers behind him, looking at the narrator together with the doctor, as if saying that it's what he prescribes too, that only in feeling pain can he feel he's alive.
3. Tyler next flickers at the testicular cancer support group that the doctor recommended, which opens with a divorced man breaking down while sharing his woes with the group. The group leader, stationed behind the man, not only reminds the men, "We give each other strength," which is what Tyler gives the narrator, his calling the next exercise, "It's time for the one-on-ones," presages the narrator's one-on-one with Tyler. Just as the leader recommends, "Let's all of us follow Thomas's example and really open ourselves up," Tyler flickers behind him. He has a supportive arm on the shoulder of the leader, who himself puts his supportive arm on the sunken shoulders of the man (Thomas) who broke down. In this flickering image of the three, one behind the other like a copy of a copy of a copy, Tyler seems to remind the narrator that he should "follow Thomas's example and really open" himself up.
4. The fourth and final flicker comes soon after Marla first walks into the testicular cancer support group just when the narrator is embraced by Bob (Meatloaf), pressed "against his tits, ready to cry." Smoking a cigarette, she asks, "This is cancer, right?" At the end of this meeting, as the narrator's gaze follows Marla walking away down the street at night, Tyler flickers on the screen. He appears midway between Marla in the background and the narrator in the foreground, just as he later comes between the two in more ways than one.

Taken together, the four flickers seem to envision Tyler's *raison d'etre*. He first flickers by the copying machine just as the narrator explains that "With insomnia, nothing's real," connecting the copy that he is with the narrator's insomnia. In flickering again behind the doctor while he emphasizes the nature of real pain, Tyler appears to show him what real pain is. His flickering behind the group leader of the support group, just as he urges the group to let's "really open ourselves up," foreshadows his pushing the narrator to "let go." His last flicker, coming after Marla "ruined everything," suggests that the narrator imagines Tyler to restore what Marla had ruined, particularly as Tyler's first act is to ruin everything for the narrator, forcing him to start anew.

Like Fincher himself, Tyler, the part-time projectionist, splices celluloid frames of his own. This we learn after he twice asks the narrator to "hit me as hard as you can," and, in a delay tactic, he jumps to "let me tell you a little bit about Tyler Durden," portraying him as a creature of the unconscious when describing him as "a night person. While the rest of us were sleeping, he worked. He had one part-time job as a projectionist." Significantly, in this episode the narrator and Tyler speak with one voice, completing each other's lines as projector and his Other. "Why would anyone want this shit job?" Tyler asks, and the narrator replies, "Because it affords him interesting opportunities," to which Tyler replies, "Like splicing a frame of pornography into family films."

While the cinematic splicings suggests that the flickers of Tyler are the narrator's projections, his explaining how the audience reacts to this splicing ("Nobody knows what they saw, but they did.") is how most of us first see *Fight Club*. We don't know what we saw, but we did. And once Tyler reveals to the narrator that *he's* his projection, we want to know what we "saw," what was projected on the screen.

All About Marla

Time-wise, the earliest we see the narrator is when he's lying in bed, informing us, "For six months, I couldn't sleep." It comes right after he interrupts his second false start with "No, wait. Back up. Let me start earlier," just as Bob, the feminized man who mirrors his masculinity, says to him at the testicular cancer support group, "Okay, you cry now." This pair of scenes (of the narrator against Bob's "bitch tits" followed by his lying in bed) is doubled by the pair that shows him in his very first support group meeting, when Bob chooses him for "one-on-one" and encourages him to cry, followed by the camera cutting to his lying in his bed in a similar shot. Only this second time, after giving expression to his pain, after letting go and opening himself up, he's sound asleep, his voice-over a lullaby. "*Babies* don't sleep this well."

But all is not well. The support groups to which he became addicted become his prescription for keeping pain at bay, his substitute for *real* human contact. As he puts it after coming out of the support group in which he first encounters, in guided meditation, his power animal, "Every evening I died. And every evening I was born again. Resurrected." With this we're back to the first *shown* support group of the narrator and Bob with which he had started his narration. "Bob loved me because he thought my testicles were removed, too. Being there, pressed against his tits, ready to cry. This was my vacation."

The narrator's "vacation" ends when he hears high-heeled footsteps echo in the stairway and in walks Marla. "And she ruined everything," the stunned narrator begrudgingly informs us. "This chick, Marla Singer, did not have testicular cancer. She was a liar. She had no disease at all." As if petrified by this dark snake-haired Medusa whose "lie reflected my lie," the narrator freezes up. "And suddenly, I felt nothing. I couldn't cry. So once again, I couldn't sleep."

With Marla ruining everything, the narrator, shown in bed once again, imagines himself confronting her in the next support group, telling her to "get out." But in the actual "next group," when the female leader takes the group on another guided meditation inside their cave to encounter the power animal, the narrator merely muses, "If I did have a tumor, I'd name it Marla. Marla, the little scratch on the roof of your mouth that would heal if only you could stop tonguing it. But you can't." Sure enough, instead of encountering the black-and-white penguin of his first entrance into his imagined cave, now (accompanied by the leader's "You feel a healing energy all around you. Now find your power animal.") he's surprised to see the black-dressed, cigar-smoking Marla, who repeats what the penguin had entreated him to do the first time: "Slide." Only unlike the sliding penguin, who demonstrated how it's done, now Marla motions for him to slide, perhaps down to the "bottom" that Tyler says Marla at least tries to hit.

Marla, of course, is Tyler's opposite. As suggested by her replacing the penguin, she's the narrator's *anima*. Where Tyler is his projected Other, Marla is a real person on whom he projects his feminine Other. What she is to the narrator is demonstrated by his picking her when the group leader, moving to the next exercise, instructs him to "pick someone special to you tonight." Coming from behind her as she's making coffee, he grabs her arm and says, "Hey, we need to talk." When he informs her, "I'm on to you," she lets him know she's on to *him*: "I saw you practicing this ... telling me off." When he threatens her with "I'll expose you," she mirrors back his projection, "Go ahead. I'll expose *you*."

As his power *anima*, his feminine Other, Marla completes the other half of his attempt to explain why he comes to these groups. "When people think you're dying, then they really really listen to you instead of just —" she reponds "— instead of waiting for their turn to speak." But despite the group leader's encouraging words, "Share yourself, completely," the narrator is far from ready. He cannot share with Marla what he shares with Bob. Marla is different. As Charles Guignon perceptively notes, all but calling Marla the feminine Other,

> Despite Marla's bizarre and seemingly co-dependent behavior, she manifests a cohesiveness and steadiness of character that goes way beyond what

any man in the film displays. Where men see their problem as needing to "complete themselves," even if that involves creating an alter to provide what is missing in the self, Marla can be seen as having already achieved a sort of completeness.... Ironic as it may be, this confused and chaotic character seems to be the most positive image we get of a stable identity in this serio-comic film.[2]

That Marla is the narrator's feminine Other, his other half, is subtly suggested by her stealing two jeans from each of the two dryers, and with the narrator remarking, "You left half your clothes." It's said more clearly by the narrator's proposed solution, "We'll split up the week," which mirrors the split in his psyche that engenders Tyler. Significantly, Marla's last words question the narrator's identity: "Who are you? *Cornelius*? *Rupert*? *Travis*? Any of these stupid names you give each night?" Just as her appearance triggered his feminine Other, now her words seem to trigger his masculine Other, Tyler Durden, the name by which she comes to know him. Following this parting, this split, which ends the movie's "feminine" segment, the unnamed narrator is not shown attending another support group.

The "split" with Marla, however, is by no means the last time the narrator encounters her. *Fight Club*, after all, is ultimately about his relationship with her, with his feminine Other. As he himself informs us at the beginning, just before he starts telling how he ended up with Tyler's gun barrel in his mouth, "Somehow, I realize all of this — the gun, the bombs, the revolution — is really about Marla Singer." Likewise, it's no accident that after his apartment is blown up the narrator first calls Marla, only to hang up, before calling Tyler. She's foremost in his mind. But to resolve his ambiguous relationship with her he needs help from Tyler Durden, his projected Other, who trains him to become more like him so that he can "let go" and share himself with his feminine Other. As Chuck Palahniuk himself had pointed out about this cinematic adaptation of his novel, "The whole story is about a man reaching the point where he can commit to a woman."[3]

Imaginary Friend

However the number of tip-offs that Marla is the narrator's feminine Other, there are many more hints that Tyler is his projected Other. Appropriately enough, where he meets his feminine Other in the more personal and emotional support groups, his masculine Other he meets during his description of his seemingly endless disorienting flights that are part of his debilitating job as recall coordinator for a major car company. But before that, unseen by the narrator, Tyler appears twice, and not only as a mere flicker. Once at an airport, when he passes by the narrator while going the *other* way on a moving walkway; once, when he appears in a TV commercial in one of the narrator's hotel rooms, opening his arms with "Welcome," together with the other waiters. Dressed in black-and-white tuxedo, like the "tuxedoed" penguin, Tyler's "Welcome" replaces both the penguin's and Marla's "Slide." In this last appearance, the narrator (apparently) sees Tyler but, like his splices, does not know it.

Underscoring that Tyler's appearance is initiated by Marla, by the feminine Other, before he "actually" appears, the narrator is shown on a plane, chatting with a black woman in the seat next to his, telling her about his job as recall coordinator. "If X is less than the cost of recall," he speaks of the *other* side of the equation (the X in $A \times B \times C = X$), "we don't do one."

Incredulous, the woman asks, "Are there a lot of these kinds of accidents?"

"You wouldn't believe," he replies, as his voice-over comes on. "Every time the plane banked too sharply on takeoff or landing, I prayed for a crash or a midair collision." Looking outside the window, he imagines his own accident as another plane is shown crashing into their plane.

For a moment, much like the imagined Tyler, the crash seems real until the narrator is shown in his seat, stunned by what he had imagined. Then, cutting to a shot that shows his profile from his right side, the camera moves to reveal Tyler, sitting next to him in the seat formerly occupied by the black woman, thus envisioning the projected Other replacing the black and black-dressed feminine Other. In their first exchange, while Tyler seems to allude to his being the narrator's illusion when speaking of "the illusion of safety," the narrator intimates they're twins when commenting on their having "the exact same briefcase," which Tyler accepts with a knowing smile. He hints who he is when offering the narrator, "You wanna switch seats?"

Tyler's first act as the narrator's projected Other is to "evict" him from his familiar but unsatisfying life by blowing up his condominium, freeing the slave he had become "to the Ikea nesting instincts." As the doorman, who functions as a threshold guardian, informs the narrator when he arrives at his apartment building and sees the burned contents of his condo in the street, "There's nothing up there. You can't go into the unit." With his option to go back now gone, he suggests the way forward. "Do you have somebody you can call?"

By magic or fate, the narrator finds Marla's phone number on a burned piece of paper among the remains of his apartment. He calls her from a nearby pay phone but, not ready for his feminine Other, hangs up when she answers. Then, finding Tyler's calling card in his coat pocket, which he gave him on the plane, he dials his number as if prompted by something more unconscious than conscious. Even though the picture on the calling card, of two winged figures facing each other from opposite sides, tells it all, the narrator is clueless: "If you asked me now, I couldn't tell you why I called him."

Besides reminding the narrator, "You called me because you needed a place to stay," Tyler explains why he called when later revealing how he came into his life: "You were looking for a way to change your life. You could not do it on your own." Not only that, in his first audible words after the call, when the two meet at Lou's Tavern, Tyler seems to suggest why the narrator called but did not speak to Marla. "You know, man, it could be worse," he refers to the exploded condo. "A woman could cut off your penis while you sleep and toss it out of the window of a moving car." Coming after the narrator's last encounter with Marla, when she grabbed his groin while emphasizing her "Yes!" to his questioning her selling the stolen jeans, his Other's words give expression to his fear of his feminine Other.

Later that evening, outside the tavern, as the narrator and Tyler stop and face each other within the symmetric entrance with the twin doors that envision their being two sides of the same being, Tyler points out the narrator's problem in asking to stay at his place: "Cut the foreplay and just ask." With the narrator finally asking, the two are shown in another symmetric shot, as Tyler asks the narrator to hit him as hard as he can. Once again, like his not asking to stay with Tyler, he has to be repeatedly coaxed into hitting Tyler. But when he finally does hit him, and Tyler hits him back, the narrator takes a step by himself when calling him to "hit me again." As with the support groups, one hit and he's hooked. Following the fight that develops between the two, which solidifies both their camaraderie and their rivalry, the narrator even proposes, while sharing a beer, "We should do this again sometime."

When the two are shown fighting a second time, again outside Lou's Tavern, their being opposite sides is mirrored by the two men, one black, one white, who observe them when coming out of the tavern. Shown a third time, with Tyler fighting a man other than the narrator, and with a bigger audience, when another man asks, "Can I be next?" the narrator and Tyler, looking at each other, realize they're on to something. "After fighting everything else in your life got the volume turned down," his voice-over comes on. "You could deal with anything."

For men only, the Fight Club is one support group that Marla cannot ruin for the narrator. "Most of the week we were Ozzie and Harriet. But every Saturday night, we were finding something out. We were finding out more and more that we were not alone.... It was right in everyone's face. Tyler and I just made it visible.... Tyler and I just gave it a name." Through the Fight Club, through physical fighting, the narrator gets to know an *other* side of himself. Or as Tyler puts it, "How much do you know about yourself if you've never been in a fight?"

Tyler's Training

After the first shown episode of the Fight Club, which becomes the focus and essence of their binary relationship, the narrator and Tyler are shown walking in the street, both smoking. The smoking, a first for the narrator, seems to be his attempt to be more like Tyler, and perhaps also like the chain-smoking Marla. But the difference between the two is highlighted in the second Fight Club episode, in which the two are each shown fighting another opponent, and a black one at that. Tyler wins his fight, by repeatedly hitting his opponent in the *groin*; the narrator loses his, by having his *head* repeatedly hit against the floor.

Before the narrator gets too deep into Fight Club, he receives a call from Marla. "Where have you been the last eight weeks?" she asks "I haven't seen you in any support groups."

"I found a new one," he informs her, dampening her excitement at the prospect of a new group, "It's for men only."

Calling with "a stomach full of Xanax," she admits, "this isn't a for-real suicide thing. This is probably a cry-for-help thing." At this stage of his training, the narrator may not want anything to do with Marla, but his Other does. No sooner does he walk away, leaving the phone off the hook while Marla keeps talking, than she and Tyler are shown in their first wild and uninhibited time in bed.

With the camera cutting to the narrator abruptly waking from what seems like a dream, there's a sense that what we saw between Tyler and Marla is his dreaming, particularly by how it's conveyed. But dream or not, when he gets up he notices that something *has* changed. "Tyler's door was closed," he notes. "I'd been living here for two months and Tyler's door was never closed." Then, on the morning after, thinking he hears Tyler coming down the stairs, he echoes his words to him after his condominium blew up without looking up from his breakfast, "You won't believe this dream I had last night. You're not gonna believe this." He's stunned when it's Marla who answers, "I can hardly believe *anything* about last night."

Just as Marla's lie reflected the narrator's lie in the support groups, her reactions to what she considers his schizoid behavior (as when he asks her, "What are you doing here?") mirrors his being Tyler's other side. Her initial disbelief stems from the fact that, as far as she knows, she has just spent the night with him. Confused by this Jekyll and Hyde transformation, particularly when he asks, "What are you doing in my house?" all Marla can say is "Fuck you!" and walk out. This explains why Tyler, who appears as soon as she's gone, doesn't want the narrator to talk to her about him. It would only confuse her. Unlike the narrator, she sees one person, Tyler Durden, which is why she's never shown together with the two of them. Or, as the narrator puts it rather uncannily, "Except for their humping, Tyler and Marla were never in the same room." This said, we do see the two together with the narrator, when he later peeks into their bedroom while they are having one of their sexual marathons.

In what can be taken as part of his training to ready the narrator for Marla, Tyler asks him as soon as she's gone, "You're not into her, are you?"

"No! God, not at all!" he answers emphatically.

"Are you sure?" Tyler asks, pressing him. "You can tell me."

"Believe me, I'm sure," he replies.

Warning the narrator, "She's a predator posing as a house pet. Stay away from her," Tyler all but calls Marla an anima. This notion is reinforced by the narrator's overreacting to the thought of being "into her." His saying, "Put a gun to my head and paint the walls with my brains" is a classic overreaction to one's projection. At this stage of his training, the narrator doesn't allow himself to do with Marla what he allows his Other.

Marla herself alludes to the narrator's two sides when, in their second morning after in the kitchen, she talks about the bridesmaid's dress she's wearing: "Someone loved it intensely for one day, then tossed it." Unconscious of what he shared with her the night before, as Tyler, the narrator is completely impervious to what he perceives as her taunting when she comes from behind him and puts her hand on his crotch, the cigarette she holds clearly a phallus.

With Marla getting too close to his projector, or perhaps because he's not ready for her, Tyler orders the narrator to "get rid of her." When the narrator protests, "*You* get rid of her," Tyler talks with his back to him, "Don't mention me." But the narrator breaks his promise and Tyler's warning when passing his message to Marla, "I really think it's time you left," inadvertently (unconsciously) alluding to the two of them when adding, "Not that we don't love your little visits." Marla's singing as she leaves, "Gotta Get Off This Merry-Go-Round," is surely meant more for the narrator than to herself.

Trying to reel the narrator back in after her eviction, Marla calls a second time, this time at his office, asking him to come over and feel her breasts for signs of cancer. As underscored by her asking him when he comes, "What happened to your hand?" (which recalls Tyler trying to get him to feel pain with the *lye*'s "chemical burn," saying "Don't shut the pain out."), Marla's asking him to feel her breasts may also be her way to get him to feel her heart. Of course, as his feminine Other, she may also be asking if he *feels* anything at all when asking, "Feel anything?" and "You feel nothing?" Reflected in the movie's only outright use of a mirror, she once again mirrors his lying to himself about his feelings for her, the feelings he can only express through Tyler.

In what can be seen as mirroring Marla's walking into the support group while the narrator was nestled in Bob's bosom, as he comes out of Marla's hotel, Bob, a voice from the past, calls out, "Cornelius!" the name he used in their support group, "Remaining Men Together." At first the narrator doesn't recognize him, but Bob reminds him, "It's me, Bob," hugging him as in the group. "We thought you were dead," he says (of testicular cancer, no doubt). But Bob is no longer in the support group. Like the narrator, he, too, has replaced it with Fight Club and has undergone a transformation, feeling "better than I've ever been in my whole life." As it turns out, the two haven't run into each other at the Fight Club meetings because, much like the split between the narrator and Marla, they go on different nights. "Congratulations," Bob repeats Tyler's commending the narrator for feeling the kiss of pain ("Congratulations. You're one step closer to hitting the bottom"). "Hey, to both of us," the narrator says to Bob, though also meaning him and Tyler, particularly as Bob subsequently asks him if he "heard about the guy who invented" Fight Club: "Do you know about Tyler Durden?"

Replacing the hugging and crying of the support group, the two are subsequently shown fighting in Bob's Fight Club, a fight which the narrator once again loses, as he had lost to Tyler, this time with Bob bear hugging him close to his bosom until he gives up. As a feminized male, a former body builder who's now missing his testicles and sporting huge breasts, Bob is the narrator's mediator between his Other and his feminine Other, much as the narrator is "passing messages between" Tyler and Marla. The narrator not only first sees Marla when he's in Bob's bosom, now he meets him immediately after feeling her breasts for cancer.

The narrator starts seeing Tyler differently after the Fight Club emerges from the unconscious basement, when, as part of Tyler's "dreamed up new homework assignments," he accompanies him to a convenience store, where Tyler threatens the clerk with his life if he does not pursue his dream, all the while showing the narrator something about himself. This threat, he thinks, is going too far, even though he has to admit, "You had to give it to him. He had a plan. And it started to make sense in a Tyler-sort of way. No fear. No distractions. The ability to let that which does not matter truly slide."

Soon after these words, which recall the "slide" of his power animal and Marla, Tyler is shown as the narrator sees him when his vision of him begins to rattle, his projection beginning to lose its power. Trying to maintain his projection, he sees Tyler muttering to himself in self-persuasion, "You are not your job. You're not how much money you have in the bank. You're not the car you drive. You're not the contents of your wallet. You're not your fucking khakis. You are the all-singing, all-dancing crap of the world."

That for the narrator the projected Other and feminine Other are diametric opposites is put forward once again when, following the rattling of his projection, Marla is shown in their house on another morning after. Accustomed to being chased out by the narrator after his Other had spent the night with her, she says "I'll be out of your way in a sec."

He then surprises her by saying, "You don't have to go."

Matching the narrator's beginning to see through his projection of Tyler, Marla begins to see through his need to project Tyler. While they talk, Tyler is heard hammering in the basement, as if signaling the narrator to watch his mouth and to obstruct his getting closer to his feminine Other.

> *Narrator*: I don't understand. I mean, why does a weaker person need to latch on to a strong person? What is that?
>
> *Marla*: What do *you* get out of it?
>
> *Narrator*: No. That's not the same thing at all. It's totally different with us. We're (he brings his two palms together) ...
>
> *Marla*: Us? What do you mean by us?
>
> *Narrator (hearing Tyler's hammering in the basement)*: I'm sorry. Do you hear this?
>
> *Marla*: Hear what?
>
> *Narrator*: You're not hearing all that noise? Hold on a second.
>
> *Marla*: No, wait! What were you saying? Don't change the subject! I want to talk about this.

As the narrator opens the basement door, Tyler cautions him from the bottom of the stairs, "You're not talking about me, are you?"

Though Marla doesn't hear Tyler's hammering or his talking, she's on to something: "That day you came over my place to 'play doctor.' What was going on there?"

With Tyler asking him, "What are you talking about?" the narrator answers each one by saying, "Nothing."

"I don't think so," Marla says confrontationally. "Come on, what do you *want*?" When the narrator looks away, Marla, repeatedly telling him to "Look at me," tries to bring him back from evading what he inadvertently (unconsciously) revealed. Her probing only changes course when she sees his scarred hand, which was bandaged the first time she asked about it in her hotel room. "Who did this?" she asks, not letting him off the hook.

But before things get too sticky, Tyler takes over from down below, putting words into the narrator's mouth, "This conversation is over!"

"I just can't win with you, can I?" Marla says, walking out in frustration. As we soon see, she can't win with him as long as Tyler is around.

No sooner is Marla out the door than the door chime rings. The narrator, going down to the basement, realm of the unconscious, asks Tyler about the bunk beds, "What is all this?"

Seeming to suggest that he should know, Tyler shoots back, "What do you think?"

The narrator gets his answer when he sees Tyler on the porch, greeting the first candidate for Project Mayhem. "What's all that?" he asks Tyler, who answers as if he knows about Project Mayhem. While with Fight Club, which he starts with Tyler, the narrator had replaced his support groups, when it's "moved out of the basement" to be "called Project Mayhem," in which he doesn't really take part, his projection of Tyler begins to fall apart.

That the narrator is getting stronger and growing away from Tyler is demonstrated in the second time he's shown fighting in *his* Fight Club, when he fights the blonde guy Tyler seems to favor, beating him to a pulp.

"Where did you go, psycho boy?" Tyler asks him.

"I felt like destroying something beautiful," the narrator replies, no doubt having Tyler himself in mind, especially after feeling rejected by him when seeing him running his hand through the guy's blonde hair and embracing his head after they assault the police commissioner. In his own words at the time, "I am Jack's inflamed sense of rejection."

About You and Me

With the narrator's first shown win in Fight Club, Tyler takes him on a prearranged "test drive," in a limousine that comes to the entrance of Lou's Tavern, the same place where the two had their first fight. The RECYCLE YOUR ANIMALS sticker on the trunk, which receives a brief close-up as the car pulls away, recalls the narrator's power animal, his feminine Other, which is about to get recycled in his psyche.

Inside the car, invoking the feminine, Tyler turns to the narrator as Ozzie to Harriet, "Something on your mind, dear?"

The narrator, unhappy about Tyler not including him on Project Mayhem, speaks to his "Ozzer," "I wanna know what you're thinking."

But Tyler, as the Other tends to do, sees it differently: "Fuck what you know! You need to forget about what you know. That's your problem. Forget about what you think you know about life, about friendship, and especially about you and me."

The narrator, unconscious of his Other, is clueless. "What's that supposed to mean?" he asks, as Tyler looks at him as if he should know.

Driving against oncoming traffic (going the *other* way), Tyler drives the narrator to the point where he screams, "Fuck you! Fuck Fight Club! Fuck Marla! I'm sick of all your shit!" These words, no doubt, are what the smiling Tyler wants to hear, words that echo his own: "It's only after we've lost everything that we're free to do anything."

"Okay, man, okay," Tyler says as he takes his hands off the steering wheel, ready to lose everything. When the narrator panics, Tyler chews him out. "Look at you! You're fucking pathetic.... Hitting bottom isn't a weekend retreat. It's not a goddamn seminar. Stop trying to control everything and just let go. Let go!" As suggested by his "All right. Fine," the narrator is more resigned than ready to "let the chips fall where they may," as Tyler called it when talking about evolving. His way of bringing the narrator to hit bottom is through the horrific accident that ensues. "We just had a near-life experience!" he rejoices as he pulls him out from the driver's seat of the rolled-over car.

Whatever the narrator experienced, when shown next, in their house, he's lying in bed once again, drifting in and out of consciousness. As if he had taken him as far as he could, Tyler leaves with the same briefcase he had when they first met on the plane. "And then Tyler was gone," the narrator's voice-over announces as he wakes up the following morning, asking himself, "Was I asleep? Had I slept?"

Without Tyler, without his projected Other, the narrator cannot find his place in their shared house, now swarming with "space monkeys," as Tyler called the men of Project Mayhem. Venturing outside, he meets Marla, who for once is not smoking a cigarette, while the narrator does, suggesting that the tables between them have turned. "Can I come in?" she asks.

Not yet realizing that he and Tyler are one and the same, he tells the surprised Marla, "He's not here."

"*What?*" she asks incredulously.

"Tyler isn't here," he says, spelling it out for her, going against his promise to Tyler by calling his name, confusing Marla, who sees Tyler before her, more than before. "Tyler went away. Tyler's gone."

However the narrator may seem to Marla as if he's back to his schizoid self, things have changed. Instead of Tyler appearing with Marla's leaving, as he had always appeared as soon as she left the house, now the narrator hears commotion coming from the house. Rushing inside, he learns that Bob has been shot and killed by the police when "on assignment ... to kill two birds with one stone," a phrase that invokes the two sides that are one, particularly as the death of the feminized male, the two genders in one, is a breaking point for the narrator, a wake-up call that starts his questioning his state of mind and initiates his desperate search for Tyler, for his Other.

Going from city to city, he asks himself once again, "Was I asleep? Had I slept? Is Tyler my bad dream, or am I Tyler's?" Not fully awake, he nonetheless starts to open his eyes. "I was living in a perpetual state of déjà vu. Everywhere I went, I felt I'd already been there. It was like following an invisible man." The "invisible man," of course, is the Tyler only he sees, the Tyler he's "always one step behind."

Finally, starting to see through his projections for the first time, the narrator walks into a restaurant that recalls Lou's Tavern. The man behind the bar, his head in a brace, echoes Tyler's TV commercial when saying, "Welcome back, sir."

In their brief exchange, the puzzled narrator finally asks two direct questions about who he is to others. His "Do you know me?" is getting warm; his "Who do you think I am?" is more to the point.

"You're Mr. Durden," the bartender informs him. "You're the one who gave me this," he shows the unbelieving narrator the scar on the back of his hand.

With this revelation, the first thing the narrator does is rush back to his hotel room to call Marla, just as he had done the first time, before he called Tyler. Only this time, in his second call, he asks who he is to her. But Marla, like the bartender asking if his questions are a test, wants to know if his question, his need to know if they ever had sex, is a trick.

> *Marla*: You mean you wanna know if I think we were just having sex or making love?
>
> *Narrator*: We *did* make love?
>
> *Marla*: Is that what you're calling it?
>
> *Narrator*: Just answer the question, Marla. Please, did we do it or not?
>
> *Marla*: You fuck me, then snub me. You love me, you hate me. You show me a sensitive side, then you turn into a total asshole. Is that a pretty accurate description of our relationship, Tyler?
>
> *Narrator (stunned)*: What did you just say? What did you just call me? Say my name.
>
> *Marla*: Tyler Durden. Tyler Durden, you fucking freak! What's going on?

What's going on, of course, is that the narrator finally realizes that something is terribly wrong. Just as Marla had "ruined" the first solution to his insomnia, now her "second opinion" ruins his other (second) solution, that of Tyler Durden. As the narrator himself had put it, "She invaded my support groups; now she'd invaded my home."

The full explanation as to what's going on, much to his surprise, the narrator gets from the Other himself, when Tyler suddenly appears as soon as he hangs up the phone. "You broke your promise," he censures his projector. "You fucking talked to her about me."

Stunned, the narrator asks Tyler what Marla had asked him.

"Tyler, what the fuck is going on here?" But Tyler only answers when the narrator finally asks directly, "Why do people think that I'm you?" Even then, just as he had first waited for the narrator to ask to stay at his place, Tyler waits for him to utter what they both know is true, that "we're the same person." Only after the narrator utters it himself does Tyler explain, to both the narrator and us. "All the ways you wish you could be, that's me. I look like you wanna look, I fuck like you wanna fuck. I am smart, capable and, most importantly, I'm free in all the ways that you are not."

With the narrator becoming conscious of what he has been unconscious of all this time, Tyler adds the finishing touch: "Little by little, you're just letting yourself become," he pauses for dramatic effect, "Tyler Durden." Shocking as this news may be, and denying it as he tries, what really gets to the narrator, what drives him to lose consciousness, is the thought of Marla.

"You're fucking Marla, Tyler?" he asks.

"Technically, *you* are," Tyler replies, adding, "but it's all the same to her."

Envisioning Marla's significance in their relationship, the brief exchange about her is the segment's only time in which the two are shown facing each other in a symmetrical shot as opposite sides, which recalls Tyler's calling card. This symmetric shot doubles for the identical shot of the narrator facing an empty chair, talking to himself, a shot followed by his first seeing himself fighting himself rather than Tyler (in their second shown fight outside Lou's Tavern). While in his "Oh, my God" the narrator thinks of Marla, Tyler thinks of her threat to Project Mayhem: "She knows too much. I think we're gonna have to talk about how this might compromise our goals." Hearing more than he can bear, as demonstrated by his "I'm not listening to this," the narrator falls unconscious on the bed. "It's called a changeover," he reverts back to the projector we now know him to be. "The movie goes on and nobody in the audience has any idea."

The changeover, as we see next when the narrator wakes up with the phone off the hook, is his changed way of seeing both Marla and Tyler. This change is suggested by the hotel receptionist's double entendre as he rushes by her on his way out, "Are you checking out?" With what he now knows, he's indeed checking out, from both the hotel and his former way of seeing the two. The list of phone calls that she needs him to initial are only the tip of the iceberg. Shown returning to their shared house on Paper Street by plane and taxi, his asking himself, "Have I been Tyler longer and longer?" comes just before he realizes what Tyler meant about Marla knowing too much. Fearing for her life, after retracing some of the calls on the list and connecting them with the plans he finds in the house, he realizes that, in order to save Marla, he must go against Tyler and his Project Mayhem.

Just as the narrator had called Marla before he called Tyler after losing his condominium, now, before he goes to the police to warn them of Project Mayhem, he takes a taxi to Marla's hotel to warn her that she's in danger. And just as he didn't want to listen to Tyler, now, when he follows her inside a restaurant, which recalls his first meeting with Tyler at Lou's Tavern, she informs him, "I don't wanna hear anything you have to say." Nonetheless, she listens long enough for the narrator to say to her, "I've come to realize something very very important."

"*What?*" Marla asks impatiently.

"The full extent of our relationship wasn't really clear to me up until now, for reasons I'm not gonna go into. But the important thing I know is that I haven't been treating you well." Having heard enough, Marla starts to leave, but the narrator isn't finished. "I'm trying to tell you that I'm sorry. Because what I've come to realize is that I really like you, Marla."

"You *do*?" she asks with unfamiliar vulnerability.

"I really do," he assures her. "I care about you and I don't want anything bad to happen to you because of me."

But things change again when the narrator tells Marla that her "life is in danger." Figuring he's back to being Mr. Jackass, she has truly heard enough, twice shouting for him to "Shut up!" As the only one who experienced his two sides, she speaks as his feminine Other when giving him her side of the looking glass, mirroring the truth with words just as her presence in the support groups reflected his lie. "There are things about you I like. You're smart. You're funny. You're spectacular in bed. But you're intolerable. You have very serious emotional problems. Deep-seated problems for which you should seek professional help."

Appropriately enough, her informing him "I'm gone" rings of Tyler's leaving. Not only that, in something that recalls the narrator's telling Tyler when first meeting him on the plane, "You are by far the most interesting single-serving friend I have ever met," after persuading Marla to get on the bus that he stops in the street, telling her to "stay out of major cities for at least a couple of days," she tells him in parting from inside the bus, "Tyler, you're the worst thing that ever happened to me."

With Marla apparently safe, the narrator tries to stop Project Mayhem, a project which mirrors the shadowy monster Tyler has become. Or as Robert A. Johnson puts it, while seeming to inadvertently describe what the narrator finds he has been doing as the autonomous Tyler in the basement of their shared house: "The shadow gone autonomous is a terrible monster in our psychic house."[4] This terrible monstrosity is given expression by the merciless brutality with which Tyler beats the narrator after he dismantles the bomb, which recalls his own brutality in his fight with the blonde guy. Significantly, the narrator realizes his part in their relationship only after Tyler hurls him down two flights of stairs.

With the narrator hitting bottom, we're back to where we first saw him with Tyler's gun in his mouth. Or as the narrator informs us, "I think this is about where we came in." Sprawled on a chair, his body beaten out of shape by Tyler, the narrator looks defeated, resigned to the inevitability of Project Mayhem. At least until he sees Marla down below in the street, brought back by Tyler's space monkeys on the same bus he had pressed her to take out of town.

"Why is *she* here?" he sits up, confronting Tyler.

"Tying up loose ends," Tyler, standing over him, speaks for the two of them when he says, "This is what we want."

Speaking for himself, the narrator finally takes a stand, taking responsibility for his words: "*I* don't want this."

Want turns to need when, talking to Tyler, to himself, the narrator asks the crucial question, "Why can't I get rid of you?"

Tyler, like a magic mirror, supplies the bottom line: "You need me."

But the narrator, realizing otherwise, speaks more to himself than to Tyler when saying, "No. I don't. I really don't anymore." From this declaration to his taking responsibility "for all of it," for what both of them had done, it's a mere step or two until he literally (and otherwise) stands up to Tyler and declares, "My eyes are open." He then kills him by putting a bullet through his own cheek, an act that mirrors his withdrawing his unconscious projection of his Other.

The narrator may not succeed in stopping Project Mayhem, but with Tyler gone for good, integrated in his psyche, the space monkeys, who up to now didn't heed his words, follow his orders to leave Marla with him and clear the room. Finally, just as the narrator had initially replaced Marla with Tyler, now she replaces Tyler in the "front-row seats for this theater of mass destruction." With the two standing side by side before the plate glass windows, holding hands, and with the narrator informing Marla, "You met me at a very strange time in my life," the story, tying up loose ends, ends with the feminine Other replacing the imaginary Other.

11

Desperately Seeking Susan: Seeking the Other

I am desperate ... sort of.—Roberta Glass

What a Pair

More than an exception among the many male-oriented movies, *Desperately Seeking Susan* is a rare feminine take on the cinematic projector and his Other. The 1985 film, starring and created by women, is also set apart by the way it "sort of" adheres to the *Gilgamesh* prototype. Whereas in the male movies that follow the prototype the Other is generally ominous and is ultimately killed by the projector at the story's end, an act that signifies its integration in the projector's consciousness, in Susan Seidelman's romantic comedy the feminine Other is admired and envied and is ultimately integrated through the pairing of the two heroines.

Desperately Seeking Susan also deviates from earlier "female double films" in the way its protagonist and her Other complement and complete, rather than oppose and contradict, one another. As Karen Hollinger notes in her book, *In the Company of Women*, while citing "two of the most prominent 1940s female double films," *A Stolen Life* and *The Dark Mirror*, both from 1946, "Double films present two women, one good and one bad, who embody oppositions or contradictions within female nature.... The plot of the female double film centers on a conflict between the two women that is eventually resolved in a simplistic but morally uplifting manner, with the good woman triumphant and the bad one defeated or destroyed."[1]

Unlike these "female double films," which are much like the male films of the Other, in *Desperately Seeking Susan* no one is "defeated or destroyed." Both women win. As fits this light comedy of *opposites attract*, this "sort of" *projector and her Other* with a wink, Roberta (Rosanna Arquette) is attracted to Susan (Madonna) because she personifies for her what Jung called the *bright* or *golden shadow*, the life-affirming aspects of herself that she represses and projects onto Susan, what David Richo calls the "positive shadow": "The positive shadow is projected onto others as admiration and envy.... The positive shadow contains all our untapped creative potential."[2]

With Susan mirroring her "positive shadow," her vibrant Other, Roberta doesn't need to see her in person to project onto her the "untapped creative potential" missing in her life as a submissive and frustrated New Jersey housewife. She imagines a kinship by merely reading her boyfriend's desperate messages in the *New York Mirror*'s personals. Susan, after all, is Roberta's projection come true, a notion suggested throughout the movie by picturing the two as mirrored opposites, as two parts of a pair, which is virtually spelled out by the movie's closing shot of the two in the front page of the *New York Mirror*, with the headline reading, "What a Pair!"

As fits Roberta calling herself "Stranger" in her message to Susan in the *Mirror* and by the repeated pairing and comparing of the two, Susan is to Roberta what Deena Metzger calls "both stranger and kin."

> To allow that there is a part of self that is both stranger and kin to us is to enter into one of the great mysteries of the psyche. This act in itself becomes a peace offering that encourages the shadow to emerge ... the shadow is a continuum of ourselves that which we become when we go to the other side. It is our other face.[3]

Shadow or Other, going "to the other side" is precisely what Roberta does when she seeks Susan, her "other face," on the other side of the Hudson River. In becoming Susan on her second crossing, she indeed "enter[s] into one of the great mysteries of the psyche," the mystery of the projector and her unconscious Other.

Mirrored Opposites

Introducing the movie's *pair* motif of the projector and her unconscious Other, *Desperately Seeking Susan*'s opening shot shows a pair of a woman's bare legs having their hair removed in a beauty salon, a "sort of" female version of the alternating shots that opened Hitchcock's *Strangers on a Train* of two pairs of legs walking toward each other from opposite directions. Particularly as Hitchcock is referenced when Roberta is later shown watching *Rebecca*, the master's 1940 film about mirrored opposites, and as Roberta's first words in this opening scene are "beautiful stranger," another name for the vibrant Other, while Susan's last words in the movie are "Good goin', Stranger," said to Roberta when the two finally meet.

In its comical and entertaining attitude, *Desperately Seeking Susan* doesn't waste time in addressing both the feminist viewpoint that women beautify themselves for men's visual pleasure and women's desire to free themselves from the "bearer of the look," as Laura Mulvey calls the "male gaze" in her seminal essay, "Visual Pleasure and Narrative Cinema." This feminine bind is underscored by the film's opening question, "Does he love me? (the opening line to Betty Everett's "The Shoop Shoop Song [It's in His Kiss]"). The song's question is answered by a woman telling her hairdresser, "If my husband calls, I'm not here," and by Roberta's own hairdresser assuring her sister-in-law about the hairstyle he has in mind for the birthday girl: "Don't worry. Her husband will love it." But as Roberta's saying that she only wants "a trim" suggests, she's already "not here" for her husband, refusing, however meekly, to be the object of his gaze. The song itself makes it clear. It's not "in his eyes ... It's in his kiss!" As Hollinger points out, "*Desperately Seeking Susan* focuses on women as both actively desiring subjects and objects of the female gaze and of female desire."[4]

In the movie's pair of mirrored opposites Susan is the empowered and liberated woman while Roberta is the traditional meek housewife. Only as suggested by her fascination with "Blackie," a name that evokes the shadowy male Other, she's looking for someone who represents her husband's Other. But while she's captivated by the shadowy name, imagining, "He could be sincere," Leslie (Laurie Metcalf), her bad sister-in-law in this urban fairy tale, sets her straight, squashing her fantasy of the male Other: "*Nobody* named Blackie is sincere."

Significantly, Roberta spots the desperate message to Susan, her real Other, in the second half of the exposition, in a rather lengthy symmetric shot that envisions the projector and her Other by showing Roberta in pink and Leslie in black, each in curlers under identical hair dryers on either half of the screen. While Roberta is enchanted by the "desperate" in the message, imagining, "It's so romantic," Leslie once again reminds her otherwise: "Everybody I know is desperate, except you."

With her mirrored fantasy momentarily shattered, Roberta lights up as she circles the message in red nail polish, letting her imagination take over. What she imagines, as Richo calls it, is "a mirror reflection" of her "long-hidden twin."

> We imagine certain traits or qualities to be in others only when they are also a mirror reflection of what is in us. Our strong reactions of awe or

envy give us the clue that we are in the picture we are looking at. The strong reaction is the result of an excitement in our psyche about seeing its long-hidden twin.[5]

Mirroring both Roberta's picturing Susan in her mind and the pair of legs that opened the beauty salon segment, Susan is first shown in an Atlantic City hotel room, holding a Polaroid camera with both hands, snapping a picture of herself. Her being Roberta's mirrored opposite is highlighted in the course of this segment by a variety of tropes of binary opposites: the 1313 room number on the door; Susan drawing a black heart with an eyeliner around the very same message that matches Roberta's red circle; and the pair of Egyptian earrings she steals from the stealer himself, an act that initiates much of the movie's comedy of errors.

Why Roberta fantasizes about Susan is revealed in the subsequent birthday party at her home. The party is for her, but the center of attention is her self-centered husband, Gary (Mark Blum), who calls "time out" for the guests to watch his TV commercial, which is preceded by the anchorman announcing, as if speaking to Roberta about seeking her Other, "The search continues for suspects in the recent robbery of ancient Egyptian artifacts." While in the commercial the "other" Gary, dressed as a white hunter and supported by four blonde bathing beauties, invites the viewers to "Gary's Oasis," Roberta, once again in pink, walks to a big plate-glass window, looking at her reflection as Gary, now in the Jacuzzi with the girls, is heard announcing, "Gary's Oasis. All your fantasies can come true." Only Mrs. Glass has other fantasies in mind. Opening the reflecting window, the looking glass, she gazes longingly at the George Washington Bridge that links New Jersey and New York, mirroring her two states of mind.

As if Roberta's projection, the camera cuts from her longing gaze to another shot of the bridge, from the other side of the river, as a Liberty bus from New Jersey to New York City is shown pulling into the Port Authority Terminal, bringing Susan to the Big Apple. Inside the terminal, evoking the pair motif, Susan is shown drying her armpits with the dryer and putting on one of the earrings in front of the mirror. Her changing from a pink blouse, Roberta's color, to a black one, foreshadows Roberta wearing Susan's "Egyptian" jacket and her imagining that she's Susan.

On the other side of the bridge, or mirror, in her New Jersey home, doubling for Gary's TV commercial in the living room, Roberta is watching Hitchcock's *Rebecca* on the television in the kitchen. The movie, whose unnamed heroine is haunted by her husband's late wife, mirrors her fascination with Susan; the scene showing the husband holding his wife's face between his two hands mirrors her relationship with Gary, who walks in, wondering why Roberta doesn't watch the movie on the television in their bedroom.

Reminding her to pick up the car radio, he reminds her that she's his wife, which explains why she desperately seeks Susan, who personifies the careless freedom she can only dream about.

Back to the other side, Susan is shown arriving at the Magic Club, whose neon sign includes a white rabbit that recalls *Alice in Wonderland*, another sign of the heroine's unconscious, the other side of the looking glass. Inside, the unconscious is evoked by the underworld that's suggested by the cigarette girl at the entrance, a "sort of" threshold guardian, who greets Susan by saying, "We all thought you were dead." As Roberta's mirrored opposite, the imagined "dead" Susan mirrors her death-in-life marriage, particularly as she answers, "No, just in New Jersey."

But Roberta not only seeks Susan, she gradually becomes her. This transformation starts with her buying Susan's jacket with the golden pyramid on the back, by which she's identified by both Dez (Aidan Quinn) and the blonde criminal (Will Patton), another set of mirrored opposites. Significantly, in the second-hand boutique, just before Susan exchanges her jacket for a pair of boots and vanishes, she briefly catches Roberta's gaze, the only time the two exchange looks before she acknowledges Roberta at the story's end when the two finally meet. As fits the theme of mirrored opposites, what Roberta undergoes between Susan's two looks, what she experiences in the span of the "female gaze," is split into two states of mind. In one state she's the unconscious Susan; in the other she's the conscious Roberta, but no longer the same Roberta she was before falling into a state of unconsciousness.

Roberta's transformation is right in line with the three phases of what Arnold van Gennep called "Rite of Passage": separation, transition, and incorporation. After her separation from her familiar world as *conscious Roberta*, in falling unconscious she undergoes a transition, a rebirth, as *unconscious Susan*. Her regaining consciousness as Roberta and retaining some of Susan's personality is the incorporation — the pairing — of the projector and her unconscious Other.

Unconscious Susan

After twice introducing Roberta on the day of her birthday — in the beauty salon and at her birthday party — showing her lost in thought in the bathtub after buying Susan's jacket suggests her rebirth, especially as her back is reflected by the mirror behind her while she studies the picture of Susan, her future identity, which she finds in the jacket together with the red Port Authority locker key and the newspaper headline that reads, MYSTERY WOMAN SOUGHT FOR QUESTIONING. As Hollinger notes, "Roberta's fascination, even obsession, with Susan clearly represents a psychologically empowering idealizing transference situation that triggers in Roberta a significant rebirth."[6]

This "transference" and "rebirth" are envisioned by cutting from Roberta's submerging herself in the tub's sudsy water to Susan (in black) writing her "name and number" to the vendor who sold her jacket to Roberta. It's yet another intimation that what we see is Roberta's unconscious projection, particularly as Susan's writing is subsequently mirrored by Roberta (in white) writing her own "Desperately Seeking Susan" message, this time "Regarding key." Rather than her back reflected in the mirror *behind* her, now she's looking at herself in the bathroom mirror *before* her. As if through the looking glass, Roberta's message transposes things. Now Susan is shown reading Roberta's desperate message in *The Mirror*, responding with "Good goin', Stranger," while Jim, Susan's boyfriend, whose desperate messages Roberta follows, is shown reading *her* message and wondering who this stranger is. The red key, of course, is not unlike Alice's "tiny golden key." Both unlock the door to another world, the magic world of the unconscious.

The change from one side of the mirror to the other is designated by Dez's changing the reels in the movie theater's projection room, and by his ending a relationship with one woman and beginning a new one, with Roberta as Susan. Dez gets into the picture when Jim (Robert Joy), Susan's boyfriend who's "stuck in Buffalo" with his band, asks him to take his place in meeting Susan at Battery Park. His answering Jim's phone call with "Projection" is another sign that what we're watching is Roberta's projection, a notion reinforced by her subsequent checking her new and more vibrant look in the mirror, on which she attached Susan's Polaroid picture, and by her wearing Susan's jacket while Jim describes her to Dez over the phone: "She's incredibly pretty, blonde hair, medium height. Oh, and she's got this green and gold jacket with a pyramid with an eye on top like a dollar bill. You can't miss it."

Wearing the pyramid jacket to her rendezvous with Susan isn't the only sign that Roberta is a second-hand Susan. Her comparison to Susan is envisioned when the blonde criminal, having also spotted her message to Susan in the *Mirror*, compares the Polaroid snapshot of Susan taken on Atlantic City's boardwalk (which he found in his partner's Atlantic City hotel room) with the real-life Roberta at Manhattan's Battery Park, waiting for Susan. Other than wearing the same jacket, their likeness is doubled by their leaning on a railing, facing two bodies of water, the ocean and the river, two common signifiers of the unconscious. As mirrored opposites, Roberta is subsequently accosted by the blonde criminal while Susan is simultaneously picked up by a policeman for not paying her cab fare when going to her rendezvous with Roberta.

11. Desperately Seeking Susan

With Susan out of the way, the coast is clear for Dez to mistake Roberta for Susan, and for Roberta to become Susan ("sort of") when falling unconscious and waking up without her memory. In this unconscious side of the looking glass, or of Mrs. Glass, each takes the other's place. Instead of Roberta seeking Susan, now Susan seeks *her*, as do all the other male characters in the movie, each for his own reason.

In becoming Susan, Roberta replaces her projecting onto her what she represses in her life with "introjecting the positive qualities she finds in Susan into her own personality."[7] Aside from wearing her jacket, this introjection is suggested by her trying to inhale one of the cigarettes she finds among Susan's belongings in the locker at Port Authority. Particularly as her *inhaling* and coughing is followed by her mirrored opposite, shown behind bars, deliberately *exhaling* the smoke in the face of the *black* policewoman who lights her cigarette before she's released from the holding tank by a *white* policewoman. Then, in Dez's apartment, under the influence of the introjected Susan, Roberta, who doesn't "know what happened," kisses Jim's stand-in. Next morning, as if through an unconscious lens, Dez watches Roberta through the fish aquarium, putting on Susan's green dress. Like Susan, she now wears the other Egyptian earring, only on the opposite ear. This transformation is reinforced by Roberta being mistaken for Susan when, following the "message" on the matchbook she finds in her suitcase, she's thrown out of the restaurant where Susan had once left without paying.

Going by a second sign, the pictured postcard, Roberta tries the Magic Club, where rather than taking Susan's place, she replaces her girlfriend, Crystal (Anna Levine), as the magician's assistant. The Magic Club, as the neon white rabbit advertises, is the magical other world of the unconscious, where things are not what they seem, or not as they're said, as demonstrated by the magician speaking in double entendre when complaining of Roberta's performance ("This one's worse than the other one"). In contrast, the more practical club host (John Turturro) gives Roberta the job, urging her to "practice a lot," so that she can be better "than the other one."

Roberta unconsciously going by her Other's name while replacing her girlfriend in the magic act fits right in with Dez thinking Roberta is Susan while taking Jim's place as her boyfriend. This mix-up is mirrored by Susan telling Gary that Roberta and the blonde criminal are trying to frame her for his partner's murder. In reality, though, the blonde criminal, after seeing Roberta wearing one of the Egyptian earrings, first follows her to the Magic Club by the postcard she dropped at the restaurant she was thrown out of when mistaken for Susan. Transposing Alice's following the white rabbit, the blonde criminal continues to follow Roberta when she leaves the club as both Susan *and* Crystal by virtue of her wearing Crystal's dress under Susan's pyramid jacket and by carrying the bag with Susan's belongings in one hand and the magic act's caged bird in the other. In this situation, as if "both stranger and kin," Roberta Glass becomes Susan-Crystal.

Roberta's unconscious state of mind is evoked by the deserted nocturnal streets in which she finds herself while trying to escape from the rather creepy criminal and by Gary's TV commercial that she sees in the night watchman's quarters where she seeks refuge. Dubbed in Spanish, a "sort of" New York *Jabberwocky* for Roberta, it seems like a message from her past, both strange and familiar. Just as the English commercial called her to make her fantasy come true as Susan, now, faintly recalling the past, it calls her to make another fantasy come true as a new Roberta. For just as her trying to get away from the blonde criminal transformed her from a conscious Roberta to an unconscious Susan, now this transformation is reversed when she wakes up as conscious Roberta after her head hits the pavement once again while trying to get away from the same blonde criminal.

Conscious Roberta

Starting the third phase in her rite of passage, *incorporation*, Roberta regains consciousness of who she is, though it doesn't stop others from mistaking her for a prostitute, the lowest point of her descent into Susan's other world. Locked up in the same cell in which Susan was detained, Roberta's having become more like Susan is mirrored by showing her Other in her New Jersey home, going through her drawers just as she went through Susan's belongings in the suitcase. The two are even released from the cooler by the same policewoman.

Also doubling for Susan, Roberta is shown packing up her Other's suitcase to leave Dez just as Susan was shown leaving her criminal boyfriend in Atlantic City. Only unlike Susan, she doesn't leave him. The two become lovebirds like the two white doves in the bird cage she carries. Significantly, they make love when Dez still believes she's Susan while Roberta *knows* she's Roberta. He believes he's replacing Jim, and in a "sort of" way he is, as now Roberta, having incorporated some of her Other's personality, is partly like Susan just as Susan has become partly like her, wearing her jacket and the Egyptian earring, now on the same ear as Roberta. The two connect when Susan writes her own message "regarding key" to Roberta, "Desperately Seeking Stranger," which Roberta spots in the *Mirror*'s personals, instructing her to "meet me Saturday night. Magic Club."

Roberta and Susan, however, are not the only ones who meet at the Magic Club. Befitting the climax, all the characters meet at the rendezvous, even Leslie and her boyfriend. Only Crystal, whom Roberta now consciously replaces as herself, is absent. Envisioning the new Roberta, she once again appears onstage wearing one of the earrings, but this time, once removed, it's attached to her stage wig rather than to her ear. In this realm of the magical unconscious, where Roberta is introduced as "Davina, Queen of the Night," the two magic tricks she assists in mirror what the movie has been conveying all along.

The first trick, with the two white doves in one cage, clearly mirrors the pairing of Roberta and Susan (behind bars), the two that are one, which is given expression by Dez's "Susan?" and Gary's "Roberta?" when seeing Roberta assisting the magician onstage; this also mirrors Dez and Jim's opposite views of Susan. The second trick, the illusion of sawing Roberta in two, mirrors the illusion of the split between the projector and her Other. These two sides are mirrored by Gary and the blonde criminal repeatedly pictured sitting back to back, even singled out in two shots during Roberta's second trick. With Gary in a light jacket and the criminal in dark, their sitting back to back mirrors what the criminal signifies in Roberta's psyche. He's her husband's *negative shadow* just as Dez is his *positive shadow*, which is why Roberta only gets together with the *positive shadow* after she knocks out this *negative shadow*.

Pandemonium erupts when, at the conclusion of the second trick, Roberta recognizes the *negative shadow*, signaling him out, "That's *him*!" His cover blown, and seeing the sparkling Egyptian earring dangling from her wig, he rushes to the stage and grabs it off her head, running backstage with Gary and Dez right behind him. Rather than pursue the blonde criminal, the two stop on either side of the sawed box, helping Roberta out while each asks about the other. One wants Roberta; the other, Susan. Finally, after introducing the two to each other, Roberta takes charge, telling Dez, "I really need to talk to Gary alone."

Roberta's situation with Gary and Dez, the old and the new, is mirrored by Susan's situation with Jim. Having earlier taken him to a side room to "talk about it in private" (when he came backstage, asking her "Who's the stranger?"), the two are discovered by the blonde criminal, who takes Susan hostage just as Gary tries to take back Roberta. Both mirrored pairs — Roberta and Gary and Susan and the criminal, of course, are temporary. Roberta tells Gary she's "not coming home" with him; and when the criminal, holding Susan at gunpoint, sticks his head through Roberta's dressing room's window, she responds to Susan's plea, "Help me," in knocking him unconscious by breaking a bottle over his head, repaying him for the two times he caused her to lose consciousness. "Nice going, Stranger," Susan both compliments and complements her projector, repeating her message's encouraging words to Roberta, this time face to face, and no longer strangers. "Susan," Roberta calls her by name, happy to finally meet her mirrored opposite.

The two's true pairing is revealed in the closing scene, which begins and ends with projections on the screen in the movie theater where Dez works as a projectionist.

"So, I guess your name isn't Susan, huh?" Dez asks Roberta when she comes up to his projection room after leaving Gary for good. "So what is it?"

"Roberta," she replies with unfamiliar confidence, happy to be who she is, happy to replace her projections with a projectionist. When the two kiss, their leaning against the movie projector stops and burns the film, while in the audience, Susan (wearing Roberta's jacket) sits next to Jim, as the two laugh over what's apparently happening in the projection room.

Signaling the change the two mirrored opposites have undergone, the projected burn on the screen dissolves into the first of *Desperately Seeking Susan*'s pair of black and white closing shots, which shows Roberta and Susan in a civic ceremony, being awarded for apprehending the criminal, the story's *negative shadow*. The two celebrate their triumph, their incorporation, by raising their joined hands high above their heads. Caught by the photographer's camera, this picture of the two appears in the front page of the *New York Mirror*, a far cry from the back pages of the personals. In this second and final shot of the epilogue, the two headlines, "WHAT A PAIR!" and "STOLEN EARRINGS RETURNED," announce that all has been restored. The pair of earrings has been returned, the pair of mirrored opposites, the projector and her Other, have been united. For all concerned, and for all intents and purposes, the desperate seeking is definitely over.

12

Apocalypse Now: The Other Story

There is no way to tell his story without telling my own.
— Captain Benjamin Willard speaking of Colonel Walter E. Kurtz

The Other Don't Surf

"I don't want to bother you much with what happened to me personally," Marlow says as he prepares his listeners for the story he's about to tell them early in Joseph Conrad's *Heart of Darkness*, the 1902 novella on which Francis Ford Coppola based his 1979 movie, *Apocalypse Now*. But bother he does. As if he can't help it, as if he has to unburden himself, he goes on with his story: "Yet to understand the effect of it on me you ought to know how I got out there, what I saw, how I went up that river to the place where I first met the poor chap." The effect the unnamed poor chap had on Conrad's Marlow is taken up early in Coppola's *Apocalypse Now* by Captain Willard (Martin Sheen), the movie's Marlow, when telling us in his voice-over, "There is no way to tell his story without telling my own."

No way, indeed. As Linda J. Dryden notes,

> Without the inspiration from *Heart of Darkness*, Coppola would have made a wholly different movie, probably less powerful and less enduring, and thus the film helps to secure the continuing presence of Conrad's novel in our culture because of the film's own enduring relevance. The popular film gains more dimensional complexity; the novel gains currency and a further reference point from which to evaluate it.[1]

Whereas Conrad's *Heart of Darkness* reveals how the imperialist Europeans projected their denied darkness onto the primitive natives of Africa, Coppola's *Apocalypse Now* envisions how America, defender of the world against communism, projected its denied darkness on Vietnam. In John Hellmann's words, "Coppola views Vietnam as the projection of Southern California into an alien landscape where even the American ideal stands at last exposed."[2] At the same time, like the Other that returns to haunt its projector, Coppola's film, and the other Vietnam movies that came out after the fall of Saigon in 1975, returned to haunt America, each movie projecting its own vision of the unpopular and tragic war. Perhaps more than anything else, these disturbing movies projected back America's real-life projection of its binary Other on the Viet Cong, the bad "gooks" to the good Americans. As David Desser notes, "It is the utter lack of recognition of 'others' ... that involved us tragically in Vietnam ... an essential cultural myopia got America into the war in the first place and clouds Americans' vision still."[3]

This "cultural myopia," this "utter lack of" recognizing the Other, is best expressed by the way Americans see "Charlie," a name which encapsulates the attempt to both demonize and familiarize the Vietnamese Other. In *Apocalypse Now* this myopia is best expressed by Colonel Kilgore's (Robert Duval) now-famous line, "Charlie don't surf." As Desser writes of this segment in his article by the same name,

> thinking that Kilgore risks his own men and slaughters the villagers near the shore merely to surf, Willard wonders why Colonel Kurtz is thought mad in the face of psychopaths like Kilgore. It is, rather, as screenwriter John Milius recognized, that America tried to import and impose its own culture into Vietnam and that cultural differences and prejudices underlay many of our government's more outrageous, thoughtless, violent, and tragic actions.... America *always* saw the war only in strictly American terms. Even the critiques of the American involvement in the war see it as a flaw in American society, a defect of character, culture, or metaphysics.[4]

Seeing "in strictly American terms" is precisely how the projector sees his Other, in his own terms of projecting. In *Apocalypse Now*, Coppola does both. With crucial contribution from cinematographer Vittorio Storaro and sound designer Walter Murch, who won Oscars for best cinematography and best sound, he projects on the silver screen both America's and Willard's unconscious projection of the Other much as Conrad portrayed it as projected by Europe and Marlow in *Heart of Darkness*.

Expovision Now

Like the many images of binary opposites that accompany the phantasmagoric *Apocalypse Now* from start to finish, the movie's *expovision*, its highly visual exposition, is divided into two distinct parts that illustrate Willard's troubled psyche. The first part, divided into three stunning segments, seems like a horrific nightmare.

Segment 1. Invoking the name of Conrad's novella in both sight and sound, *Apocalypse Now* opens with the rhythmic sound of whirring helicopter blades over a dark screen. Gradually, in a stationary long shot, a lush green forest fades in, tainted only by sparse white smoke rising from below. With the blades' whirring sound coming closer, a chopper crosses the screen from left to right, followed by a cloud of yellow smoke, which thickens as a sinuous electric guitar comes on — the instrumental opening to The Door's "The End," the song that accompanies the *expovision*'s beginning and end. With the sound of another approaching helicopter, a throbbing bass begins to accompany the guitar, soon followed by the jangling rattle of a tambourine. The second helicopter also crosses the screen from left to right, though now, much closer to the camera, only its landing skid is visible. Then, immediately after the chopper has crossed the screen, the whole forest, the whole screen, bursts into flames just as the singer Jim Morrison, as if announcing Willard's binary friend, begins to sing "This is the end, beautiful friend."

Shedding light on this opening shot in his book *Apocalypse Now*, Karl French cites Murch.

> There was something about that, the green jungle, flattened by the telephoto lens, looking very calm and peaceful and then having it suddenly erupt in red fire. It was something that, for Francis, had to do with what the whole Vietnam experience was about. It encapsulated what had happened in Vietnam.[5]

This stunning long shot of the green jungle, which changes before our eyes, indeed envisions in one encapsulated picture America's increasing involvement in Vietnam. The gorgeously green forest may well represent the Vietnam before American's entrance, and the sparse white smoke the American forces that came first, mostly advisors and special forces. Likewise, considering helicopters were key weapons of the Vietnam War, the first helicopter crossing the screen and the yellow smoke that follows signal the American escalation, while the second helicopter and the napalm bombing of the forest that directly follows represent the inflaming of the war.

Whereas up to now the camera was stationary, showing the same "postcard" picture of the forest, once the forest erupts in flames, it begins to slowly pan from left to right, revealing more of the inflamed jungle. Opposite the camera's movement, two helicopters cross the screen from right to left, followed by another chopper crossing from left to right. These five helicopters, shown before Willard's face is superimposed on the screen, may well represent the five soldiers that start out on the PBR that takes Willard up the river to Kurtz (Marlon Brando). Like the two pairs of helicopters flying in opposite directions, the four-man crew are themselves two sets of pairs, two sets of binary opposites that mirror Willard and his unconscious Other. Perhaps to underscore the significance of this pattern of five helicopters, it's repeated two more times, once in each of the *expovision*'s next two segments.

Segment 2. The *expovision*'s second segment starts with an overhead shot of Willard's upside-down face superimposed on the left side of the screen over the background of the burning forest as two helicopters crisscross each other and are replaced by the superimposition of the rotating ceiling fan. The segment ends with the superimposing of a primitive stone statue of a human face on the right side of the screen, opposite Willard's upside-down face, accompanied by "The End." As part of Kurtz's old temple, this statued icon of the Other mirrors Willard's troubled psyche.

Segment 3. In the *expovision*'s third segment, the rotating of the camera gradually brings Willard's face right side up, superimposed with the rotating ceiling fan once again. At the end of the segment, just as the first part of "The End" fades out, Willard's face is once again shown up-side down and on the left side of the screen, while the other half of the screen is completely dark. With only the sound of the approaching helicopter blades, he opens his eyes and looks up. Then, in the second shot of this four-shot sequence, the camera cuts to the whirling fan on the ceiling, shown from Willard's point of view, its whirling shadow projected on the ceiling. In the third shot, with the camera returning to Willard on the left side of the screen, now the dark half of the screen, like the ceiling fan's projected shadow, is revealed to be his very own shadow. With his eyes seeming to follow the sound of the helicopter, the camera returns to his point of view, coming in toward the window with the venetian blinds together with Willard, shown parting two blinds and peering through them at the bustling city street outside. As if surprised, or disappointed, he utters his first words: "Saigon. Shit."

Where up to now Willard's state of mind was envisioned by a myriad of images, the second part of the *expovision*, divided into two distinct segments, mostly with no superimpositions and accompanied by his voice-over, shows him in his hotel room, breaking down while "waiting for a mission."

Segment 1. The first segment combines images with the first part of Willard's voice-over narration, revealing a tormented man of two minds. "Every time I think I'm gonna wake up back in the jungle. When I was home after my first tour, it was worse. I'd wake up, and there'd be nothing." Just as the helicopters of the first part are replaced by the ceiling fan, the earlier smoke and the subsequent burning of the picturesque jungle is doubled by Willard smoking in bed, picking up his wife's picture and putting it against his burning cigarette as if burning his bridges behind him. Once again, his words reveal an inner split: "I hardly said a word to my wife until I said yes to a divorce. When I was here, I wanted to be there. When I was there, all I could think of was getting back into the jungle."

Willard's binary state of mind is further revealed by his comparing himself to "Charlie," who at this stage of his story, before he hears of Kurtz, personifies his Other. "Every minute I stay in this room," he says, "I get weaker. And every minute Charlie squats in the bush, he gets stronger." He ends his opening monologue with words that reveal his claustrophobic, if not paranoid, state of mind: "Each time I looked around, the walls moved in a little tighter."

Segment 2. The second segment, accompanied by a rather frenzied part of "The End," reveals what's perhaps best expressed by the song's "wilderness of pain." This part of the song, which replaces Willard's narration, is taken up again when he kills Kurtz toward the story's end. In fact, following a shot that shows the intoxicated Willard going through some martial-arts moves, and a second shot that shows his face lost in dark brooding, his camouflaged face, the same one shown just before he kills Kurtz, is briefly superimposed on his present face. This shot is followed by a close-up of (what seems like) Kurtz's profile as he waits for his end. Then, after a shot of Willard looking directly into the camera while extending his fist, he suddenly smashes the full-size mirror in his room, injuring his hand, the same hand he stares at and repeatedly flexes before killing his mirrored Other. Last shown writhing in pain, Willard smears his bloodied hand on his face as if going native, sinking to the floor in agonizing despair.

Binary Opposites

In what may be seen as a transitional two-shot *expovision* of the movie's binary opposites, two military men, one blond, the other dark-haired, come with orders for Willard. The first shot follows the "binary" pair as they climb the stairs to Willard's second-story room, accompanied by his renewed narration, which explains why they've come: "Everyone get everything he wants. I wanted a mission. And for my sins, they gave me one. Brought it up to me like room service." Envisioning Willard's words, the two men are last shown in this first shot in a twofold image of binary opposites. With the screen itself divided into two parts, the left side is dark while the right side — the side in which the two men are shown — is light. The blond man, on the left, is in light; the dark-haired one, on the right side, is in darkness, only his silhouette shown. This double splitting of the screen, which envisions Willard's split psyche, recalls the shot showing his face up-side down on the left side of the screen, while the other half of the screen is completely dark.

The second shot, continuing the imagery of binary opposites, shows the two men at Willard's door. With the screen once again divided into dark and light halves, the blond soldier stands against the dark background of the room's door while the dark-haired one, shown once again in silhouette, stands on the left side against the light background of the wall.

Knocking on the door, the blond soldier calls out, "Captain Willard, are you in there?"

"Yea, I'm coming," Willard is heard from *in there*, as his narration continues: "It was a real choice mission. And when it was over, I'd never want another." Still in the same shot, Willard opens the door, but only the blond soldier enters the room, verifying Willard's identity. The "shadowed" dark-haired soldier, the "Other" of the two, remains outside. He only enters when Willard, inviting his "binary buddy" inside, calls out, "Hey, buddy, are you gonna shut the door?"

Inside his room, the paranoia suggested in the *expovision* is reinforced by Willard's pair of questions, "What are the charges?" and "What'd I do?" When told the two have come "to escort you to the airfield" for his "orders to report to Com-Sec Intelligence at Nha Trang," Willard, "not feeling too good," prefers to return to bed. Seeing they have "a dead one," the two wake him back to life by giving him a cold shower, foreshadowing the rain shower that comes after Willard carries out his mission in killing Kurtz. Willard's wailing in pain under the cold shower that awakens him from the "dead," which ends this brief segment, mirrors his writhing in pain that ended the *expovision*.

Along with this segment's revealing cinematography, Willard's narration tells its own story. The first part suggests reminiscence, as if the mission has already been carried out. The second part, particularly his "when it was over, I'd never want another," reinforces the notion that his story is told after the fact, much like Marlow's telling his tale in *Heart of Darkness*.

Willard's arrival at Nha Trang, by helicopter and escorted by the two "binary" soldiers, once again opens with two shots and is accompanied by his narration that mentions Kurtz for the first time, suggesting a preordained connection between the two, not unlike the one between the projector and his Other. "I was going to the worst place in the world and I didn't even know it yet," he mentions in the first shot. "Weeks away and hundreds of miles up a river that snaked through war like a main circuit cable, plugged straight into Kurtz." Likewise, his second mention is in the second shot: "It was no accident that I got to be the caretaker of Colonel Walter E. Kurtz's memory any more than being back in Saigon was an accident. There is no way to tell his story without telling my own. And if his story is really a confession, then so is mine."

Once inside the general's (G. D. Spradlin) office for his orders, Willard's identity is questioned a second time. Despite his "waiting for a mission," as suggested by his turning down a cigarette offered by the young colonel (Harrison Ford) and by his not eating the food before him, he has no appetite for the mission he's about to get. The significance of "appetite" is underscored by the general's pair of double entendres: "I hope you brought a good appetite, Captain," and his offering Willard a bowl of shrimp while practically calling it the *Other*, "Captain, I don't know how you feel about this shrimp, but if you'll eat it, you'll never have to prove your courage in any other way." He says this after suggesting they pass the food "both ways."

To familiarize Willard with Kurtz, the general asks the colonel to play his recorded messages, those "monitored out of Cambodia." Naturally, there are two messages, each one revealing another side of Kurtz. The first one, the more personal of the two, speaks of the two sides of the razor's edge: "I watched a snail crawl along the edge of a straight razor. That's my dream. It's my nightmare." The second message speaks of dealing with the collective Other: "But we must kill them. We must incinerate them, pig after pig, cow after cow, village after village, army after army." Then, all but pointing out his being the receptacle of others' projections, Kurtz adds, "And they call me an assassin. What do you call it when the assassins accuse the assassin?"

Kurtz's conflicting sides in particular, and man's two sides in general, are given expression by the general: "There's a conflict in every human heart, between the rational and the irrational, between good and evil. And good does not always triumph. Sometimes the dark side overcomes what Lincoln called, 'The better angels of our nature.' Every man has got a breaking point. You and I have them. Walt Kurtz has reached his, and very obviously he has gone insane." In the silence that follows, Willard's eventual response ("Yes, sir. Very much so, sir. Obviously insane.") is hardly enthusiastic. He's even less so when he learns that his mission is to "terminate the colonel's command." Nonetheless, as suggested by his now taking a cigarette offered by the civilian, whose only line in the movie ("Terminate with extreme prejudice.") ends the scene, Willard accepts the mission.

In terms of *binary opposites*, which Coppola takes great pains to plant throughout the movie, the civilian's curious overstating is not unlike the common overreacting to one's projected Other. Just as it was "no accident that [Willard] got to be the caretaker of Colonel Walter E. Kurtz's memory," it's no accident that the civilian is the only one who eats. At this stage of the story, as his "extreme prejudice" underscores, he's the only one with a "good appetite" for terminating the Other. A final intimation that the mission is an unconscious one is the young colonel's reminder that "this mission does not exist, nor will it ever exist," after which Willard starts smoking the cigarette lit by the civilian as if already introjecting Kurtz as his Other.

In the subsequent series of aerial shots, Willard is transferred by helicopter to his mission's river patrol boat (PBR), wondering if he had bitten off more than he can chew. "How many people have I already killed?" he asks rhetorically. "There were those six that I knew about for sure. Close enough to blow their last breath in my face." With the PBR heading out to sea, his voice-over mirrors his second thoughts about his mission and his will to carry it out. "But this time it was an American and an officer. That wasn't supposed to make any difference to me, but it did. Shit, charging a man with murder in this place was like handing out speeding tickets at the Indy 500. I took the mission. What the hell else was I gonna do? But I really didn't know what I'd do when I found him."

Much like the numerous images of binary opposites that dominate the first part of the movie, once on the PBR Willard's state of mind is mirrored by the binary pairings of the four crewmen. Alluding to this pairing right from the start, Willard introduces the four, one after the other, starting with the crew's pair of whites: "The machinist, the one they called Chef, was from New Orleans. He was wrapped too tight for Vietnam. Probably wrapped too tight for New Orleans. Lance, on the forward 50s, was a famous surfer from the beaches south of L.A. To look at him, you wouldn't believe he'd ever fired a weapon in his life." Then, shown sitting next to Clean, Willard introduces the crew's pair of blacks: "Clean, Mr. Clean, was from some South Bronx shithole, and I think the light and space of Vietnam really put the zap on his head. Then there was Phillips, the chief. It might have been my mission, but it sure as shit was the chief's boat." As the most responsible member of the crew, Chief (Albert Hall) warns Willard when telling him of another man he had taken up the same river: "About six months ago, I took a man who was going up past the bridge at Do Luong. He was regular army, too. I heard he shot himself in the head."

Aside from being paired as binary opposites of white and black, the four crewmen are also paired by their names. These pairings' "critical drama," as Louis Greiff calls it in his essay "Conrad's Ethics and the Margins of *Apocalypse Now*,"

> is enacted at the margins of *Apocalypse Now*— among a grouping of lesser figures with decidedly un–Conradian names.... The black man, Chief Phillips, is presented as a model of discipline and self-control, to the point of seeming cold and unfeeling at times. By contrast, the white man, a

would-be New Orleans saucier, overreacts to everything that happens on the PBR and is never far from hysteria.... If Chief represents the precise discipline of craftsmanship, then Chef represents its artistic or imaginary core.[6]

Like the homophonic names of the older Chief and Chef (Frederic Forrest), the other pair, the younger Clean (Laurence Fishburne) and Lance (Sam Bottoms), is suggested by their anagrammatically sharing the letters in their names. This pairing is underscored by showing Clean singing and dancing to the Rolling Stones' "Satisfaction" and Lance's waterskiing behind the PBR, while Chef cheers on the two and Chief enjoys it from the sidelines. Disassociated from the pairs, Willard is shown opening Kurtz's dossier and looking at his pictures, learning more about the man whose voice already hooked him just as the Other hooks its projector: "I had heard his voice on the tape and it really put the hook in me, but I couldn't connect up that voice with this man."

Another of *Apocalypse Now*'s binary pairs, of course, is the two Colonel Ks, Colonel Kilgore and Colonel Kurtz, who appear at opposite ends of Willard's journey up the river, each one projecting his own madness in the way he fights the war. Like the significant names of the four crewmen, as Margot Norris points out in her essay, "Modernism in Vietnam,"

> Kilgore's allegorical name points to a one dimensionality that itself has philosophical significance, that makes him — in contrast to the brooding, introspective Kurtz — a Conradian and Eliotian "hollow man" with no interiority, no self-consciousness, no conscience, no powers of *anagnorisis*. His insanity is of a different order than that of Kurtz — who sees his own perversity as the interiorization of the perversity of war.[7]

Just as the four crewmen's skin color and names point to the binary opposites that govern the movie, the change each one undergoes as they travel farther away from civilization and ever closer to Kurtz mirrors Willard's changing apprehension, as in both *seeing* and *fear*, of his Other. This mirroring is doubled by Willard's voice-over narration, which is always about his relationship with his Other.

Outer Station

Foreshadowing the transformation Willard undergoes on his journey up the river, when first shown picking up Willard in their PBR (as silhouettes), all four crewmen are in full uniform. Next morning, only the two black soldiers are fully dressed. Clean, like his nickname, is shown brushing his teeth; Chief, also like his name, is steering the boat, refusing Willard's proffered cigarette. In contrast, the two whites, both bare chested, are enjoying themselves as if on a vacation cruise. Chef is reading Henry Miller's *Sexus* with a beer can at his side; Lance is tanning his face with a triptych aluminum reflector.

The real deterioration of the crew's military orderliness begins as soon as they part from Kilgore and his air cavalry and start their journey up the river, when three of the men, the less responsible Chef, Lance, and Clean, "light up" and "get high." They invite Willard to join them, but he turns them down, only to turn to his own poison, as shown by his emptying his liquor bottle into his canteen and drinking its last drops. Having witnessed Kilgore attack the Vietnamese village so he can see Lance surf, Willard now reflects on the two colonels: "If that's how Kilgore fought the war I began to wonder what they had against Kurtz. It wasn't just insanity or murder. There was enough of that to go around for everyone." What they had against him, of course, is his personifying and mirroring their denied Other.

The first crewman to start losing his bearings is the machinist Chef. Imagining he's "not here," that he's "walking through the jungle, gathering mangos," he tries to fulfill his fantasy by venturing into the unconscious jungle, breaking the cardinal rule of never getting off the boat. Rather than finding mango's, however, he's stunned by a pouncing tiger, barely getting back on the boat in one piece. But the damage, as his uncontrollable hysterics testify, has been done. Once confronted by the unconscious, he's never the same.

"Never get out of the boat," Willard, who got off the boat with Chef, repeats the mantra Chef repeats to pacify himself, projecting it onto Kurtz: "Absolutely goddamn right. Unless you were going all the way. Kurtz got off the boat. He split from the whole fucking program. How did that happen? What did he see here that first tour?" Shown at night lighting a cigarette and shining a flashlight on the various documents in Kurtz's dossier, Willard's initial picture of his Other grows less negative. As he says himself, "The more I read and began to understand, the more I admired him."

Whereas Willard has been rather passive up to now, a first sign of his growing impatience with the military "bullshit," as he calls it, is his physically manhandling the sergeant at the supply camp along the river (identified by the sign as Transportation Company in SVC HAU PHAT), where they stop for fuel. Accompanying him, Chef, Lance, and Clean are happy to see the captain come alive when asserting himself. Soon, they're witnesses to "a bizarre sight," as Clean calls this station when they approach it, a surreal staging of Playboy Playmates appearing before the troops, which ends in total mayhem, much like the war itself. Witnessing the disastrous ending of the three-playmate circus, Willard's voice-over (silent during this stop at the first station) returns with growing appreciation of the enemy's determination to win the war: "Charlie didn't get much USO. He was dug in too deep or moving too fast. His idea of great R&R was cold rice and a little rat meat. He had only two ways home, death or victory." As does Willard himself.

Central Station

Willard's voice-over returns as they leave the first station on the morning after, taking sides with Kurtz in his fight with the military powers that be. "No wonder Kurtz put a weed up Command's ass. The war was being run by a bunch of four-star clowns who were gonna end up giving the whole circus away."

The circus continues as two friendly PBRs pass by Willard's boat, going the other way. The first one plays chicken, coming as close to the PBR as possible; a flare is thrown from the second boat, burning the PBR's canopy. Lance and Chef's replacing it with the palm leaves, accompanied by Clean's drumming, is another sign of their leaving civilization behind, the closer they get to the heart of darkness. This change, this going native, is mostly mirrored by Lance, who is shown applying camouflage on his face, telling Chief, "So they can't see you. They're everywhere, Chief." His deterioration is accompanied by Willard's reading about Kurtz's not "unjustified" killings of the four "double agents," *two* of whom "were colonels in the South Vietnamese army," and his letter to his son explaining his actions. Finding a picture of a shadowy silhouette, believed "to be Col. W. E. Kurtz," Willard is shown looking at the shadowy Other that Kurtz represents for him, and is transfixed by what he sees.

The closer they get to Kurtz, the more signs they see of the war's mayhem. Chief, who tries to keep his crew in line, goes too far when, going by the book, he stops a sampan for "a routine check." Willard tries to talk him out of it, saying, "Let's forget routine now and let them go." But Chief cannot forget routine, he says, letting Willard know who's really in charge: "Until we reach your destination, Captain, you're just on for the ride." With Chef once again off the boat and Chief insisting that he check everything, their search turns into a horrific massacre, a literal *search and destroy*, as the nervous and trigger-happy Clean opens fire when a woman suddenly runs toward something in the boat. Once again, it's the irresponsible trio of Clean, Chef, and Lance who open fire.

All crew members are clearly horrified by their action, particularly when realizing the woman was running after a puppy. The incident is also a turning point for Willard, who finally asserts himself on the PBR when shooting the wounded woman Chief wants to take for medical treatment, telling him, "I told you not to stop. Now let's go." As he says afterward, this change is linked to his getting to know his Other: "Those boys were never gonna look at me the same way again. But I felt like I knew one or two things about Kurtz that weren't in the dossier."

Reinforcing the notion that Willard's shooting the woman is a turning point, it's followed by the fade-out and the rather lengthy dark screen that signals a new chapter. Just as the movie opened with the sound of helicopters over a dark screen, now we hear the chugging of the PBR as its silhouetted form fades in, sailing up the river under the sunset's fiery red sky, reflected in the river's water as if sailing infernal waters. Willard's narration, which foreshadows Kurtz's "There's nothing that I detest more than the stench of lies," completes the picture. "It was the way we had over here of living with ourselves. We'd cut them in half with a machine gun and give them a Band-Aid. It was a lie, and the more I saw of them, the more I hated lies."

Approaching the second station of the Do Luong Bridge, the "last army outpost on the Nung River," Willard and the crew seem to have arrived at what seems like Dante's *Inferno*. They're stunned by the devastation and desolation they witness, particularly the desperate soldiers who wade in the river like the doomed and tormented souls in Dante's Hell, begging to be taken home by the PBR, which sails by like Dante and Virgil crossing the Acheron River. As the lieutenant who delivers their mail informs Willard, "You're in the asshole of the world, Captain!"

Willard, accompanied by Lance, goes ashore looking for fuel and information. The overall chaos they encounter, part of which is conveyed as experienced by Lance high on the acid he had dropped earlier, envisions what's meant by *war is hell*. But however horrific, it's purgatory compared to the hell Willard finds at Kurtz's compound. Hell, of course, is the unconscious underworld, dwelling place of the Other. As Willard speaks of this central station, "Beyond that, there was only Kurtz."

Inner Station

The brief dark screen that separates their leaving behind the Do Luong Bridge and their moving farther up the river into the primeval Cambodian interior announces the uncharted territory into which they're crossing. At first, while all but Chief are preoccupied with the mail they received, it's almost as if they're back home. Chef reads how his woman "pictures me at home having a beer and watching TV"; the stoned Lance thinks that where they are is "better than Disneyland"; Clean plays the cassette tape he received from his mother. Willard, on the other hand, is informed by the message he received of "a new development regarding" the captain, who had taken the "identical" mission before him and was now "with Colonel Kurtz," as though under his spell.

For a while, all is peaceful. But considering what follows, it's merely the proverbial calm before the storm. As if made to pay for the senseless massacre (Clean for opening fire on the sampan's occupants, Chief for deciding to stop and search it in the first place), the two black crewmen, the "shadowy" others in the white-black pairings, are killed in two attacks, one after the other. Clean is killed in the first attack from the river bank while the tape from his mother, in which she hopes he'd "stay out of the way of the bullets," keeps playing. Except for the delirious Lance, who's concerned with losing his puppy during the attack, the others are stunned by his death. The usually tough Chief, like his binary opposite before him, undergoes his own breakdown.

Following Clean's death, they enter yet another circle of hell, this one signaled by the thick impenetrable fog and the distant voices coming from the river bank. Their crossing ever deeper into the jungle's primitive darkness is best conveyed by Lance's animal-like howling. Having crossed to the other side, he doesn't utter a word for the remainder of the movie. His going native, dancing in loin cloth and all, is truly, in Conrad's words, "go[ing] ashore for a howl and a dance."

Chief, who "can't see nothing" in the thick fog, announces, "We're stopping." Only this time, no longer the man he was before they stopped to search the sampan, or before Clean was killed, Willard takes charge. "You're not authorized to stop this boat," he says.

Chief tries a second time: "I said I can't see a thing, Captain. I'm stopping this boat. I ain't risking more lives."

But Willard, no longer "just on for the ride," reminds him in no uncertain terms, "I'm in command here, goddamn it. You'll do what *I* say."

As if saying the magic words, the fog clears to reveal the carnage and mayhem on the river banks, allowing Willard a glimpse of his Other: "He was close. He was real close. I couldn't see him yet, but I could feel him, as if the boat were being sucked upriver and the water was flowing back into the jungle. Whatever was going to happen, it wasn't gonna be the way they called it back in Nha Trang."

Just as they're out of the fog, they're attacked by a barrage of arrows, an attack which ends with a spear piercing Chief's chest, shot in such a way that it gives a fleeting impression that it hits Willard, as if Chief catches what was meant for Willard. Perhaps that's why he grabs Willard with his remaining strength, trying to choke him for getting "us into this mess," as he yelled at him just before he's hit. Or else, perhaps he sees the horror in Willard's face just as earlier he had said to him about where they're going, "One look at you and I know it's gonna be hot, wherever it is."

With Chief's death and Kurtz "real close," Willard decides to get off the boat and head into the jungle alone, though not before informing Chef of his mission. "That's fucking typical," Chef says in disbelief. Nonetheless, not wanting to be without the commanding officer, or alone with the delirious Lance, he proposes, "We'll go with you. We'll go up there, but on the boat." Now, with Chief killed by a spear, or lance, which is underscored by Lance wearing a broken arrow on his head (as if pierced through it) when ceremoniously putting Chief to rest in the river, Willard is the only one with his Other alive.

Heart of Darkness

Farther up the river, one after the other, Willard and the two remaining crewmen are each superimposed over the infernal spectacle they encounter on both sides of the river, revealing each one's reaction to what they see. Accompanied by eerie sounds, their awestruck looks suggest they've entered a strange and horrifying world. Willard, sensing his Other's closeness, is shown tossing the dossier's documents into the river, page by page, once again of two minds as he contemplates his *binary friend*: "Part of me was afraid of what I would find and what I would do when I got there. I knew the risks, or imagined I knew. But the thing I felt the most, much stronger than fear, was the desire to confront him."

Then, as if entering yet another circle in hell, the PBR is shown passing through a narrow strait in the fiery river that mirrors another sunset. This entrance is envisioned by the superimposition of the giant stone face on the left side of the screen. As a gargoyle of sorts, this iconic image of the Other recalls both the superimposed stone face at the movie's beginning and Willard's upside-down face on the same side of the screen.

Judging by the reception the three receive when approaching Kurtz's compound, particularly by the American photojournalist (Dennis Hopper), who informs them that "it's all been approved," Kurtz, the Other who "knew more about what I was going to do than I did," knows of Willard's arrival. He not only makes Willard wait, he puts him through a series of rituals taken straight from James Frazer's *The Golden Bough* and Jessie L. Weston's *From Ritual to Romance*, the two books singled out later when Willard's eyes wander over his captor's belongings, two books about rites of sacrificial death and redemption that inspired T. S. Eliot's *The Wasteland*, two books that explain why the ailing and mentally unsound Kurtz accepts what Weston called "the ceremonial slaying of the monarch."[8] Kurtz himself all but ties it together by quoting from Eliot's "The Hollow Men," a poem whose epigraph, "Mistah Kurtz — he dead," cites Conrad's *Heart of Darkness*.

When Willard asks to speak to the colonel, the unnamed photojournalist informs him, "You don't *talk* to the Colonel. You *listen* to him." Indeed, more than a physical presence, Kurtz is a voice, the voice of the Other that had "put the hook" into Willard in the first place. But instead of meeting his Other in his first venture off the boat (with Chef), Willard is confronted by his own predecessor, Captain Colby (Scott Glenn), who looks as if he had confronted the Other's horror and has been petrified ever since.

The second time Willard goes ashore, this time with the far-gone Lance, his voice-over describes the madness he sees: "Everything I saw told me that Kurtz has gone insane. The place was full of bodies: North Vietnamese, Vietcong, Cambodians. If I was still alive, it was because he wanted it that way." Having said that, he's surrounded by Kurtz's "children," who turn him upside-down (recalling how he was first shown in his hotel room in Saigon) and roll him in mud. Only after this primeval baptism, this symbolic rite of death by hanging, is he taken to Kurtz. Willard himself alludes to death (by malaria?) when, in one continuous shot, he's brought to Kurtz and made to kneel with his hands tied behind his back. "It smelled like slow death in there, malaria, nightmares," he says. "It was the end of the river, all right."

Like the ailing Fisher King in the Grail legend, before we (and Willard) hear Kurtz's voice, we hear his coughing, the first sign of his illness. As the camera moves in toward Kurtz lying in his bed, shrouded in darkness, he addresses his visitor by name: "Where are you from, Willard?" Hearing he's from Ohio, and that he lived 200 miles from the Ohio River, Kurtz connects the two by recounting an experience he had while going "down that river when I was a kid," where for "about five miles you'd think that heaven just fell on earth in the form of gardenias," which evokes Willard's other river, the "river that snaked through war like a main circuit cable, plugged straight into Kurtz." The connection between the two is envisioned by Kurtz's partly shown bald head at the left side of the screen, the same side in which Willard was initially shown.

The connection made, Kurtz sits up and sprinkles water on his (feverish?) head before continuing, "Have you ever considered any real freedoms? Freedoms from the opinion of others? Even the opinions of yourself?" Once again addressing Willard by name, he gets to the point. "They say why, Willard, why they wanted to terminate my command?" When he asks directly, "Are you an assassin?" Willard (who had heard the recorded Kurtz ask "What do you call it when the assassins accuse the assassin?") evades the question by claiming he's "a soldier." But Kurtz doesn't relent. "You're neither. You're an errand boy, sent by grocery clerks to collect the bill." Coming from his Other, he may well be saying, "You're far from free when you serve others' projections, even the projections of yourself."

Kurtz's train of thought continues in the subsequent scene, which opens with the camera following the photojournalist as he heads toward a narrow bamboo cage in which Willard is now imprisoned. Giving Willard water, he rephrases Kurtz's words, "Why would a nice guy like you wanna kill a genius?" As Kurtz's errand boy, the "dying" king's fool informs Willard, "He's got something in mind for you." But Willard isn't ready for that "something." At least, not yet. He still has to undergo another rite. The photojournalist's observation, "He is clear in his mind but his soul is mad," a line straight from Conrad, alerts Willard to the Other he's up against.

Come nighttime, with rain falling and Willard tied to a stake as if to a cross, to his great horror, Kurtz tosses Chef's decapitated head in his lap. Not without poetic irony, the severed head recalls the photojournalist's reciting the beginning of Kipling's famous poem, "If," while sharing the frame with Chef, "If you can keep your head when all about you / Are losing theirs ..."

"Oh, Christ!" Willard cries out when seeing the head, which evokes the severed head of John the Baptist, his body collapsing as if surrendering to a more powerful force. That this is part of a ceremonial rite is suggested by Kurtz's face, for once fully shown but under a mask of camouflage, thus mirroring his clear mind but mad soul. On the one hand, he kills Chef before he radios for the airstrike; on the other, the act itself is mad. For Kurtz it may be just another decapitated head, but for Willard it's horrifying. As he had said about Kurtz, "This time it was an American."

That for Willard this horrifying experience signals a new chapter, a new life, is suggested by the subsequent shot of the dawn upon which his anguished face is superimposed. Now, the golden light reflected in the river, replacing the former fiery red of hell, suggests a resurrection, particularly as, coming after his "Oh, Christ," Willard is carried to a bed in Kurtz's living quarters in a manner that recalls the Pieta.

After some time, when Willard has recuperated, Kurtz is shown reciting from Eliot's "The Hollow Men," the poem's "We" standing in for the two of them. Having done his part as a go-between, the photojournalist, paraphrasing another Eliot poem, "And with a whimper I'm fucking splitting," departs and is never seen again. Now it comes down to Willard and Kurtz, to the projector and his Other. But as Willard discovers, it's one thing to imagine his Other; it's another thing to confront him face to face. "On the river, I thought that the minute I looked at him, I'd know what to do, but it didn't happen," he admits. "I was in there with him for days, not under guard — I was free — but he knew I wasn't going anywhere. He knew more about what I was going to do than I did."

Kurtz himself may well be speaking of the Other when saying to Willard, "I've seen horrors, horrors that you've seen." Likewise, he alludes to Willard's projections when saying, "You have a right to kill me. You have a right to do that. But you have no right to judge me." Having reached his end, all he wants is to be seen for who he is, without judgment, without projections. To make his point, he returns to the *binary friend*: "Horror has a face, and you must make a friend of horror. Horror and moral terror are your friends. If they are not then they are enemies to be feared. They are truly enemies." Then, speaking from another personal experience, of the Viet Cong's hacking off the children's inoculated arms, he all but tells Willard that he can only kill his Other by withdrawing his projections: "You have to have men who are moral and at the same time who are able to utilize their primordial instincts to kill without feeling, without passion, without judgment. Without judgment. Because it's judgment that defeats us."

In his last will and testament, Kurtz appeals to Willard as one who could understand him, as one who could see him beyond judgment and lies, beyond his and others' projections. "I worry that my son might not understand what I've tried to be. And if I were to be killed, Willard, I would want someone to go to my home and tell my son everything you saw. Because there is nothing I detest more than the stench of lies. And if you understand me, Willard, you'll do this for me."

Shown next, the whole preparation of the sacrificial rite is sandwiched between two similar shots of Kurtz standing by the temple's entrance, overseeing the whole thing like a high priest. With Lance clad only in loincloth and taking part in the sacrificial ritual, his going completely native mirrors Willard's *getting off the boat*. Or as he puts it after not replying to headquarters on the radio and literally slipping off the PBR and into the river, "They were going to make me a major for this and I wasn't even in their fucking army any more."

That terminating Kurtz for Willard represents his killing his own unconscious Other is suggested by his last words in the movie, in which he realizes that Kurtz "really took his orders from" the unconscious jungle. "Everybody wanted me to do it, him most of all. I felt like he was up there, waiting for me to take the pain away.... Even the jungle wanted him dead, and that's who he really took his orders from anyway." Willard's readiness to kill Kurtz is mirrored by Lance smearing blood on the sacrificial animal's head, which is followed by a shot of Willard's head emerging from the river's dark water. Both their faces are masked by camouflage, as was Kurtz's face when tossing Chef's decapitated head into Willard's lap. Kurtz himself, having overseen the preparations for the sacrifice from the entrance to his temple, turns around and heads inside.

Underscoring the significance of Willard's killing Kurtz, it's juxtaposed with the sacrificial slaughtering of the bull and accompanied once again by

The Door's "The End." As in Conrad's *Heart of Darkness*, Kurtz's dying words, "The horror! The horror!" are the words of one who had more than a glimpse of his own mad soul, his own heart of darkness. That by killing his Other Willard has come to terms with his own heart of darkness is envisioned by his taking Kurtz's journal, his last will and testament, back to civilization under one arm and taking the deranged Lance back to the PBR by the other.

Shown leaving Kurtz's compound in the PBR, Willard's camouflaged face fades in at the center of the screen, his state of mind mirrored one last time by showing Lance's camouflaged face cleansed by the falling rain. No longer "in their fucking army," no longer at the service of their projections, Willard, after silencing the voice of his Other, turns off the radio, the voice of the "Almighty."

In one final shot, and one final envisioning of the unconscious Other, after the PBR is shown on the river, heading back, the face of the stone statue fades in on the right side of the screen. Then, as Willard's camouflaged face fades in at the center of the screen, the superimposed PBR on the river is replaced by superimposing the *expovision*'s burning forest and helicopters. Finally, Willard's superimposed face merges with the superimposed face of the stone statue as Kurtz's final words, "The horror! The horror!" echo in his mind. As his face fades from the scene, the face of the stone statue, icon of the Other, is all that remains on the right side of the screen until it, too, fades out, thus ending with the same dark screen that opened the movie, envisioning both America's and Willard's heart of darkness.

13

The Lives of Others:
The Others of Our Lives

The shock is not that an Other exists, but that you realize that you are an Other for other Others.
— Morris Berman, Coming to Our Senses

Wiesler's Other

The double entendre that clinches *The Lives of Others*, Gerd Wiesler's "It's for me," sums up Florian Henckel von Donnersmarck's movie in more ways than one. The book Wiesler is buying, *Sonata for a Good Man*, is both intended for and dedicated to him. Its author, as the movie suggests from start to finish, is Wiesler's Other, the personified part of himself he denies and suppresses in his perfunctory semblance of life, what Daniel Deardorff calls "the 'Other' who stands at the margin within society and at once at the edge of consciousness within each individual."[1]

The Other, of course, or the *Doppelgänger*, is no stranger to German cinema. Borrowed from the Romantic literature of the early 19th century, it was one of the central motifs in early German films, which pioneered the use of the double. A prime example of this motif, as Otto Rank had pointed out in *The Double*, is *The Student of Prague*, both the Stellan Rye's 40-minute version discussed by Rank and Henrik Galeen's feature from 1926. At this early stage of the cinematic *Doppelgänger*, the two silent movies followed the *Jekyll and Hyde* formula. Much as Hyde is Jekyll's other *side*, the student Balduin's *Doppelgänger* is his mirror reflection, an autonomous being who steps out of his mirror. But where Hyde changed into Jekyll when shot dead, Balduin dies when shooting "the other" (as it's called in both films) who vanishes as if it had never existed.

The German *Lives of Others* from 2006 is another story. Like the title character in *Desperately Seeking Susan*, Georg Dreyman personifies Wiesler's bright shadow, mirroring the other person he could be. In dedicating the book to Wiesler, Dreyman all but echoes Susan's words to Roberta, "Good goin', Stranger." Bearing in mind the film's recurring pairs of light and dark and other tropes of binary opposites, this dedication from Wiesler's Other is the movie's final sign that *The Lives of Others* is essentially about the Others of our lives.

Bookend One (Exposition)

Following the dark screen that opens *The Lives of Others*, the story's pairs of binary opposites are introduced by the sound of two distinct pairs of footsteps before two figures are shown from behind, one in uniform, the other in civilian clothing, walking down a corridor (identified as the Stasi's Temporary Detention Center), whose two-toned walls match the colors of their clothing. The uniformed man, walking erect, is escorting the comparatively stooped civilian by the arm as they pass from the corridor's lighted area to a shadowy one, then to another lighted one. However subtle, this sequence of light, shadow, and light foreshadows the three chapters of Wiesler's life: (1) idealistic young student; (2) the "bad" man he is when we first meet him; (3) the "good" man he becomes in the course of monitoring his Other. In fact, like the name of Georg Dreyman's book, *Sonata for a Good Man*, *The Lives of Others* is structured like the sonata's three-part form: exposition, development, and recapitulation.

Still in the opening shot, as the two men pass through the corridor's shadowy area, the subtitle "November 1984" appears briefly on the screen, bringing to mind Orwell's futuristic novel of Big Brother. When the red lights along the corridor come on accompanied by a loud buzzer, the uniformed man stops the civilian. This "double" warning signals that another pair of military man escorting a civilian is crossing the other (perpendicular) corridor. These two pairs, one in the foreground, the other in the background, foreshadow the binary opposites that are at the heart of the movie: Wiesler and Dreyman at center stage; Wiesler and Grubitz in the backdrop. Once the other pair is out of sight, the military man continues leading the civilian down the corridor. When they stop by one of the corridor's many doors, the civilian is instructed to address the person on its other side as "Captain."

13. The Lives of Others

The binary images continue on the other side of the door as a hand (of the Captain) is shown switching on the reel-to-reel tape recorder that dominates the screen, and by the two men — the interrogating captain in military uniform and the civilian undergoing interrogation — who face each other from opposite sides of two tables. As binary opposites, the two are repeatedly shown in symmetrical shots. Moreover, suggesting that Captain Gerd Wiesler (Ulrich Muhe) is ostensibly interrogating his mirrored Other, the initials of the name he gets the suspect to reveal, W.G., are his own initials in reverse.

In keeping with the opening shot's twos and pairs, the interrogation sequence is conveyed in two parts, both opening with a close-up of two reel-to-reel tape recorders, cinematically perpendicular to each other. While the real interrogation commences with Wiesler turning on the first tape recorder, the lesson that uses the interrogation as a teaching tool is taken up as he presses the other machine's "stop" button. This jump from the actual interrogation to the one played back transports us to the second part of the exposition, itself divided into two parts: the classroom and the replayed interrogation. Underscoring their difference, the classroom sequences are shown in natural light (like the original interrogation) while the replayed segments of the interrogation are envisioned in a golden light that evokes the theater.

Surveying the classroom's students, the camera pans from left to right, coming to a pair of young students sitting at the end of the second row. The student on the left is wearing a dark turtleneck sweater; the one on the right is in a light shirt. Shown together twice, in the second shot the student in the light shirt questions Wiesler's humanity in using sleep deprivation to break down a suspect. Wiesler, noting the student, marks a tiny "x" next to his name in the name map. The marked student, singled out in two identical shots, seems to remind Wiesler of himself as he was 20 years before. The first shot shows him with his eyes looking down, as if bowing to Wiesler's interrogation tactics. In the second shot, he speaks the teacher's mind in answering his "Do you notice anything about his statement?" with, "It's the same as at the beginning."

The other student, sitting to the marked student's left, may well remind Wiesler of young Grubitz (Ulrich Tukur), who appears at the end of his lesson, applauding as if in a theater, reminding his long-time friend that 20 years earlier they sat where his students sit today. The next time they're shown together in the Stasi headquarters, in the cafeteria, Grubitz takes down a young man's name for telling a joke about party boss Erich Honecker. This young man, whom Grubitz forces to continue the joke he started telling his co-workers, seems to remind Grubitz of the young, rebellious youth he had once been. But more than making fun of Honecker's inflated egoism and illustrating how others in the party really see him, Honecker's three greetings to the sun in the morning, noon, and evening (like the three areas of light and shadow in the opening shot) are another allusion to the three chapters of Wiesler's life.

The way Wiesler is repeatedly shown looking at Grubitz in this episode, particularly the rather long shot that closes the segment, is not so very different from the way Honecker is depicted in the young man's joke. Revealing a marked difference between the two old friends, this second meeting is the beginning of their falling out, as Wiesler's eyes are increasingly opened over a period of days as he "watches" his Other, until he ends up, banished, in the same basement as the young joker.

Following the classroom scene, the theater segment also begins with a dark screen, in which the audience is heard settling into their seats. The opening shot showing Wiesler and Grubitz sitting down in two box seats, which mirrors the shot of the two students in Wiesler's classroom, reinforces the notion that one pair stands for the other. Now Wiesler is on the left side in a dark suit; Grubitz, shown straightening his tie, is on the right in a light suit.

Having given Wiesler a "ticket of passage" to the theater, a place where he first sees his Other, Grubitz hands him the binoculars as soon as they're seated, so he can have a closer look at Minister Hempf, who's sitting "at one o'clock." As Grubitz is quick to point out, Hempf "really cleaned up the theater scene," much as Wiesler has cleaned up his now-sterile life. But as demonstrated by the applause given to Dreyman upon entering a side gallery, no one else notices Hempf, particularly Wiesler, who is at once struck by the sight of the playwright, sitting (apparently) at *two* o'clock. His labeling Dreyman "an arrogant type, the kind I warn my students about," underscores his immediate suspicion and his uncomfortable identification with the playwright.

Wiesler's suspicion, of course, is not surprising. Georg Dreyman (Sebastian Koch) is everything he's not. He's handsome, admired, and successful. He's his binary opposite, his Other. That's why Wiesler reacts so negatively when he sees him. Binary opposites may attract, but for Wiesler, rather than love, it's suspicion at first sight. Just as "psychoanalysis has long been disposed to regard the voice of the dream as the utterance of a true self, the Other interpreter of our being, and to regard our conscious subjectivity with suspicion,"[2] Wiesler regards his Other with immediate suspicion, never suspecting his own "conscious subjectivity," his own conscious projections.

As the lights dim and the curtain opens on Dreyman's play, Grubitz invites Wiesler to see for himself that Dreyman is not the person he suspects him to be. But more than seeing *for* himself, Wiesler sees *himself*, mirrored in the play penned by his Other, a situation not unlike what Christopher

Bollas calls "the dream space as a night theatre involving the subject in a vivid re-acquaintance with the Other ... offering a place for this interplay of self and Other."[3] Turned around, as reflected in a mirror, with the "drama space" replacing the "dream space," for Wiesler Dreyman's play is "where the Other takes the subject's day narrative and transforms it into a night fiction, so that the subject is compelled to re-experience his life according to the voice of the unconscious."[4]

That the play is about the "interplay of self and Other" is evoked by the two prominent fluorescent lights that hang high above center stage and by the two-shot ending of Marta, played by Christa-Maria (Martina Gedeck), dancing with the play's older lead female. Like Dreyman's book, the play itself speaks both *to* and *for* Wiesler, particularly the part in which Marta speaks of the big wheel and her inescapable visions in a four-shot sequence sandwiched between the two shots of his watching. The import of her words, "Why am I not spared these visions?" is highlighted by the close-up she receives, the sole close-up shown of the play. Like her, Wiesler is also "not spared these visions" in the course of monitoring her partner in life. *Hearing* Dreyman ("voice of the unconscious") through the headphones rather than *seeing* him, Wiesler can only *envision* him in his imagination, in his "night theater," where the unconscious Other comes to life.

In the second theater segment, the play's after party, the opening shot of Christa-Maria dancing with Dreyman, just as she had danced with the older woman at the end of the play, continues the pair motif that opened the preceding segments. But whereas the theater segment focused on Wiesler's fascination with Dreyman, the after party focuses on Hempf's (Thomas Thieme) obsession with Christa-Maria. Recalling the pairing of Wiesler and Grubitz in the theater, the minister and his driver are singled out in two shots which show them glaring at the dancing couple, their legs open wide in a rather suggestive (obscene) pose, particularly Hempf, whose folded hands may be covering his desire for the actress. Doubling for these two shots, Wiesler and Grubitz are paired in the scene's last two shots, once again observing as if it's all part of the drama.

As a an epilogue to this opening night, Wiesler and Grubitz are paired one last time when they're shown heading home in the latter's car. Once Wiesler arrives in his apartment, we see its functional lifelessness that mirrors his sterile life. This is contrasted by the very next sequence that shows Dreyman playing street soccer with three neighborhood children. Of course, with Wiesler starting his surveillance, the two boys and girl may very well anticipate the "binary" *ménage à trois* that develops as he monitors the couple. His seeing Dreyman and Christa-Maria (through their apartment window) embracing and kissing, much as he had seen them through the open door in the theater, marks the end of the movie's *opening bookend* and the beginning of the "night fiction," the middle part, in which Wiesler monitors his Other. The next time he *sees* the two lovers together, in an event that marks the end of the surveillance, it's from practically the same spot in the street, thus ending the "night fiction" where it starts.

Night Fiction (Development)

The "night fiction" segment, like the scenes in the opening "bookend," is divided into two parts. The first part focuses on Wiesler's relationship with Dreyman; the second, on his relationship with Christa-Maria. As if he has "night fiction" on his mind, the more Wiesler gets involved in his Other's life in the course of his surveillance, the more *fictional* he makes his typed reports.

Developing what was introduced in the opening bookend, the "night fiction" segment conveys the binary opposition between Wiesler and his Other through a number of cinematic props. The most prominent one, no doubt, and the one that best depicts the dichotomy between the two, is the emblematic tie, which is already evoked in the opening interrogation, when only the uniformed Wiesler wears a tie. While in the course of the story Wiesler doesn't wear a tie on two occasions (during his appointment with the prostitute and when he buys Dreyman's book), his Other is twice shown wearing his tie, at his birthday party and at Albert Jerska's (Volkmar Kleinert) funeral, two opposite occasions that mark birth and death.

As the best interpreter of Dreyman's plays, as one who had once brought his words to life on the stage, Jerska is Dreyman's Other just as Dreyman is Wiesler's. This relationship is underscored in their two meetings, the only two occasions in which Jerska is shown (*sans* tie). In the first meeting, in his room, Jerska all but points to being Dreyman's Other when confiding in him, "I can't bear those fat, dressed-up people at premieres anymore.... In my next life, I'll simply be an author. A happy author who can write whenever he wants. Like you." On the second occasion, at the birthday party in Dreyman's apartment, Jerska's Otherness is largely conveyed by how the two are envisioned while sharing a couch. Whereas one is wearing a tie and one is not, each is shown against another half of the giant picture in the background, occupying opposite sides of both the picture and the movie screen, with the two lamps on either side of the screen recalling the two fluorescent lamps in the play while adding to the *mise en scène* of binary opposites.

When Dreyman asks Jerska, "Did you really come here to read?" and Jerska replies, "It is Brecht," the camera cuts to the listening Wiesler, who's shown writing down what his Other's Other pointed out. The fact that the

Brecht book finds its way to Wiesler, who becomes a behind-the-scenes director of Dreyman's life, suggests that the director's role is passed on to him, particularly as Dreyman is shown receiving the news of Jerska's suicide immediately after Wiesler is shown reading the stolen book.

With all that's *tied* to the tie, its outright significance is made clear in the exchange between Christa-Maria and Dreyman before the guests arrive for his birthday party, an occasion in which the playwright is the only one shown wearing a tie.

> *Christa-Maria*: Don't forget, you promised to wear a tie for your birthday.
>
> *Dreyman*: I would, but I don't have one.
>
> *Christa-Maria (presenting him with her gift)*: Happy birthday.
>
> *Dreyman*: A tie?
>
> *Christa-Maria*: You said you didn't want any books. Or can't you tie a tie, you working-class poet?
>
> *Dreyman*: What? I was born wearing a tie! I had to "fight my way out of my middle-class fetters."
>
> *Christa-Maria*: Then put those fetters on again, just for me.

But the "working-class poet" doesn't know how to tie a tie. By chance, or by *deus ex machina*, he hears his next-door neighbor coming up the stairs, and asks her to tie his tie for him. "It'll be our secret," he tells her when seeing (in the mirror) the tie tied around his neck. "You can keep a secret, right?" he asks the woman, who earlier was advised by Wiesler to keep her mouth shut about seeing his men coming out of Dreyman's apartment after installing the secret microphones. Shown twice, this sharer of the two's secrets is another connection between the two "secret sharers." That's why, immediately following Wiesler's knocking on her door and ringing the buzzer, Dreyman is shown pressing the buzzer of Jerska's apartment. Underscoring its significance in Wiesler's transformation, the tie segment falls on his first surveillance shift.

Another prop that illustrates the binary opposition between Wiesler and Dreyman is the masculine tie's counterpart, the round (feminine) ball, shown twice (once with each of the two). Where the playful playwright plays ball with the neighborhood children, Wiesler is not as playful when a little boy from his apartment building, following his rolled ball, gets into the elevator with him, though their brief exchange shows him playing ball as best he can. Ironically, precisely when he doesn't act as a "bad man," when he asks for "the name of your ball" rather than the name of the boy's father, the boy all but calls him such, holding up a mirror which shows how others see him. Nonetheless, confronted by the innocent boy, it's the first time Wiesler is shown not playing the "bad man."

Linking Dreyman's *playing* ball with the children, this second time in the elevator for Wiesler follows his hearing the playwright *playing* on the piano the *Sonata for a Good Man* score he had received from Jerska for his birthday, which he plays after hearing of the director's suicide. While Jerska's suicide initiates Dreyman's waking up, his "taking action," Wiesler's brief encounter with the boy depicts the inner transformation he's undergoing.

Wiesler's not intervening as a "bad man" is directly opposite to his intervening as a "good man" in Dreyman's life, when he sees (for the second time) Christa-Maria getting out of Hempf's black limousine. Warned by Grubitz (after the first time) that he cannot report such things about their superiors, Wiesler sides with his Other by "calling" Dreyman to the entrance door so that he may witness Christa-Maria's betrayal. As she enters the building, Dreyman stands next to the entrance wall so as not to be seen. Later on, in his last intervention (and the last sign of his transformation), when he saves Dreyman by lifting the typewriter from its hiding place ahead of Grubitz, Wiesler hides in the exact same place when Dreyman enters the apartment building.

Much like the revealing tie and ball, Wiesler's inner transformation is revealed by two works of art, both associated with Jerska: the Brecht book and the *Sonata for a Good Man*. The book Wiesler gets immediately after his tryst with the prostitute, when he's last shown reclining on his couch, spent but unfulfilled, seeming to compare his situation with Dreyman in bed with Christa-Maria. What's more, as if wanting to share this intimacy a second time, upon entering the two's apartment to lift the book, he's shown by the couple's bed, touching the linen. When shown next, immediately after Dreyman asks Christa-Maria if she saw his Brecht book, Wiesler is lying on the same couch in his apartment, captivated by one of the book's poems. Wiesler's inner transformation is further advanced by the second work of art, the score for the *Sonata for a Good Man*, which he hears in his subsequent shift, when Dreyman's playing moves him to tears.

Even though (or perhaps because) the two are binary opposites, Wiesler never meets Dreyman face to face in the course of the movie. But in the second part of the "night fiction" he meets his partner in life, the actress who gives voice to the playwright's words. In fact, true to form, he meets her twice. Once as "a good man," as she calls him in the pub; once as a "bad man," when he interrogates the actress in the Stasi Temporary Detention Center.

In the first encounter, deeply disturbed by what he had heard between Dreyman and Christa-Maria (the playwright pleading with her not to go to meet the un-named Hempf), Wiesler enters a pub and asks for soda water but quickly changes it to "Vodka. Double." The doubles continue when, just as he picks up his second double, Christa-Maria, in a light shirt, enters and sits down at an adjacent table to Wiesler, who is wearing a dark coat. When the actress downs her cognac in one shot, Wiesler, as if working up the nerve after her drink, approaches her table, addressing her as "Ms. Sieland."

Looking up, Christa-Maria asks, "Do we know each other?"

Wiesler, looking down at the sitting actress and echoing Dreyman, speaks like her knowing shadow: "You don't know *me*, but *I* know *you*. Many people love you for who you are." Allowing himself to sit at her table, Wiesler, facing the actress from the other side, continues speaking as her knowing shadow: "I've seen you on stage." He shakes uncontrollably, barely getting the words out. "You were more who you are than you are now."

"So, you know what I'm like," Christa-Maria counters.

"I'm your audience," he speaks in double entendre.

When the actress has heard enough and gets up to leave, Wiesler, back to his familiar interrogating self, asks, "Where to?" Christa-Maria, feeling she owes her audience an answer, repeats the lie she told Dreyman, that she's "meeting an old classmate."

But Wiesler, speaking as her "true self, the *Other* interpreter of [her] being," stops her with his piercing words: "You see? Just now you weren't being yourself."

The actress, sitting back down and removing her sunglasses, retorts, "So you think you know her well, this Christa-Maria Sieland. What do you think? Would she hurt someone who loves her above all else? Would she sell herself for art?"

"For *art*?" Wiesler replies. "You already have art. That'd be a bad deal. You are a great artist. Don't you know that?"

The actress, after a brief pause, repays Wiesler while foreshadowing his Other's very same words: "And you are a good man."

Wiesler learns what his words to Christa-Maria had put into action when, in his next surveillance shift, he reads his assistant's latest report. Glad to learn that the actress had returned to Dreyman, and apparently still under the influence of her calling him "a good man," he commends the surprised and bewildered assistant, "Good report." Only as things turn out, Wiesler's words initiate the machinations that bring the two together for their second encounter, under entirely other circumstances. Her choosing Dreyman over Hempf prompts the minister to have the actress arrested and brought before Grubitz for questioning regarding Dreyman. Though Grubitz fails to get the desired results from the actress, he's sharp enough to order Wiesler to the interrogation center and has him sit on the same sweat-stained chair (which receives a close-up) in which his suspect sat at the story's opening. Suspecting Wiesler of covering up for Dreyman, whom he suspects of writing the *Spiegel* article about East Germany's unreported suicides, Grubitz asks the "good man," "Are you still on the right side?" But as Wiesler's long-time friend, he offers him "one last chance" to redeem himself by getting the truth out of Christa-Maria, not without adding a warning, "Don't screw it up again."

In the second interrogation for both Wiesler and Christa-Maria, and with the tables turned in more ways than one, the "good man" reveals his "right side." Hearing approaching footsteps in the corridor, he turns on his swivel chair so that his back is to the door when Christa-Maria is escorted into the interrogation room and sits down in the same chair he had occupied earlier. "So you're my commanding officer? Then command me," she says with what can be taken as either arrogance or resignation, or both. But the slight smirk on her face changes when Wiesler, slowly turning around in his chair, reveals his face. Despite his position of power, his expression betrays his anxiety in meeting his idol under these completely different circumstances. Christa-Maria looks down in double disappointment — disappointment in herself and in the man who seemed so direct and truthful in their first encounter. Whereas then, Wiesler had told the "great actress" the truth about herself, now he threatens that she may never appear onstage again.

As shown in the opening interrogation, Wiesler once again peels away Christa-Maria's resistance layer by layer, until she seems to have fallen under his spell, ready to follow his command to reveal the whereabouts of Dreyman's incriminating typewriter. Drawing his second map of Dreyman's apartment, he orders her to mark the spot with "a cross."

Though not shown, Wiesler redeems himself not by getting Christa-Maria to reveal where the typewriter is hidden but by removing it from its hiding place before Grubitz and his men can find it. As he's about to leave through the door of Dreyman's apartment, Wiesler spots the playwright outside and hides against the wall precisely as Dreyman had done when he had sent him to the door as Christa-Maria was returning from her tryst with Hempf. As that was Wiesler's first intervention in the life of his Other, now, in his final and most penetrating intervention, he takes his Other's place in this one-sided relationship, momentarily becoming one with his Other.

Whereas the whole surveillance was initiated by Hempf because he wanted the playwright out of the way so he can have Christa-Maria for himself, Wiesler's intervention has the opposite results. Shown returning home from the interrogation before Grubitz and his men arrive, and immediately taking a shower (her second), the actress comes out in a white bathrobe precisely when Grubitz, in his second search of the apartment, is about to remove the doorsill. "Could it be a secret compartment?" he asks the stunned Dreyman, who's shown looking accusingly at Christa-Maria. In a brief but tense four-shot sequence, in which each one is shown twice, the two face each other without a word, their expressions alone speaking volumes.

Unable to face Dreyman, Christa-Maria runs out of the apartment before

Grubitz can lift the doorsill, only to find the secret compartment empty. Ironically, and tragically, Christa-Maria is spared this vision. But Dreyman is not, and the look on his face changes from accusatory to gratitude as he imagines that rather than betray him, Christa-Maria had saved him by removing the incriminating evidence. While the two shots, the before and after, reveal the two sides of Dreyman, in both shots one side of his face is in light, the other in shadow.

Cutting to the street outside, showing Wiesler standing by his car parked across the street from Dreyman's apartment, he's surprised to see the actress walk out in her white bathrobe. But he's utterly stunned when he sees her stop in the middle of the street before an oncoming truck. Wiesler sees the actress (to borrow a line from her play) "crushed by the mighty wheel."

Horrified by what he has just witnessed, Wiesler rushes to the dying Christa-Maria, whose last words are her true confession: "I was too weak. I can never put right what I've done wrong."

Wiesler, trying to show her that he's "a good man" after all, assures her, "There's nothing to put right," as *he* had moved the typewriter. But hearing Dreyman coming, he stops in mid-sentence and steps aside so that his Other can take his place.

"Forgive me," Dreyman cries repeatedly (four times), holding Christa-Maria in his arms as she lay dying.

Bearing in mind the *two* that informs the movie, and Dreyman's replacing Wiesler with the dying actress, perhaps he speaks for the two of them, two "forgive me's" for each one. Particularly as the two comes up in the "twofold" mirrored image reminiscent of the Pieta, suggesting that the actress with the two significant names is "crucified" so that the two, Wiesler and Dreyman, may live as each other's Other.

The subsequent scene shows Wiesler driving Grubitz in his car just as Grubitz was shown driving Wiesler home following the play's after party. Whereas during the first ride Wiesler was eager to begin Dreyman's surveillance, now, with the surveillance finished, he emerges from the "night fiction" a changed (albeit disturbed) man. Wiesler's relationship with Grubitz, running diametrically opposed to his one-sided relationship with Dreyman, also comes to an end.

"There's one thing you should understand, Wiesler," Grubitz says. "Your career is over. You'll end up in some cellar, steam-opening letters until you retire. That means the next twenty years. Twenty years. That's a long time."

Only as suggested by the headline (and the picture) in the newspaper that Grubitz tosses on the car's front seat, announcing Gorbachev's election, times indeed "are a-changing." There's a resurrection after all, which perhaps explains Wiesler instructing Christa-Maria to put "a cross" on the spot where the incriminating typewriter was hidden.

Bookend Two (Recapitulation)

Four years and seven months later, Wiesler is indeed in "some cellar, steam-opening letters," which functions as the tomb in this East German passion play, while sitting behind him is the same young man who told the Honecker joke in the cafeteria, whose dark jacket counters Wiesler light one. Shown listening to the radio via his earphone, in this brief scene the young man embodies the former eavesdropper's binary opposite. At the same time, suggesting that the opposites are no longer divided, he announces, "The Wall has come down." Then, pausing to listen again, he confirms the news a second time: "Yes, the Wall has come down," as he hands Wiesler the earphone so he too can, to echo Grubitz, *hear* it for himself: "The border guards have opened the gates. The excitement is enormous! People are streaming out in thousands! It's unbelievable! Dear listeners, November ninth, nineteen-eighty-nine, will go down in history!" Wiesler doesn't share the announcer's excitement, at least not outwardly. But hearing the unbelievable news, exactly five years after he was shown in his first interrogation, he gets up and walks out of the basement, a man resurrected.

Shifting from one to the Other, the subsequent segment, two years later, focuses on Dreyman just as up to now the movie had focused on Wiesler. As a mirrored version of the first theater segment, in a recapitulation of sorts, it opens with a surveillance of the theater audience, reminiscent of the earlier shot of Wiesler's classroom. In both scenes, the camera pans from left to right until it comes to Dreyman, who's accompanied by another woman, while onstage a black actress is playing the part formerly played by Christa-Maria. Only now, perhaps because the name Marta is too much like Maria, she's called Elena. As she delivers the very same line in which the original actress received a close-up, "Why am I not spared these visions?" Dreyman, overcome with emotions, starts heading out. His hearing these words from a black actress, which recalls Christa-Maria's line as witnessed by Wiesler, is another sign of their being binary opposites, particularly as neither was spared the vision of the actress's tragic end.

In the theater's foyer, as he tries to collect himself, Dreyman hears another voice from the past, coming, significantly enough, from behind his back: "Too many memories, huh?" Dreyman turns to see Hempf, who confesses, "I couldn't stay in there either." Doubling for their encounter at the after party, and following the former minister's reminding him, among other things, that he has "not written since the Wall fell," the utterly stunned Dreyman has a rude and most shocking awakening.

> *Dreyman*: There is one thing I do need to ask you.... Why was I never under surveillance? Everyone else was. Why not *me*?

> *Hempf:* You were under full surveillance. We knew everything about you.
>
> *Dreyman:* Full surveillance?
>
> *Hempf (leaning towards Dreyman, as if sharing a secret):* Every inch was bugged. The full program.
>
> *Dreyman:* Impossible.
>
> *Hempf (leaning even closer):* Take a look behind your light switches. We knew everything. We knew that you couldn't give our little Christa what she needed.
>
> *Dreyman:* To think that people like you once ruled a country.

Dreyman leaves the premises a disturbed man, as Hempf is shown grinning to himself and uncomfortably straightening his tie.

Back in his apartment, Dreyman looks behind the light switches, discovering and pulling out the wires inside the walls, uncovering and undoing what Wiesler and his men had installed seven years earlier. But tracing the hidden wires inside the wall is only the beginning of Dreyman's retracing Wiesler's surveillance. In the subsequent scene he's shown arriving at the former Stasi Headquarters, now a Research Site and Memorial open to the public, the very place where the series of events that resulted in Christa-Maria's death were put into motion. Requesting to see his file, Dreyman is amazed to see two tall stacks of documents carted in through two swinging two-toned doors. That these documents chart Wiesler's surveillance from start to finish is underscored by the woman's explanation, "I ordered them chronologically. Old ones on top and the newer ones underneath," her words evoking the conscious and the unconscious, the unconscious Other that Wiesler became conscious of in the course of his surveillance.

The first page Dreyman opens has his name and identity number, which, like two binary bookends, starts and ends with the number two. As he learns, the lead for "Operation 'Lazlo,'" as he's called, "came from Minister Bruno Hempf." Reading Wiesler's reports from the top, Dreyman is confounded by the falsified reports, which substitute his article about East Germany's unreported suicides with "a play that Hauser and Lazlo" will write for the GDR's 40th anniversary." Ironically, in another case of binary opposites, while Dreyman was writing to reveal the truth, Wiesler was covering it up in his fictional reports.

To get to the bottom of it all, Dreyman, skipping over the "night fiction," pulls out the stack's bottom file, which reveals Christa-Maria's betrayal. Her confession, "Georg Dreyman wrote the Spiegel article, 'One Who Made It to the Other Side,'" suggests that the article's title speaks for his "secret sharer," who, by falsifying his reports, has truly "made it to the other side," the side opposite the one Grubitz calls "the right side."

Retracing the last day of Wiesler's surveillance through his reports, Dreyman puts two and two together, finally understanding what his "shadow" was doing, particularly when he comes to the final page and sees the two crossed (perpendicular) red fingerprints from the typewriter's red ribbon, shown twice, which doubles for his own blood-stained article (with two red stains). Just as Wiesler was more curious about the playwright than his play, Dreyman is most curious about the man who wrote the reports, whose code name has two X's, as if to mark the binary opposites.

"Who is HGW XX/7?" Dreyman asks the man sitting at the head of the former classroom, who looks for Wiesler's file card (as Wiesler was earlier shown looking for Jerska's card after hearing he gave Dreyman the score of *Sonata for a Good Man*). Finding the card, he holds it up with two hands in a mirrored image of his holding his blood-stained article. His seeing Wiesler's picture not only recalls Wiesler's seeing the playwright's picture in the play's program, his identity number, like Dreyman's two binary bookends, begins and ends with the same number. Only where the playwright's is two, Wiesler's is one.

Seeking to see the real man for himself, Dreyman is subsequently shown through a reflecting car window as he surveys the street from inside a cruising cab, looking for the man who saved him, who now works as a mailman. Significantly, his spotting and following the man who had him under surveillance, now towing his mail cart in the street, is the movie's last change of roles and turning of the tables. "Stop," he orders the driver (recalling the military man's order to the civilian in the opening), rolling the car's window halfway down. Unseen by Wiesler, he gets out and starts walking toward him, but soon stops, as though feeling things are best left as they are.

Coda

In a fitting ending to the movie's many twos, another two years later, in the movie's coda, the camera follows Wiesler towing his mail cart in the street in one continuous shot, just as it followed the two figures in the opening shot. Dressed in precisely the same uniform in which he was last shown through Dreyman's eyes, he passes a bookstore with three identical show windows, the last one displaying a bigger-than-life picture of Dreyman on the cover of his new book. Unaware of this display, Wiesler walks by. But the camera stops precisely when the window and the book are at center frame, just as it had stopped at the opening shot in the corridor. After a second or two, in a double take of sorts, Wiesler comes back into view, into the frame, returning to look at what he had glimpsed from the corner of his eye. There, reflected in the glass, he sees both himself and his pictured Other, who seems to be looking at him. With the "mirror" between them, this quintessential image of binary opposites is the closest the two come to facing each other.

The show window itself, like the movie, is divided into three parts. While the middle and biggest part, which corresponds to the movie's "night fiction," displays Dreyman's picture and the name of his book, the matching outer parts are not unlike its two bookends, especially with the advertised book between them. What's more, the book itself, *Sonata for a Good Man*, with two figures on its cover, is the movie's second work of art with the same name. Dedicated to the tieless (and unshaven) Wiesler (who now resembles Jerska), the book is his Other's acknowledgment in more ways than one.

When the salesman asks if he wants the book wrapped as a gift, and Wiesler replies, "It's for me," the hint of a smile on his face in the movie's closing freeze-frame says it all. Combining the two works of art that so moved Wiesler, the Brecht book and the *Sonata for a Good Man*, Dreyman's book surely marks a new chapter in his life with his Other. Holding the book, which apparently tells his story, Wiesler realizes he's an Other for his Other.

Chapter Notes

Introduction

1. John Gardner and John Maier, *Gilgamesh* (New York: Vintage, 1984), p. 4.
2. Ibid., p. 78.
3. Rivkah Scharf Kluger, *The Archetypal Significance of Gilgamesh* (Einsiedeln, Switzerland: Daimon Verlag, 1991), p. 16.
4. Ibid., p. 27.
5. Ibid., p. 29.
6. Morris Berman, *Coming to Our Senses* (New York: Bantam, 1990), p. 28.
7. Kluger, pp. 42–43.
8. Berman, p. 36.
9. Christian Metz, *The Imaginary Signifier* (Bloomington: Indiana University Press, 1977), p. 4.
10. Gardner and Maier, p. 30.
11. Kluger, pp. 207–8.
12. Valdine Clemens, *The Return of the Repressed* (Albany: State University of New York Press, 1999), p. 9.
13. Leo Braudy, *The World in a Frame* (Garden City, NY: Anchor, 1976), p. 20.
14. Richard Kearney, *Strangers, Gods and Monsters* (New York: Routledge, 2003), p. 77.
15. Sharon Packer, *Movies and the Modern Psyche* (Westport, CT: Praeger, 2007), p. 28.
16. Otto Rank, *The Double* (Chapel Hill: University of North Carolina Press, 1971), p. 4.
17. Ibid., p. 7.
18. Braudy, pp. 227–29.

Chapter 1

1. Adrian Danks, "Dr. Jekyll and Mr. Hyde," *Sense of Cinema*, Issue 60, www.sensesofcinema.com, 2002.
2. Tom Milne, *Rouben Mamoulian* (Bloomington: Indiana University Press, 1969), p. 17.
3. Ibid., p. 45.
4. Ibid., p. 41.

Chapter 2

1. Thomas M. Leitch, *Find the Director and Other Hitchcock Games* (Athens: University of Georgia Press, 1991), pp. 132–33.
2. Paul Gordon, *Dial "M" for Mother* (Madison, NJ: Fairleigh Dickinson University Press, 2008), p. 17.
3. Robin Wood, *Hitchcock's Films Revisited* (New York: Columbia University Press, 1989), p. 300.
4. William Rothman, *Hitchcock—The Murderous Gaze* (Cambridge, MA: Harvard University Press, 1982), pp. 185–86.
5. Gordon, p. 35.
6. Ibid., p. 41.
7. James McLaughlin, "All in the Family: Alfred Hitchcock's *Shadow of a Doubt*," in *A Hitchcock Reader*, Marshall Deutelbaum and Lealand Pogue, eds. (Chichester, UK: Blackwell, 2009), p. 142.
8. Gordon, p. 39.
9. Ibid., p. 47.

Chapter 3

1. Donald Spoto, *The Art of Alfred Hitchcock* (New York: Anchor, 1992), p. 195.
2. Robin Wood, *Hitchcock's Films Revisited* (New York: Columbia University Press, 1989), pp. 87–88.
3. Ibid., p. 86.
4. T. S. Eliot, "The Love Song of J. Alfred Prufrock," in *The Complete Poems and Plays* (New York: Harcourt, Brace, 1950), pp. 5 and 7.
5. Ibid., p. 3.
6. Spoto, p. 193.
7. Wood, p. 95.

Chapter 4

1. Laurent Bouzereau, "The Making of *Cape Fear*," *Cape Fear* DVD Supplement, Universal Pictures, 2001.
2. Edward C. Whitmont, "The Evolution of the Shadow," in *Meeting the Shadow*, Connie Zweig and Jeremiah Abrams, eds., (New York: Jeremy P. Tarcher/Puntam, 1991), p. 17.
3. Marie-Louise von Franz, "The Process of Individuation," in *Man and His Symbols* (London: Aldous, 1964), p. 178.
4. Marie-Louse von Franz, *Projection and Re-Collection in Jungian Psychology* (London, Open Court, 1980), p. 3.
5. William A. Miller, "Finding the Shadow in Daily Life," in *Meeting the Shadow*, Connie Zweig and Jeremiah Abrams, eds. (New York: Jeremy P. Tarcher/Puntam, 1991), p. 40.
6. Marie-Louise von Franz, *Shadow and Evil in Fairy Tales* (Boston: Shambhala, 1995), p. 5.
7. von Franz, *Projection and Re-Collection in Jungian Psychology*, p. 13.

Chapter 5

1. Andrew J. Rausch, *The Films of Martin Scorsese and Robert De Niro* (Lanham, MD: Scarecrow Press, 2010), p. 145.
2. Ellis Cashmore, *Martin Scorsese's America* (Malden, MA: Polity Press, 2009), p.164.
3. M. J. Sunderland, "Saul Bass: Great Designer of Movie Titles," *Cinemarolling*, December 19, 2010, http://cinemaroll.com.

4. Laurent Bouzereau, "The Making of *Cape Fear*," *Cape Fear* DVD Supplement, Universal Pictures, 2001.
5. Kirsten Moana Thompson, *Apocalyptic Dread* (Albany: State University of New York Press, 2007), p. 40.
6. Bouzereau.
7. Ken Wilber, "Taking Responsibility for Your Shadow," in *Meeting the Shadow*, Connie Zweig and Jeremiah Abrams, eds. (New York: Jeremy P. Tarcher/Puntam, 1991), p. 274.
8. Rausch, p. 157.
9. Thompson, p. 39.

Chapter 6

1. Laurence F. Knapp, *Directed by Clint Eastwood* (Jefferson, NC: McFarland, 1996), p. 43.
2. Paul Smith, *Clint Eastwood* (Minneapolis: University of Minnesota Press, 1993), pp. 134–35.
3. David Cremean, "A Fistful of Anarchy," in *Clint Eastwood, Actor and Director*, Leonard Engel, ed. (Salt Lake City: University of Utah Press, 2007), p. 70.
4. Dennis Bingham, *Acting Male* (New Brunswick, NJ: Rutgers University Press, 1994), p. 226.
5. David Rico, *Shadow Dance* (Boston: Shambhala, 1999), pp. 184–85.
6. Drucilla Cornell, *Clint Eastwood and Issues of American Masculinity* (Fordham University Press, NY, 2009), pp. 61–62.

Chapter 7

1. Jerry Hogrewe, "Making *Blood Work*," Warner Home Video, 2002.
2. Edward C. Whitmont, *The Symbolic Quest* (New York: Harper Colophon, 1969), p. 21.
3. John P. Conger, "The Body as Shadow," in *Meeting the Shadow*, Connie Zweig and Jeremiah Abrams, eds., (New York: Jeremy P. Tarcher/Puntam, 1991), p. 85.
4. Connie Zweig and Jeremiah Abrams, eds., *Meeting the Shadow* (New York: Jeremy P. Tarcher/Puntam, 1991), p. 239.
5. Whitmont, p. 36.
6. Walter Metz, "The Old Man and the C: Masculinity and Age in the Films of Clint Eastwood," in *Clint Eastwood, Actor and Director*, Leonard Engel, ed. (Salt Lake City: University of Utah Press, 2007), pp. 207–8.

Chapter 9

1. Robert A. Johnson, *Owning Your Own Shadow* (New York: HarperCollins, 1991), p. 4.
2. Nancy Qualls-Corbett, *The Sacred Prostitute* (Toronto: Inner City Books, 1988, p. 102–4.
3. Philip Charles Crawford, "The Legacy of Wonder Woman," *School Library Journal*, January 2006.

Chapter 10

1. George M. Wilson and Sam Shpall, "Unraveling the Twists in *Fight Club*," in *Fight Club*, Thomas E. Wartenberg, ed. (New York: Routledge, 2012), p. 92.
2. Charles Guignon, "Becoming a Man," in *Fight Club*, Thomas E. Wartenberg, ed. (New York: Routledge, 2012), pp. 48–49.
3. Chuck Palahniuk, interview on *Chat Books*, http://edition.cnn.com/chat/transcripts/palahniuk.html, October 1999.
4. Robert A. Johnson, *Owning Your Own Shadow* (New York: HarperCollins, 1991), p. 5.

Chapter 11

1. Karen Hollinger, *In the Company of Women* (Minneapolis: University of Minnesota Press, 1998), p. 31.
2. David Richo, *Shadow Dance* (Boston: Shambhala, 1990), pp. 12–13.
3. Deena Metzger, "Writing About the Other," in *Meeting the Shadow*, Connie Zweig and Jeremiah Abrams, eds. (New York: Jeremy P. Tarcher/Puntam, 1991), pp. 299–300.
4. Hollinger, p. 91.
5. Richo, p. 99.
6. Hollinger, p. 86.
7. Ibid.

Chapter 12

1. Linda J. Dryden, "'To Boldly Go': *Heart of Darkness* and Popular Culture," in *Heart of Darkness*, Norton Critical Edition, 4th ed., Paul B. Armstrong, ed. (New York: W. W. Norton, 1991), p. 500.
2. John Hellmann, *American Myth and the Legacy of Vietnam* (New York: Columbia University Press, 1986), p. 203.
3. David Desser, "Charlie Don't Surf," in *Inventing Vietnam*, Michael Anderegg, ed. (Philadelphia: Temple University Press, 1991), p. 97.
4. Ibid., p. 82.
5. Karl French, *Apocalypse Now* (London: Bloomsbury, 1998), p. 17.
6. Louis K. Greiff, "Conrad's Ethics and the Margins of *Apocalypse Now*," *Literature/Film Quarterly* 20, 1992, pp. 191–92.
7. Margot Norris, "Modernism in Vietnam," in *Heart of Darkness*, Norton Critical Edition, 4th ed., Paul B. Armstrong, ed. (New York: W. W. Norton, 1991), pp. 498–99.
8. Jessie L. Weston, *From Ritual to Romance* (Garden City, NY: Doubleday Anchor, 1957), p. 60.

Chapter 13

1. Daniel Deardorff, *The Other Within* (Berkeley: North Atlantic Books, 2004), p. xv.
2. Christopher Bollas, *The Shadow of the Object* (London: Free Association Books, 1987), p. 78.
3. Ibid., p. 68.
4. Ibid., p. 70.

Bibliography

Two film supplements were also of value: Laurent Bouzereau's "The Making of *Cape Fear*" (*Cape Fear*, DVD Supplement, Universal Pictures, 2001) and Jerry Hogrewe's "Making *Blood Work*" (*Blood Work*, DVD Supplement, Warner Home Video, 2002).

Berman, Morris. *Coming to Our Senses*. New York: Bantam, 1990.
Bingham, Dennis. *Acting Male*. New Brunswick, N. J.: Rutgers University Press, 1994.
Bollas, Christopher. *The Shadow of the Object*. London: Free Association Books, 1987.
Braudy, Leo. *The World in a Frame*. Garden City, N. Y.: Anchor, 1976.
Cashmore, Ellis. *Martin Scorsese's America*. Malden, MA: Polity Press, 2009.
Clemens, Valdine. *The Return of the Repressed*. Albany: State University of New York Press, 1999.
Conger, John P. "The Body as Shadow." *Meeting the Shadow*. Connie Zweig and Jeremiah Abrams, eds. New York: Jeremy P. Tarcher/Puntam, 1991.
Crawford, Philip Charles. "The Legacy of Wonder Woman." *School Library Journal*, January 2006.
Cremean, David Cremean. "A Fistful of Anarchy." *Clint Eastwood, Actor and Director*. Leonard Engel, ed. Salt Lake City: University of Utah Press, 2007.
Danks, Adrian. "Dr. Jekyll and Mr. Hyde." *Sense of Cinema*, Issue 60, www.sensesofcinema.com, 2002.
Deardorff, Daniel Deardorff. *The Other Within*. Berkeley: North Atlantic Books, 2004.
Desser, David. "Charlie Don't Surf." *Inventing Vietnam*. Michael Anderegg, ed. Philadelphia: Temple University Press, 1991.
Dryden, Linda J. "'To Boldly Go': *Heart of Darkness* and Popular Culture" *Heart of Darkness*, Norton Critical Edition, *4th ed.*, Paul B. Armstrong, ed. New York: W. W. Norton, 1991.
Eliot, T. S. "The Love Song of J. Alfred Prufrock." *The Complete Poems and Plays*. New York: Harcourt, Brace, 1950.
French, Karl. *Apocalypse Now*. London: Bloomsbury, 1998.
Gardner, John, and John Maier. *Gilgamesh*. New York: Vintage, 1984.
Gordon, Paul. *Dial "M" for Mother*. Madison, NJ: Fairleigh Dickinson University Press, 2008.
Greiff, Louis K. "Conrad's Ethics and the Margins of *Apocalypse Now*." *Literature/Film Quarterly* 20, 1992.
Guignon, Charles. "Becoming a Man." *Fight Club*. Thomas E. Wartenberg, ed. New York: Routledge, 2012.

Hellmann, John. *American Myth and the Legacy of Vietnam*. New York: Columbia University Press, 1986.
Hollinger, Karen. *In the Company of Women*. Minneapolis: University of Minnesota Press, 1998.
Johnson, Robert A. *Owning Your Own Shadow*. New York: HarperCollins, 1991.
Kearney, Richard. *Strangers, Gods and Monsters*. New York: Routledge, 2003.
Kluger, Rivkah Scharf. *The Archetypal Significance of Gilgamesh*. Einsiedeln, Switzerland: Daimon Verlag, 1991.
Knapp, Laurence F. *Directed by Clint Eastwood*. Jefferson, N.C.: McFarland, 1996.
Leitch, Thomas M. *Find the Director and Other Hitchcock Games*. Athens: University of Georgia Press, 1991.
McLaughlin, James. "All in the Family: Alfred Hitchcock's *Shadow of a Doubt*." *A Hitchcock Reader*. Marshall Deutelbaum and Lealand Pogue, eds. Chichester, UK: Blackwell, 2009.
Metz, Christian. *The Imaginary Signifier*. Bloomington: Indiana University Press, 1977.
Metz, Walter. "The Old Man and the C: Masculinity and Age in the Films of Clint Eastwood." *Clint Eastwood, Actor and Director*. Leonard Engel, ed. Salt Lake City: University of Utah Press, 2007.
Metzger, Deena. "Writing About the Other." *Meeting the Shadow*. Connie Zweig and Jeremiah Abrams, eds. New York: Jeremy P. Tarcher/Puntam, 1991.
Miller, William A. "Finding the Shadow in Daily Life." *Meeting the Shadow*. Connie Zweig and Jeremiah Abrams, eds. New York: Jeremy P. Tarcher/Puntam, 1991.
Milne, Tom. *Rouben Mamoulian*. Bloomington: Indiana University Press, 1969.
Norris, Margot. "Modernism in Vietnam." *Heart of Darkness*, Norton Critical Edition, 4th ed. Paul B. Armstrong, ed. New York: W.W. Norton, 1991.
Packer, Sharon. *Movies and the Modern Psyche*. Westport, CT: Praeger, 2007.
Palahniuk, Chuck. Interview, *Chat Books*. http://edition.cnn.com/chat/transcripts/palahniuk.html. October 1999.
Qualls-Corbett, Nancy. *The Sacred Prostitute*. Toronto: Inner City Books, 1988.
Rank, Otto. *The Double*. Chapel Hill: University of North Carolina Press, 1971.
Rausch, Andrew J. *The Films of Martin Scorsese and Robert De Niro*. Lanham, MD: Scarecrow Press, 2010.
Rico, David Rico. *Shadow Dance*. Boston: Shambhala, 1999.
Rothman, William. *Hitchcock—The Murderous Gaze*. Cambridge: Harvard University Press, 1982.
Smith, Paul. *Clint Eastwood*. Minneapolis: University of Minnesota Press, 1993.
Spoto, Donald. *The Art of Alfred Hitchcock*. New York: Anchor, 1992.
Sunderland, M. J. *Saul Bass: Great Designer of Movie Titles. Cinemarolling*, December 19, 2010, *http://cinemaroll.com*.
Thompson, Kirsten Moana. *Apocalyptic Dread*. New York: State University of New York Press, 2007.
von Franz, Marie-Louise. "The Process of Individuation." *Man and his Symbols*. London: Aldous, 1964.
_____. *Projection and Re-Collection in Jungian Psychology*. London: Open Court, 1980.
_____. *Shadow and Evil in Fairy Tales*. Boston: Shambhala, 1995.
Weston, Jessie L. *From Ritual to Romance*. Garden City, N.Y.: Doubleday Anchor, 1957.
Whitmont, Edward C. "The Evolution of the Shadow." *Meeting the Shadow*. Connie Zweig and Jeremiah Abrams, eds. New York: Jeremy P. Tarcher/Puntam, 1991.
_____. *The Symbolic Quest*. New York: Harper Colophon, 1969.
Wilbur, Ken. "Taking Responsibility for Your Shadow." *Meeting the Shadow*. Connie Zweig and Jeremiah Abrams, eds. New York: Jeremy P. Tarcher/Puntam, 1991.
Wilson, George M., and Sam Shpall. "Unraveling the Twists in *Fight Club*." *Fight Club*. Thomas E. Wartenberg, ed. New York: Routledge, 2012.
Wood, Robin. *Hitchcock's Films Revisited*. New York: Columbia University Press, 1989.
Zweig, Connie, and Jeremiah Abrams, eds. *Meeting the Shadow*. New York: Jeremy P. Tarcher/Puntam, 1991.

Index

Abrams, Jeremiah 102
Acting Male 83
adversary(ies) 53, 62, 87, 89, 96, 99
Alice in Wonderland 163
All My Sons 125
anima 83, 86, 111, 133, 145; autonomous 124; dark 124
animal(s) 2, 61, 74, 80, 132, 134; power animal 144, 151, 153; world 4
animus 111
Anthony, Bruno (*Strangers on a Train*) 35–50, 52
Apocalypse Now 169–171, 176–177
Apollo 46
appetite, sexual 58
Archetypal Significance of Gilgamesh 3, 5
archetype 5; archetypal struggle 80
area, shadowy 188
arousal, sexual 17; excitement 73; promiscuity 16; tension 71, 74; theories 17
Arquette, Rosanna 160
assassin(s) 175, 183
assassination 85–86, 92
assimilating 5
attack, sexual 53
autonomy 7, 157; being 187; person 141

Babylonian epic 4
Bach, J. S. 11, 19
Baker, Joe Don 67
Balsam, Martin 56, 64
bank 29–30
Barkin, Ellen 125
Bass, Elaine 66

Bass, Saul 65–66
Becker, Harold 125–126
Bergen, Polly 55
Berman, Morris 4, 187
Bible 67–68
bicycle 28, 30
Bingham, Dennis 83
The Birds 51
Blood Work 82–83, 98–99, 108, 110
body double 109
Bollas, Christopher 191
Bonham Carter, Helena 140
bookends, binary 199
Bowden, Danielle (*Cape Fear*) 68–81
Bowden, Leigh (*Cape Fear*) 69–81
Bowden, Sam (*Cape Fear*) 52–62, 65–81
Boyle, Robert 51
Brando, Marlon 172
Braudy, Leo 8
Brecht, Bertolt 192–194, 201
Breur, Josef 8
buddy, binary 174
Byrne, David 111

Cady, Max (*Cape Fear*) 52–62, 65–81
camera movement 172
cameras 21, 41, 43, 52, 55–56, 59, 66–69, 72–73, 75, 78, 81, 85, 87, 96, 99, 111, 116–117, 120, 122–123, 129–130, 133, 147, 149, 162, 171–173, 184, 189, 192, 198, 200; subjective 11–13, 141
candle, phallic 20
Cape Fear (1962) 51, 54, 64, 67, 81, 110
Cape Fear (1991) 64–65, 81

210   Index

Carew, General (*Dr. Jekyll and Mr. Hyde*) 15, 17–18, 19, 20–21
Carew, Muriel (*Dr. Jekyll and Mr. Hyde*) 15–19, 21
Carroll, Leo G. 41
Cashmore, Ellis 65
Cerberus 45
cigars 23, 25, 27, 47, 52, 57, 59–60, 69, 78; phallic 69; smoking 25, 145
Cinderella 101–102
Cinderella 101
cinema 2, 7–8, 35; screen 4
Ciotat Station 8
Collinge, Patricia 25
Coming to Our Senses 4, 187
Confessions of a Justified Sinner 7
Conger, John P. 101
Conrad, Joseph 7, 169–171, 181–182, 184, 186
conscious 18, 42, 48, 59–60, 62, 66, 69, 73, 95, 99–100, 105, 120, 124, 126, 147, 199
consciousness 5, 34, 45, 50, 54, 60, 63, 83, 101, 154, 156, 187
content, sexual 76
Coppola, Francis Ford 169–170, 175
Cornell, Drucilla 96
Cotten, Joseph 22
counterpart: feminine 103; shadowy 116
creatures, primeval 80
Cremean, David 82
crime 47, 76, 80, 99; monstrous 20
crime scene 99, 103, 105
criminals 1, 41, 108, 163–167
crisscross 41, 46, 50, 172

Daniels, Jeff 98, 110
Dante, Alighieri 68, 179
dark half 172
The Dark Mirror 159
dark side 83
darkness 170, 181
daughter 55, 57, 60–63, 65, 67, 69, 72–74, 76, 78, 81, 88
Deardorf, Daniel 187
De Jesus, Wanda 98
Demme, Jonathan 110, 126
De Niro, Robert 64–66
desire(s) 26, 41, 113; dark 39; illicit 77; incestuous 72; object of 30, 74; repressed 61; sexual 63; women's 161
Desperately Seeking Susan 159–161, 168, 188
Desser, David 170
Dewars, double 129, 136–137, 139
Dial "M" for Mother 23
Dirty Harry 82, 86
divorce 47, 50, 139, 173

Dr. Jekyll and Mr. Hyde (film) 8–9, 11–21, 22, 140, 187
The Doors 171, 186
Doppelgänger 1, 72, 82, 96, 187; as narrative device 82
double(s) 1, 5–7, 9, 13, 15, 20, 29, 33, 35–38, 41–42, 45, 49–50, 52, 55, 58–60, 62, 67, 70, 72, 74, 80, 96, 98–99, 102–105, 107, 109–111, 119–121, 124, 128, 131, 135, 156, 187, 194, 200; mirrored 108; motif of 27, 33, 35, 68; shadowy 52–23, 52, 102; unconscious 102, 106
The Double 9, 187
double agents 179
double bass 36
double cross(ing) 35–36, 39, 46
Double Down 98, 102, 104, 106–107
double entendre 54, 65, 99, 103, 127–128, 132, 156, 165, 175, 187
double meaning(s) 18, 37, 39–40, 42, 74, 104, 111, 137
double strategy 38
doubled 49, 62, 68, 79, 85, 101, 144, 164, 172
doubling 13, 41, 44, 47, 61, 86, 96, 105, 121, 191, 198
Dracula, Count 28, 34
dream(s) 1, 5, 78, 81, 104, 149, 154, 163; interpretation 4; significance of 5; symbolic 4
Dreyman, Georg (*The Lives of Others*) 188, 190–201
Driggs, Charlie (*Something Wild*) 110–124
Dryden, Linda J. 169
Durden, Tyler (*Fight Club*) 141–158
Duval, Robert 170

Eastwood Clint 82–83, 98, 108–110
Ego 3, 12, 19; inflated 4–5
Electra complex 26
Eliot, T. S. 37, 182, 184
The End 171–173, 186
Enkidu 1–4, 6–7, 16, 81
Epic of Gilgamesh 1–7, 141; as prototype 2, 7–8, 10, 16, 22, 35, 140–141, 159
evil 14–15, 103
excitement, sexual 18
eye(s) 12, 69
eyeglasses 44

faces, split 104
fairy tale 75; fantasy 115; urban 161
family 26, 32–33, 59, 63, 69, 109, 115
family picture 113, 115, 122
fantasy(ies) 162, 166; mirrored 161
father 18, 21, 22, 26–29, 31, 39, 41, 43, 46, 58, 70, 77, 132, 135, 137, 193

father figure 28; shadowy 33
father-son conflict 17
female desire 161
female double films 159–160
female gaze 161, 163
feminine 133, 153; half 110; Other 109, 131–133, 135–138, 145–148, 151–153, 157–159; side 68, 111, 133
Fight Club 10, 140–142, 144, 146
figure, shadowy 7, 66
The Films of Martin Scorsese and Robert De Niro 64
Fincher, David 10, 140–142, 144
Find the Director and Other Hitchcock Games 22
Fisher King 183
The Following Sea 98, 102–103
Ford, Harrison 175
forest 3, 75, 76
Frankenstein 7
Frazer, James 182
French, Karl 171
Frenzy 23
Freud, Sigmund 5, 7–8, 26
Freudian psychoanalysis 9
Freudian slips 18
Freudianism 9
friend(s), binary 95, 140, 171, 182, 185
From Ritual to Romance 182
frustration, sexual 16

The Game 141
Gilgamesh (King) 2–7, 81
Glass, Roberta (*Desperately Seeking Susan*) 160–168, 188
glasses 40, 43
The Golden Bough 182
Goodman, John 129
Gordon, Paul 23–4
Gothic period 6; tales 7
Granger, Farley 35
Grant, Cary 71
Great Dane 45
Greiff, Louis 176
Griffith, Melanie 110
Guignon, Charles 145
guns 43–44, 46, 58, 62, 78, 92, 107, 109, 134, 138, 142, 146, 157
Guns of Navarone 51

Hackman, Gene 82
Haines, Guy (*Strangers on a Train*) 35–50
handcuffs(ed) 113–116, 122
heart 98, 102–103, 108–109, 120, 134, 150
heart attack 83, 106
Heart of Darkness 7, 169–170, 174, 182, 186

heart transplant 83, 108
Helen (*Sea of Love*) 125–126, 131–139
Henkel, Lulu/Audrey (*Something Wild*) 110–124
Herbert, Holmes 14
Herrmann, Bernard 51, 64–66
Hitchcock, Alfred 9, 22, 27, 35, 37, 40, 51–52, 64–66, 91, 160
Hitchcock, Patricia 41
Hitchcock—The Murderous Gaze 24
Hobart, Rose 15
Hobbes, Halliwell 17
Hogg, James 7
Hollinger, Karen 159, 161, 163
The Hollow Men 182, 184
Honecker, Erich 189–190, 198
Hopkins, Miriam 15
Hopper, Dennis 182
Horrigan, Frank (*In the Line of Fire*) 83–97
horse(s) 11–12, 16
Humbaba 3
hunger, sexual 57
Hyde, Edward 6, 15–16, 18–21, 140

Id 12, 19
If 48, 184
images, binary 189
In the Line of Fire 82–83, 98–99
incorporation 115–116, 163, 166; other 120; other half 124
individuation 5, 83, 109
Inferno 179
initiation rite 113–114, 119
inner split 1, 173
innuendos, sexual 18
instincts, primordial 185
integration 40, 45, 50, 54, 60, 62, 63, 139, 158, 176
The Interpretation of Dreams 5
introjection 165
Ishtar 3
Ivy (*Dr. Jekyll and Mr. Hyde*) 15–16, 18–19

Jackson, Michael 118
Jekyll, Henry 6–7, 11–21, 140
Jenkins, Richard 127
John the Baptist 184
Johnson, Robert A. 157
Jung 22, 83, 109, 111, 133, 160

Kael, Pauline 82
Kahlo, Frida 111
Keller, Frank (*Sea of Love*) 125–139
Kelly, Grace 71
Kennedy, President 84–85, 87–88, 91, 96, 107

key(s) 42, 46, 53–54, 70–71, 139; red 164
Kilgore, Colonel (*Apocalypse Now*) 170
killer 99–103, 105–108, 125–126, 129–130, 132, 135, 138
king 2–3, 5
Kipling, Rudyard 48, 184
Knapp, Laurence F. 82
Koch, Sebastian 190
Kurtz, Walter (*Apocalypse Now*) 170–186

Lacan, Jacques 4
Lange, Jessica 66
Lanyon, Dr. 13–16, 20
Leitch, Thomas 22
Lewis, Juliette 65
Lifford, Tina 103
lighter 38–39, 48–50
Liotta, Ray 116
"Little Red Riding Hood" 75–76
The Lives of Others 187–188
Lone Ranger 104
Look Homeward Angel 71
looking glass 6, 157, 162–165
Lorne, Marion 39
Louis, Joe 128–129
love 19–20
love-making 155
The Love Song of J. Alfred Prufrock 37
Lumière Brothers 8

Madonna 160
Magnum Force 82
Malkovich, John 83
Mamoulian, Rouben 9–11, 16–18, 22
man, feminized 144, 151, 154
manhood 19, 115
March, Fredric 12
Marlow (*Heart of Darkness*) 169–170, 174
Marnie 51
marriage 19, 121–122; conscious 50; failed 125, 133; unconscious 50
Martin, Lori 55
Martin Scorsese's America 65
Masculine Other 146
match, verbal 38
maternal figure(s) 25, 31; as therapist 30
maturation, sexual 30
McCaleb, Terry (*Blood Work*) 98–109
McDermott, Dylan 84
McGuffin 22
McLaughlin, James 27
Meatloaf 143
Medusa 145
Meeting the Shadow 102
ménage à trois 191
Mesopotamia 2

message(s) 43, 45, 47, 61, 70, 92, 97, 100–101, 103–104, 106, 113, 136, 150, 160–162, 164, 166–167, 175; coded 100, 104–106; desperate 160–161, 164;
metaphoric devices 11
metaphors, visual 10
Metz, Christian 4
Metz, Walter 108
Metzger, Deena 160
Miller, Arthur 125
Miller, Henry 78, 178
Miller, William 62
Milne, Tom 13, 17
mirror(s) 4, 6–7, 11–13, 16–19, 25, 37, 47, 57, 63, 72–73, 107–108, 115, 120, 123, 128, 141, 144–145, 150, 157–158, 162–163, 167, 174, 176–177, 182, 185, 191, 193; bathroom 123; full-size 173; one-way 73; reflection 161; stage 4
mirroring 4, 6, 13, 32, 57, 8, 87, 104, 148, 150, 162, 164–166, 176, 177–178, 179, 184, 185, 188, 190
Mitchum, Robert 51, 64–65
monster 1, 3, 20, 69, 72, 91, 157
monstrosity 157
Morrison, Jim 171
mother 4, 17–20, 25–29, 32, 39, 46–47, 58, 69, 73, 75–77, 81, 115–116, 131–132, 137; as confessor 19; conscious 18; symbolic 44; unconscious 18, 20–21
Mother Earth 19
Mother Nature 4
Movies and the Modern Psyche 8
Muhe, Ulrich 189
Mulvey, Laura 161
Murch, Walter 170–171
murder 39, 41, 43–44, 45, 46–48, 105, 130, 134, 176
myth 1

name, shadowy 161
nature, dual 5, 9, 11
Netherworld 76
Never Been Kissed 142
New York 40
Newton, Charlie (*Shadow of a Doubt*) 22–34
Newton, Emma (*Shadow of a Doubt*) 23–34
Nietzsche, Friedrich 67
Ninsun 4
Nolte, Nick 65–66
Noone, Buddy (*Blood Work*) 98–109
Norris, Margot 177
North, conscious 60, 66–67
North by Northwest 23, 51, 66

Index

Norton, Edgar 12
Norton, Edward 140

Oakley, Charlie (*Shadow of a Doubt*) 22–34, 52
obsession 30
Oedipal desire(s) 20, 23–24, 30; drama 17, 20–21, 24–25, 23, 30; dreams 26; inescapable 78; problem 31; relationship 39; subtext 23; triad 17
Oedipus 17, 21, 23, 24, 27, 28, 31
Oedipus complex 26
opposite(s) 107, 160–165, 167–168; binary 1, 10–11, 53, 84, 93, 100, 124, 162, 171–176, 188, 190, 192–193, 194, 198–201; diametric 151; ear 165; genders 22; male 111; mirrored 107, 160; sides 7, 18, 73, 88, 90, 189
oppression 3
Orwell, George 188
Other: autonomous 40; binary 170; collective 175; demonic 78; denied 76, 178; enigmatic 22; escaping 79; feminine 109, 131–133, 135–138, 145–148, 151–153, 157–159; half 110–112, 114, 116, 119, 122–124; icon of 186; image of 182; imaginary 140, 158; inescapable 39; investigation of 84; knowing 85, 87, 97; male 160, 161; masculine 146; mirrored 173; monstrous 107; motif of 52; negative 78; people 4; pictured 201; primordial 81; projected 65, 69, 77, 141, 146–147, 151, 154; relentless 119; repressed 103, 137; self 16–19, 21; simulated 142; shadowy 12, 66, 79, 101, 129, 179, 181; side 19, 88, 199; sidekick 104; unconscious 27, 31, 36, 42–45, 47–50, 52, 54, 56, 59–65, 67, 70–71, 73, 77, 83–86, 91–93, 98–100, 104–106, 108, 124–126, 130, 134–135, 139, 158, 185–186, 191, 199; unrepressed 75; vibrant 160; voice of 183, 186; wronged 65, 80–81; young 135
other half 110–111, 118, 122–124
overreact(ing) 58, 62, 76–77, 88, 93, 135, 150, 175
Ozzie and Harriet 148, 153

Pacino, Al 125
Packer, Sharon 8
pair(s) 13, 15, 41, 99, 110, 134, 144, 160, 173, 177; of binoculars 85, 87, 89, 121; of claws 37, 44; of doubles 38; of eyes 66, 103; of hands 39, 44; of marble columns 14; of legs 160, 162; of men 13; of messages and visits 45; motif 134, 160, 162; of shoes 36; twin 13
pairing 159, 163, 167–168

Pandora's box 30
partner(s) 85, 93, 97, 99–100, 104–106, 128, 130, 132, 137, 164
partnership 104–105, 130
Peck, Gregory 52, 61, 64
persona 83, 131
personality: dual 12; split 141
personification 7
Peterson, Wolfgang 83
Phillip, Phil 126
photographs 29–30
Picasso 134
picture 54–55, 59–60, 63, 89
The Pictures of Dorian Gray 7
Pieta 184, 197
Pitt, Brad 140
Pluto 40, 45
Poe, Edgar Allan 7
policemen 30, 32–33, 41, 49, 57, 73, 103, 121, 126–128, 153–154, 164
policewomen 165–166
Poole (*Dr. Jekyll and Mr. Hyde*) 6, 12–13, 16, 19, 21
prison 59–60, 68, 73, 78; psychic 63
Problem Child 69
project(s) 1, 4–5, 10, 12, 52, 127, 129–130, 141–142, 145, 152
projection(s) 26, 47, 48, 54, 56, 62, 74, 88, 103–104, 125–126, 130, 132, 135–136, 141, 144, 151–153, 155, 160, 164, 165, 168, 170, 175, 178, 183, 185–186
Projection and Re-Collection in Jungian Psychology 63
projector, cinematic 34, 49, 62, 74, 78–79, 104, 155, 159, 170, 177; and her (unconscious) Other 160–161, 163, 167–168; and his (unconscious) Other 7, 16, 22, 35–37, 41, 48, 50, 66, 69, 71, 86, 95, 99–100, 108, 123, 126, 128, 130, 136, 141, 144, 147, 170, 174–175, 184
prostitutes 17
protagonists 7–8
psyche 13, 15, 28, 33, 83, 90, 99–100, 108, 124, 132, 136, 141–142, 146, 153, 158, 160, 162; split 174; troubled 142, 171–172
Psycho 51, 66
psychoanalysis 8, 190
psychoanalytic concept 8; Freudian 9; perspective 24; theory 4
psychological obstacle 98–99; prism 65; terms 34; thriller 65
psychology 1, 35
purgatory 179

Qualls-Corbett, Nancy 133

Index

Rank, Otto 9, 187
Rausch, Andrew J. 64, 74
Rear Window 51
Rebecca 160, 162
rebirth 163–164
reflection 16, 162
rejection 101
relationship, binary 149
repression 4, 6, 14–16, 18, 30, 34, 63, 71, 124, 160, 165; of desire 61; of the Other 56, 103, 126, 137; rage 130; return of the repressed 7, 19, 57, 59, 65, 76, 85, 100, 118, 136, 138–139; revenge of the repressed 79; unconscious 7, 54
resurrection 184, 198
ring 23, 33; of smoke 23; wedding 121
rite: ceremonial 113, 184; initiation 114; of passage 110, 114, 119, 163, 166
Rivers, Graciella (*Blood Work*) 98, 101–109
Roberta, conscious 163, 166
The Rolling Stones 177
Roman, Ruth 41
Rothman, William 24
Russo, Rene 83
Rye, Stellan 9, 187

The Sacred Prostitute 133
Satisfaction 177
Saturday Night Fever 117
scapegoat 40
Scharf Kluger, Rivkah 3, 5
Scorsese, Martin 64–67, 69, 81
Sea of Love (film) 125–126
Sea of Love (song) 126–127, 129, 132, 134, 136, 138
The Secret Sharer 7
Seidelman, Susan 159
self: good 13; indecent 15; lesser 82; other 13, 15, 21; and Other 191; recognition of 4; schizoid 154
separation 4, 115–116, 163
Sexus 78, 178
shadow 1, 11–12, 33, 41–43, 45–47, 50, 53–54, 70, 76, 83, 105, 127, 129, 160, 190, 197, 200; bright 120, 160, 188; golden 160; helping 120; knowing 195; life 126; negative 167–168; positive 160, 167; projection of 41, 46, 62; self 22; work 102
shadow boxing 70, 129
Shadow of a Doubt 9, 22–25, 27, 30, 34–35, 51–52, 110
shadowing 33, 87, 90, 139; Other 79
Shelley, Mary 7
Shpall, Sam 141
Sieland, Christa-Maria (*The Lives of Others*) 191–199

Sinclair, Ray (*Something Wild*) 116–124
Singer, Marla (*Fight Club*) 140, 143–158
smoking gun 48
soldiers, binary 174
Something Wild 110–111, 125–126
Sonata for a Good Man 187–188, 194, 200–201
South, unconscious 60, 66–67
split 15, 66, 146; binary 4
Spoto, Donald 35, 40
Spradlin, G. D. 175
Standard Babylonian Version (*of Gilgamesh*) 3
Stevenson, Robert Louis 2, 5–8, 11, 17
Stewart, James 91–92
A Stolen Life 159
Storaro, Vittorio 170
The Strange Case of Dr. Jekyll and Mr. Hyde 2, 5–7, 9, 11
Strangers in the Night 136
Strangers on a Train 35–36, 51–52, 160
Strick, Wesley 72
The Student of Prague 9, 187
Studies of Hysteria 8
subconscious 7
subjectivity, conscious 190
subtext 8, 22, 64–65, 111; Freudian 12; symbolic 8; unconscious 105
suicide(s) 193–195
sunglasses, mirrored 73
Superego 12, 19
surveillance 103
Susan (*Desperately Seeking Susan*) 160–168, 188
symbol, phallic 150
symmetry 93; head 29; lectern 13; mise-en-scene(s) 12; painting 128; picture 20; shot(s) 19–20, 36, 93, 97, 128, 148, 156
synchronicity 5

theme, double 9
Thompson, J. Lee 51–52, 54, 64–65, 67, 69, 71, 81, 110
Thompson, Kirsten Mona 72, 81
threshold 46, 116, 121; guardian of 85, 118, 128, 147, 163
Thus Spake Zarathustra 68
Tight Rope 82–83
To Catch a Thief 71
Toccata and Fugue in D Minor 11
Tomasini, George 51
Torn Curtain 64
train 27, 34, 36, 40–41, 43, 47–50
train station 28
transformation 4–5, 13, 16, 116–117, 163, 166, 193–194

Index

transition 115–116, 123, 163
trauma 4, 84
Travers, Henry 25
Travolta, John 118
The Troggs 114
The Trouble with Harry 51
twin(s) 33; claws 36; doors 148; pairs 54; pictures 29

uncanny 2, 58
unconscious 7, 18, 44–46, 48, 53, 58–60, 62, 65–66, 69, 72–73, 76, 78–82, 95, 99–101, 103, 105, 109, 111–112, 118–120, 124, 126, 132, 136–137, 147, 150, 153, 156, 163–164, 167, 178, 199; alibi 41; basement 134, 151; collaborator 50; collective 5; complex 63; contents 63; creature of 37, 57, 144; crime 76, 78; culprit 46; darkness 138; desire(s) 37, 40–41, 61–62, 65, 76; double 102, 106; drama 138; falling 101, 163, 165; fear 104; figure 3, 58; heroine's 163; images 8; ingenious 47; invitation 56; jungle 178, 185; lens 165; lust 62; magic world of 164–165; magical 167; marriage 50; mechanism 8; message 20, 92, 104; mother 18, 20–21; Other 27, 31, 36, 42–45, 47–50, 52, 54, 56, 59–65, 67, 70–71, 73, 77, 83–86, 91–93, 98–100, 104–106, 108, 124–126, 130, 134–135, 139, 158, 185–186, 191, 199; personality 1; projection(s) 141–142, 164, 190; realm of 49, 61, 103, 127, 152; reference 18; repressed 7; river 81; sea 109, 126; son 21; South 60; state of mind 166; story 8; subtext 105; Susan 163, 166; symbol of 108; theater of 79; voice of 191; wild man 81; working of 5
unconsciousness 163
underworld 40, 45–46, 163
Unforgiven 82
Union 60, 67
Uruk 2–3, 5–6

vampire 29
Van Gennep, Arnold 114, 163
Varden, Norma 44
Vertigo 51, 66, 91
Victoria, Queen 20
Victorian England 6; London 6
Vietnam 170–171
Vietnam War 171
Virgil 179
visit(s) 42–43, 45, 47; nocturnal 41
voice, feminine 132
Von Donnersmarck, Florian Henckel 187
Von Franz, Marie-Louise 56, 63

Waits, Tom 139
Walker, Robert 35
The Wasteland 182
Webb, James R. 64
Weston, Jessie L. 182
Whitmore, Edward C. 54, 99
Wiesler, Gerd (*The Lives of Others*) 187–201
wife 41, 55–58, 60, 63, 69, 117, 119, 127–128, 133, 138–139, 173; ex-wife 125–127, 129–131, 134–139
Wilber, Ken 74
Wild Thing 114
Wilde, Oscar 7
The Will to Power 68
Willard (*Apocalypse Now*) 169–186
William Wilson 7
Wilson, George M. 141
witch 1, 75
Wolfe, Thomas 76
Wonder Woman 134–135
Wood, Robin 23, 36, 45
Woods, primeval 78
Wright, Theresa 22

Yankee Stadium 128
Yankees (New York) 126–127

Zweig, Connie 102

www.ingramcontent.com/pod-product-compliance
Lightning Source LLC
Chambersburg PA
CBHW032054300426
44116CB00007B/740